Jesus Darkly

Rafael Rodríguez

Foreword by Joel B. Green

Remembering Jesus with the New Testament

Abingdon Press™

Nashville

JESUS DARKLY:
REMEMBERING JESUS WITH THE NEW TESTAMENT

Copyright © 2018 by Abingdon Press

This book is printed on acid-free paper.

Library of Congress Cataloging-in-Publication Data has been requested.

978-1-5018-3911-5

Unless otherwise indicated, Scripture quotations are taken from the Common English Bible, copyright
2011. Used by permission. All rights reserved.

Scripture quotations noted NRSV are from the New Revised Standard Version Bible, copyright © 1989
National Council of the Churches of Christ in the United States of America. Used by permission. All
rights reserved worldwide. http://nrsvbibles.org/.

18 19 20 21 22 23 24 25 26 27—10 9 8 7 6 5 4 3 2 1
MANUFACTURED IN THE UNITED STATES OF AMERICA

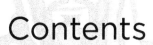

Contents

Foreword

"Who do you say that I am?" As the Gospels of Matthew, Mark, and Luke tell the story, Jesus's question to his disciples is haunting. This is because, first, we hear that lots of people had widely divergent, even conflicting views of Jesus. Is he John the Baptist, come back to life? Maybe he's one of Israel's prophets, resuscitated. And then, second, when one of the disciples, Peter, speaking for them all, responds to Jesus's question, he gets it right, and wrong. He uses the right words—"You are the Christ, the Son of the living God" (Matt 16:16), "You are the Christ" (Mark 8:29), "The Christ sent from God" (Luke 9:20)—but he seems not to understand what he's saying. Or, perhaps better, he apparently has a different dictionary to define those terms than Jesus uses. Who is Jesus?

For those of us concerned with the question of Jesus's identity and significance, *Jesus Darkly* is an exciting book. Here, Rafael Rodríguez changes the conversation about what we know about Jesus and how we know it. This is due above all to the way he takes advantage of a ground shift in the way we understand memory—and, therefore, the way we grasp what it means to represent history.

For two or three centuries, the Holy Grail of historical inquiry has been "Jesus as he really was." This meant stripping away layers of interpretation, like peeling back the layers of an onion, in order to discover a nontheological Jesus (or, maybe, a pretheological Jesus). Scholars sought to reconstruct what actually happened from a range of sources—the New Testament Gospels, to be sure, but also Paul's writings and writings from outside the Bible. However, anyone who has peeled an onion knows that an onion is simply layer upon layer, and study of any historical moment or person is the same. There is no "historical core" that stands apart from its interpretation. Every sentence is an organic fusion of event and interpretation. The quest to find "Jesus as he really was" turns out to be like that old quest for the mythological unicorn. There's no such thing. Jesus is always known *in relation to*—say, in relation to the story of Israel, in relation to the woman taken ill, in relation to problems when the Corinthians gather at the table, or in relation to believers concerned with the seemingly ever-present encroachment of evil in the world.

That's because memories of people and events are being formed before the historian shows up to form a historical record. Oral history nurtures a community of memory, so that history-telling precedes and shapes history-writing. In this process, memories are constantly changing, some brought to the surface and others suppressed, shaped and reshaped, and pressed into service in relation to their perceived importance.

Jesus Darkly recognizes that memory is never an act of simple recall. Instead, it is a complex process in which the past is reconstructed in light of present interests that are defined and shaped in community. Decades of neuroscientific study have emphasized the degree to which memory is malleable and dynamic, especially as our recollections of people and events are cast within a narrative that runs from the past into the future. Accordingly, social memory studies, on which Rafael Rodríguez builds, rejects old ways of trying to divorce *history* from *theology*, while acknowledging that all memory is an indissoluble concoction of *past* and *present*, of *event* and *interpretation*.

Bringing this approach to the study of Jesus means that we want to explore what Jesus's person and mission *mean* within the narrative frameworks we find already in the New Testament and, indeed, within the whole of the Scriptures. This approach allows us to get a toehold on how early Christians understood Jesus's significance in relation to their own present challenges and needs. This approach focuses on how the representations of Jesus we have in the New Testament make sense of Jesus of Nazareth, and presses us to consider who Jesus was and what Jesus did that accounts for the particular interpretations of Jesus we read in the Gospel of John, 2 Corinthians, 1 Peter, and the rest.

Jesus Darkly is profound for the way it sets up conversations about study of the historical Jesus, study of the New Testament Gospels, and study of New Testament Christology. It's also important for the way it situates Jesus's significance within the overarching drama of the Bible. Its importance, though, is matched by its accessibility, the way it welcomes readers to this journey of exploration. We are indebted to Rafael Rodríguez for this rare accomplishment. And we hope for the widest possible readership.

Joel B. Green

Preface

When the word of the Lord came to Abram and promised that he would have a child and his descendants would be as numerous as the stars in the night sky, Abram "believed the LORD; and the LORD reckoned it to him as righteousness" (Gen 15:6 NRSV). It would be six chapters and as many as twenty-five years before Abram and his wife, Sarai, gave birth to a son (Gen 21:1-7). And yet Abram believed the Lord; and the Lord reckoned it to him as righteousness.

Joel B. Green and David Teel first invited me to write this book over a cup of coffee in Atlanta in November 2015. In the three years since, David has been a constant encouragement—persistent, yet patient—through multiple delays. Writing this book didn't take anything like twenty-five years. Even so, Joel and especially David believed me when I told them the book was making progress, and while reckoning their faith as righteousness is well above my paygrade, I am nevertheless grateful. Thank you.

Others read parts of or even the whole manuscript and offered helpful suggestions that improved the final product. Here Joel Green deserves special mention (as well as thanks for his wonderful foreword). But I would also like to thank Alan Bradford, Paul Franklyn, Heather Gorman, Jamey Gorman, Shawn Grant, Kevin Harvey, Daniel Overdorf, Sue Stratton, Griffin Swihart, Jon Weatherly, Jeff Wischkaemper, and Katie Wischkaemper. I also benefited from conversations with and suggestions from Mark Nelson, Ken Schenck, Gary Stratton, Travis Williams, Kenny Woodhull, and Mark Ziese. Finally, a number of friends weren't necessarily helpful as I wrote this book, but they made life better during the process: Matthew and Amanda Broaddus, Dave and Becky Eveland, Chris Keith, Anthony Le Donne, Brian and Tricia Leslie, Brandon and Jamie Perry, Sean and Beth Ridge, Chris Skinner, Judy Stack, and Matthew Thiessen. Thank you.

I reserve my deepest and most profound gratitude to a small group of women: my wife, Andrea, and our daughters Janelle, Josephina, and Nam Daosodsai. In this time of knowing Jesus darkly, waiting for the day when we know him face-to-face, the best parts of my life are Andrea's fault. In the autumn of 2004 she said she wanted to have a baby. I didn't have the energy to oppose her, and in 2005 Janelle was born. In the spring of 2007 she said she wanted to adopt a baby. I didn't have the energy to oppose her, and in 2010 we brought Josephina home. In the spring of 2018 she said she wanted to host a foreign exchange student. I didn't have the energy to oppose her, and earlier this month we met Nam, our newest-but-oldest daughter. I didn't ask for any of these blessings, and now I can't imagine my life without all of them. Thank you, Andrea.

PS, Josephina reminds me I neglected one last female in our house. In the spring of 2016 Andrea said she wanted a dog. As always, I didn't have the energy to oppose her, and so we brought home Holly Shih Tzu. Holly didn't help with this book, but she does make life lovelier.

Rafael Rodríguez
August 2018

An Introduction to Memories of Jesus

Then Jesus said to them, "You foolish people! Your dull minds keep you from believing all that the prophets talked about. Wasn't it necessary for the Christ to suffer these things and then enter into his glory?" Then he interpreted for them the things written about himself in all the scriptures, starting with Moses and going through all the Prophets. (Luke 24:25-27)

Cleopas's Folly

The story of two disciples walking to Emmaus (Luke 24:13-35) is my favorite moment in scripture.[1] Luke revels in the irony of Jesus's conversation with Cleopas and an unnamed disciple walking with their backs to Jerusalem. The disciples know what happened to Jesus; indeed, it seems *everyone* in Jerusalem knows what happened to Jesus. The two disciples can't but talk about these events, so when a stranger joins them on the road, he asks what they're talking about. The disciples stop, held fast by their sorrow. Cleopas replies, "Are you the only visitor to Jerusalem who is unaware of the things that have taken place there over the last few days?"

Luke must have been smiling as he explained that Cleopas and his companion were initially prevented from recognizing Jesus. Jesus asks the

---

1. I have written about the Emmaus episode (Luke 24:13-35) in two places; see Rafael Rodríguez, "Textual Orientations: Jesus, Written Texts, and the Social Construction of Identity in the Gospel of Luke," in *T&T Clark Handbook to Social Identity in the New Testament*, ed. Coleman A. Baker and J. Brian Tucker (London: T&T Clark, 2014), 205–8; idem, "'According to the Scriptures': Suffering and the Psalms in the Speeches in Acts," in *Memory and Identity in Ancient Judaism and Early Christianity: A Conversation with Barry Schwartz*, ed. Tom Thatcher, SemeiaSt 78 (Atlanta: SBL Press, 2014), 205–7.

disciples what they're talking about, and Cleopas, ignorant of the one he's addressing, accuses Jesus of a singular ignorance. Cleopas doesn't know what the reader knows, that in fact *Jesus is the only one* in or near Jerusalem who knows "the things that have taken place there over the last few days." But Luke doesn't yet resolve the tension between Cleopas's folly and his accusation against Jesus. Quite the opposite: Luke heightens that tension by having Jesus ask, "What things?" Jesus has just invited Cleopas to fill him in on recent events, but we—the reader—already know that Cleopas himself has no idea what is going on!

The irony is palpable. In verses 19-24, Cleopas explains recent events to Jesus, focusing especially on the women's peculiar report of the empty tomb and angelic vision. This report, Cleopas admits, "left us stunned," and even though "some of those who were with us" went and verified the women's report, Cleopas is left on the verge of acknowledging that, in fact, he has no idea what has actually happened.

At this point Jesus moves to resolve the tension. Although his identity won't be revealed until he breaks bread and distributes it to the disciples in verse 30, he identifies and corrects their ignorance in verses 25-27. Jesus doesn't confirm the women's testimony; neither does he reveal his identity, thereby confirming the truth of the angels' announcement that Jesus is alive. Instead, he chastises the disciples for their failure to understand and believe "all that the prophets talked about" (Luke 24:25). Jesus then redresses this failure by "interpreting for them the things written about himself in all the scriptures, starting with Moses and going through all the Prophets" (Luke 24:27).

This, then, is the point. The disciples know what happened to Jesus: his crucifixion as well as the reports of the empty tomb and the angelic announcement. They misunderstand those events, however, because they are ignorant of Moses and the Prophets. According to Luke, knowing the facts of Jesus's life and teachings ("the events" Luke refers to in the opening of his Gospel; see Luke 1:1) isn't enough to prevent the disciples from being "foolish people" and having "dull minds."

The disciples need the proper framework for understanding those facts. That framework is supplied by Moses and all the Prophets, "the scriptures" that Luke mentions three times in this chapter (see 24:27, 32, 45). Recall that Luke, in the opening verses of his Gospel, refers to "the events that have been fulfilled among us" (1:1). From beginning to end, Luke tells the story of Jesus as the culmination, the climax, or the *resonant theme* of the larger story of Moses and the Prophets, of Israel and her God. These key moments of the gospel—from Jesus's life and teachings to his death and resurrection—resonate with the hopes, promises, and dramatic movements of Israel's biblical traditions. Ideas like *mercy, forgiveness, reconciliation (atonement)*, as well as others that are associated with peculiarly Christian theology, don't contrast with the Christian Old Testament. Instead, these ideas find their truest significance in light of their long trajectory from Abraham, Israel, Moses, and David, and on through Jesus and his followers.

✱ Consensus across the Canon

Luke isn't alone. The authors of the New Testament (hereafter NT) often exhibit different perspectives on a variety of subjects, but on this point they agree: *To understand Jesus rightly means to understand him in relation to Israel's scriptures.* The Hebrew Bible, containing the five books of the Torah, the Prophets, and the Writings and which Christians call the Old Testament, provides the story—the setting, the plot, the characters, the conflict, and the resolution—within which Jesus makes sense.[2] In fact, apart from the story of the Hebrew Bible, Jesus makes little sense (or worse, the *wrong* sense). Jesus himself, of course, is never mentioned in the Hebrew Bible, though the early Christians would quickly find and imagine him throughout its pages, whether as the "offspring" in Genesis 3:15 who will strike the serpent's head, as the exalted but disfigured servant in

---

2. The term *Hebrew Bible* has its problems but is, nevertheless, my preferred term for the Old Testament. For some, the idea of a *New* Testament makes sense primarily in relation to—even in contrast to—an *Old* Testament, though the language of *new testament* (or *new covenant*) predates the ideas of an *Old* or a *New Testament* (see Jer 31:31-37; 1 Cor 11:25; 2 Cor 3:6; Heb 8:8 [quoting Jer 31:31]; 9:15; among the Dead Sea Scrolls, see CD VI, 19; VIII, 21; 1QpHab II, 3). Of course, our New Testament authors primarily cited biblical traditions and texts in Greek, in Septuagintal forms, so those traditions were not "Hebrew" (at least, not in terms of their language). Throughout *Jesus Darkly*, the term *Hebrew Bible* (instead of *Old Testament*) will help us remember that the texts of the Jewish Bible—the Tanakh—defined the concept "scriptural" or "biblical" without being completed or supplanted by other, "new" texts.

Isaiah 52–53, as the "fourth man" in the fiery furnace in Daniel 3:25, and in many, *many* other places.

The authors of the NT unanimously present their various and sundry texts as in some sense related to the stories, traditions, prophecies, and hopes of the Hebrew Bible. The four Gospels, or Paul's letters, or the Catholic Epistles all present themselves as commentary on and the fulfillment of the Hebrew Bible, what rabbinic scholar Martin Jaffee calls "text-interpretive traditions."[3] Some examples:

> In the Gospel of John, Jesus defends himself to "the Jews," who are increasingly antagonized both by Jesus's actions and by his words. He had healed a man on a Sabbath, and some of the Jews were unhappy about this potential violation of Sabbath regulations. At the end of John 5, Jesus drops a bombshell on his interlocutors: "Don't think that I will accuse you before the Father. Your accuser is Moses, the one in whom your hope rests. If you believed Moses, you would believe me, because Moses wrote about me. If you don't believe the writings of Moses, how will you believe my words?" (John 5:45-47).

> In the opening to his most influential letter, the Apostle Paul introduces the broad themes of the gospel he preached throughout Asia Minor, Greece, and Macedonia, and which he hoped to preach also in Rome, with these words: "God's good news, which he promised ahead of time through his prophets in the holy scriptures concerning his son, who was descended from David" (Rom 1:1-3).[4] In light of the very close connection between Paul's gospel and the holy scriptures, no wonder he claimed that his proclamation of faith "confirmed the Law" rather than cancelled it (Rom 3:31)!

---

3. "By the term *text-interpretive tradition* I mean a body of interpretive understandings that arise from multiple performances of a text (written or oral). They come to be so closely associated with public renderings of a text as to constitute its self-evident meaning. As a tradition, the text-interpretive material exists in the memories of both the textual performers and their auditors. The public readers deploy the text selectively in light of their judgment of their audiences' capacities, while audiences supply it in their reception of the reading" (Martin S. Jaffee, *Torah in the Mouth: Writing and Oral Tradition in Palestinian Judaism 200 BCE–400 CE* [Oxford: Oxford University Press, 2001], 9).

4. The CEB translates Romans 1:2-3, "God promised this good news about his Son ahead of time through his prophets in the holy scriptures. His Son was descended from David." The Greek text does say, "God promised this good news…ahead of time," but it does not say the good news is "about his Son." Paul's claim is much more dramatic: the holy scriptures themselves are "about his Son"!

The Gospel of Matthew is famous for, among other things, its frequent notices that this or that event in Jesus's life fulfilled something said by the Lord through one of the prophets.[5] These notices, called "fulfillment quotations," appear across the breadth of Matthew's Gospel; the first occurs in chapter 1 and the last in chapter 27, though half of them occur in Matthew 1–4. In addition to the fulfillment quotations, when Jesus is betrayed by Judas and arrested, Jesus declares twice that these events must take place "so that what the prophets said in the scriptures might be fulfilled" (Matt 26:56; see also v. 54). All of this recalls Jesus's words early in his first extended teaching, the Sermon on the Mount: "Don't even begin to think that I have come to do away with the Law and the Prophets. I haven't come to do away with them but to fulfill them" (Matt 5:17).

In the letters of Revelation 2–3, the exalted Jesus offers promises to "those who emerge victorious" from the seven churches in Asia Minor. Those promises use the language of scripture to communicate the reward for those who remain faithful to the gospel. To the church in Ephesus, Jesus will allow the faithful "to eat from the tree of life, which is in God's paradise" (Rev 2:7; see Gen 3:22, 24).[6] To the church in Pergamum, Jesus will give the faithful "some of the hidden manna to eat" (Rev 2:17; see Num 11). To the church in Thyatira, Jesus promises authority to rule the nations "with an iron rod and smash them like pottery" (Rev 2:27; see Ps 2:8-9). In fact, each of the promises to the seven churches resonates with biblical themes and imagery, though these three use the language of scripture most overtly. For the author of Revelation, scripture defines what it means to be faithful to Jesus and to be recognized as such by him.

The anonymous author of Hebrews, who repeatedly contrasts Jesus with the figures and events of Israel's scriptures, nevertheless turns to the scriptures in order to describe Jesus. For example, in his description of Jesus the high priest, the author turns to the mysterious Melchizedek, mentioned in Genesis 14 and Psalm 110, to justify a Judahite (instead of Levitical) priesthood (Heb 7:11-17). Similarly, he briefly describes the tabernacle and its system of sacrifices (Heb 9:1-10) in order to provide his readers with the necessary perspective for understanding Christ,

---

5. See our discussion of "fulfillment formula" in chapter 2.

6. The Greek word *paradeisos* means "garden" or "orchard" and is used in the Septuagint (LXX), the Greek translation of the Hebrew Bible, to refer to the garden of Eden (Gen 2:8, and throughout Gen 2–3).

who "entered the holy of holies once for all by his own blood, not by the blood of goats or calves, securing our deliverance for all time" (Heb 9:11-28; v. 12 quoted). Even Hebrews, which is interested in *contrasting* Jesus with his biblical antecedents, cannot but portray Jesus using biblical terms and imagery.

These examples—drawn from Luke, John, Paul (Romans), Matthew, Revelation, and Hebrews—demonstrate that the writers of the NT, for all their differences, agree that *understanding Jesus rightly means understanding him in relation to Israel's scriptures.* The church would eventually develop language and imagery for talking about Jesus apart from the Hebrew Bible. But in the NT, our writers—*all of them!*—turn to Israel's scriptures to interpret, explain, and proclaim Jesus. Therefore, if we have any hope of understanding Jesus as the NT authors understood him, we must pay special attention to the ways they drew upon the narratives, prophecies, and theology of the Hebrew Bible in order to perceive and talk about Jesus. As we trace the memory of Jesus across the NT canon, we will pay special attention to the connections between that memory and the narratives, prophecies, and promises of Israel's scriptures.

The Story of Scripture: A Basic Sketch

I was raised to think of Jesus as the solution to the problem of my sin. I was—and still am—a sinner, and sin was a problem I was ill equipped to handle on my own. In fact, every person is a sinner (here I'm supposed to invoke the Apostle Paul: Rom 3:23), a condition or status we all have in common with the first person, Adam (again, Paul: Rom 5:12-17). Jesus came to solve the problem of my sin (here I could invoke the second Gospel: Mark 10:45), both by living a sinless life and then, in obedience to the will of his Father, by dying on a cross as the finally efficacious sacrifice that would atone for my sin and reconcile me with God.

I still believe all of this. However, I no longer think this is the most helpful way of explaining either the problem of sin or Jesus as the solution for that problem. Surprisingly, "sinners in need of forgiveness" may not be the most useful lens for understanding "the human condition." Perhaps the

---

most fundamental problem with this lens is that it focuses our gaze at the wrong place. Genesis 3 tells the story of the inaugural sin, through which the first Man and Woman realize their nakedness, experience shame, and hide from the One they have disobeyed. But Genesis 3 isn't the beginning of the story, and sin isn't the essence of humanity. What we need, then, is a wider lens to help us see the story the Bible *actually* tells.

To better appreciate the Bible's story, let's consider it as a drama, a play in multiple acts in which later scenes develop and advance the plot of earlier scenes. No one would expect to understand the second half of a play without first having followed the action of the first half. In the same way, we should not expect to understand rightly the NT apart from the story of the Hebrew Bible.[7] We can represent the Bible's full story in six scenes:[8]

Scene 1: God Establishes the Kingdom: Creation

Scene 2: Rebellion in the Kingdom: Fall

Scene 3: The King Chooses Israel: Redemption Initiated

Scene 4: The Coming of the King: Redemption Accomplished

Scene 5: Spreading the News of the King: The Mission of the Church

Scene 6: The Return of the King: Redemption Completed

These scenes don't correlate to particular parts of the Bible. Instead, they suggest different ideas found throughout the Bible. For example, Scene 2 ("Fall") is narrated most obviously in Genesis 3, but we also find it in the stories of the Flood, of Israel's repeated violations of the covenant, and of divisions or failures in the church. Scene 5 ("The Mission of the Church") is most clearly the subject of the Acts of the Apostles, but we

---

7. The "scripture-as-drama" metaphor is found, for example, in N. T. Wright, *The New Testament and the People of God, Christian Origins and the Question of God 1* (Minneapolis: Fortress, 1992), 140; see also Craig G. Bartholomew and Michael W. Goheen, *The Drama of Scripture: Finding Our Place in the Biblical Story* (Grand Rapids: Baker Academic, 2004).

8. I am following Bartholomew and Goheen, *Drama of Scripture*, who also include an "Interlude: A Kingdom Story Waiting for an Ending: The Intertestamental Period" (see pp. 113–27).

see it also in the letters and other texts written by Jesus's earliest followers. And so on. When we read the Bible, we don't move through these six scenes in sequence. Instead, we move between them, back and forth between the poles of brokenness and wholeness, awaiting a time when God will bring an end to the back-and-forth and complete the work of redemption.

The rest of this introduction will sketch the main plotlines of Scenes 1–3 through the Hebrew Bible. In the following chapters, we will take up the ideas of "Redemption Accomplished," "The Mission of the Church," and "Redemption Completed," but we will not narrate them in sequence. In other words, don't expect (for example) Scene 4 to correlate with the Gospels, Scene 5 with Acts and the epistles, or Scene 6 with Revelation. As we said above, these ideas are intertwined throughout the NT texts. Throughout *Jesus Darkly*, we will see that understanding the narratives and images and rhetoric of the NT requires us to read those narratives, images, and rhetoric as part of an overarching plotline spanning the creation of the world, the fall of humanity, and the covenants with Israel.

Before we turn to our sketch of the Bible's drama, let's consider two related ideas that serve, individually and together, as helpful metonyms for the Bible's story of redemption and reconciliation. According to Craig Bartholomew and Michael Goheen, "'covenant' (in the Old Testament) and 'the kingdom of God' (in the NT) present a strong claim to be the main door through which we can begin to enter the Bible and to see it as one whole and vast structure."[9] I like this for two reasons. First, both "covenant" and "the kingdom of God" are helpful lenses through which to read the whole biblical story, more helpful than, say, "sin" or "judgment" or "how to get into heaven" or some other lenses. Second, "covenant" and "kingdom of God" are related concepts, two sides of a single coin,[10] nearly (but not quite) synonymous. At the heart of Scene 3 is a promise repeated throughout scripture: "I'll take you as my people, and I'll be your God"

---

9. Bartholomew and Goheen, *Drama of Scripture*, 24.

10. Bartholomew and Goheen use exactly this phrase: "covenant and kingdom are like two sides of the same coin, evoking the same reality in slightly different ways" (Bartholomew and Goheen, *Drama of Scripture*, 24).

(Exod 6:7).[11] This reciprocating idea—YHWH as the God of Israel; Israel as the people of God—is at the heart of the biblical covenants, whether the covenant between God and Abraham (Gen 17:7), between God and Israel (Lev 26:12), or the Jeremian promise of a new covenant (Jer 31:33). This is the covenant of God. We will see in the following chapters (esp. chapter 2) that the "kingdom of God" refers to the sphere in which this covenant has been fulfilled.

Scene 1: God Establishes the Kingdom: Creation

Even before they sin and experience death, the first Man and Woman are *created in the image of God*. This is the most important and fundamental thing to say about human beings. Before we are sinners, we are created in the image of God.[12] The Man and the Woman, as primordial or paradigmatic human beings, were set in the midst of creation as the image of the living God, in the same way that temples of other gods featured images of their lifeless deities. And they were given a job: fill creation with life and tend to what God has made. "Be fertile and multiply; fill the earth and master it. Take charge of the fish of the sea, the birds in the sky, and everything crawling on the ground" (Gen 1:28). Humanity's defining feature is its relationship with the creator God, not its experience of rebellion from God.

Even when the God who creates is moved to bring divine creation to the brink of destruction (because of humanity's unrelenting sinfulness, brokenness, and evil), God relents, preserving a male/female pair of every living species and four pairs of humans.[13] Just as important, however, is God's renewed commandment for humanity after Noah to "be fertile, multiply, and fill the earth. All of the animals on the earth will fear

---

11. See also Lev 26:12; Jer 7:23; 11:4; 30:22; 31:33; 32:38; Ezek 11:20; 14:11; 36:28; 37:23, 27; Zech 8:8. The same idea appears in the New Testament; e.g., 2 Cor 6:16; Heb 8:10; Rev 21:3, 7.

12. This sequence is easily overlooked. For example, "Strange as it may seem, the history of the human race begins with the sin of our first parents and their expulsion from the Garden of Eden" (Walter C. Kaiser Jr., *The Messiah in the Old Testament*, Studies in Old Testament Biblical Theology [Grand Rapids: Zondervan, 1995], 38). This reading of the human story is incomplete because it begins in the wrong place.

13. But see Genesis 7:2-3, where Noah is instructed to take seven pairs of every kind of clean animal and of every kind of bird, and one pair of every kind of unclean animal.

you and dread you—all the birds in the skies, everything crawling on the ground, and all of the sea's fish. They are in your power. . . . As for you, be fertile and multiply. Populate the earth and multiply in it" (Gen 9:1-2, 7). God's covenantal command outlives and outlasts the exercise of his wrath against sin. Rebellion, of course, comes early in humanity's story and affects all of its later chapters. But this rebellion isn't the story's opening chapter. It isn't even the second chapter. Sin and the serpent enter a story well underway, a story already defined in terms of face-to-face fellowship, peace, order, and right relationships. A story of wholeness, of peace, of *shalom*. A story that is good, even supremely good (Gen 1:4, 10, 12, 18, 21, 25, 31).

Despite occupying only two chapters, Scene 1 performs a crucial function: it provides the setting in which the rest of the Bible's story will take place, "When God began to create the heavens and the earth" (Gen 1:1). As setting for the drama, Genesis 1–2 "provide the conditions—the possibilities and the limitations—within which the characters chart their destinies."[14] The Bible's story is set within creation, not outside or beyond it. As Bartholomew and Goheen explain: "The Bible depicts this created, material world as the very theater of God's glory. . . . Like an orchestra, it produces a symphony of praise to the Creator."[15]

Christians have an unfortunate tendency to anchor the story of God somewhere else: in "heaven." I can understand why. The night before his arrest and crucifixion, Jesus prepares his disciples for his departure, saying: "My Father's house has room to spare. If that weren't the case, would I have told you that I'm going to prepare a place for you? When I go to prepare a place for you, I will return and take you to be with me so that where I am you will be too" (John 14:2-3). It certainly sounds as though Jesus is going somewhere else, like he expects the disciples to join him *there* rather than wait for him *here*. When Paul anticipates Jesus's return and says, "we who are living and still around will be taken up together with them in the clouds to meet with the Lord in the air. That way we will always be with the Lord" (1 Thess 4:17), it's natural for Christians to

14. David Rhoads, Joanna Dewey, and Donald Michie, *Mark as Story: An Introduction to the Narrative of a Gospel*, 3rd ed. (Minneapolis: Fortress, 2012), 63.

15. Bartholomew and Goheen, *Drama of Scripture*, 39.

picture God's kingdom as an otherworldly place, a place somewhere else, a place no longer contained or contaminated by this broken world.

It's natural, but it's also mistaken. From beginning to end, salvation is a matter of the body and the world in addition to the spirit and the soul. Remember John 14, where Jesus announced that he was going and preparing a place for his disciples? Just a few verses later Jesus clarifies that the home he and his Father share with his friends isn't somewhere else but is here, in the world: "Whoever loves me will keep my word. My Father will love them, and *we will come to them and make our home with them*" (John 14:23, emphasis added). In the same way, Paul anticipates that creation will be "set free from slavery to decay"—not destroyed!—when God's family is finally revealed (Rom 8:18-25). Even in 1 Thessalonians 4, which has led some Christians to suppose that God's people would be raptured away from earth and taken to heaven, Paul imagines not humanity's abandonment of creation but Jesus's return to and renewal of the earth. "Paul does *not* say that at Jesus' *Parousia* his people will be taken up into heaven to live with him there.... The point of Jesus coming 'from' heaven is that he will change both this old world and our present bodies."[16] Even that most otherworldly of NT texts, the Revelation of John, looks forward to "a new heaven and a new earth" and a day when "God's dwelling is *here with humankind*" (Rev 21:1, 3, emphasis added), rather than a snatching away of God's people from this world to somewhere else.[17]

So the story of God takes place in and is inextricably tied to *this* world, which God created and which is only and repeatedly good. As the story's setting, creation will experience real degradation and conflict (see the next section). It will, in Paul's words, be "subjected to frustration" (Rom 8:20). But the hope of redemption is not, ultimately, a hope for freedom *from* the world God created but rather freedom *for* that world. And as the image of God in the world, our future and our fate are inseparably intertwined

---

16. N. T. Wright, *Paul: In Fresh Perspective* (Minneapolis: Fortress, 2005), 141–45 (p. 143 quoted).

17. The Greek text of Revelation 21:3 does not contain the word *here* (*hōde*). Nevertheless, the text clearly says "God's dwelling is *with humankind*" (*meta tōn anthrōpōn*) rather than that the dwelling of humankind is with God. While John goes up into heaven to see God's throne (Rev 4:1-2), the New Jerusalem descends to earth from God, which explains why the prayer in Revelation 22 is "Come!" (22:17, 20).

with the future and fate of the world around us. The story of the world is a good story, one of wholeness, of peace, of *shalom*.

Scene 2: Rebellion in the Kingdom: Fall

Earlier I suggested that "sinners in need of forgiveness" isn't the best way of summarizing the story of the whole Bible. Don't misunderstand this observation. The Bible tells many stories that are variations of "sinners in need of forgiveness." When the prophet Isaiah is granted a glimpse into the throne room of God, he cries out, "Mourn for me; I'm ruined! I'm a man with unclean lips, and I live among a people with unclean lips. Yet I've seen the king, the LORD of heavenly forces!" (Isa 6:5). Isaiah's reaction is similar to Peter's (who was also called Simon, or sometimes Simon Peter), when Jesus told him to drop his nets into deeper water:

> Simon replied, "Master, we've worked hard all night and caught nothing. But because you say so, I'll drop the nets." So they dropped the nets and their catch was so huge that their nets were splitting. They signaled for their partners in the other boat to come and help them. They filled both boats so full that they were about to sink. When Simon Peter saw the catch, he fell at Jesus' knees and said, "Leave me, Lord, for I'm a sinner!" (Luke 5:5-8)

If Isaiah and Peter were sinners, Paul was remembered as worse than both: "This saying is reliable and deserves full acceptance: 'Christ Jesus came into the world to save sinners'—and I'm the biggest sinner of all" (1 Tim 1:15). "Sinners in need of forgiveness" is *a* story the Bible tells, even if it isn't the Bible's *central* story. "Sin" (including the story of the fall) is a concept easily misheard, especially when we let it define the Bible's larger drama. For our purposes in understanding Jesus, I will refer to "brokenness" in order to sidestep problems with the way some of us experience the word *sin*.

In the Bible's good story of a world wrought by God's creative power, creation does indeed experience brokenness. In the midst of God's abundant provision of all that life requires, the Man and the Woman disregard God's voice and heed the serpent's instead. In the middle of the garden, God grew two trees: one of life and one of the knowledge of good and evil. God offered the Man to eat from every tree but one, saying, "Eat your fill from all of the garden's trees; but don't eat from the tree of the knowledge of good and evil, because on the day you eat from it, you will die!" (Gen 2:16-17). The instructions seem simple enough. Apparently, they were not.

In Genesis 3, the serpent promises the Woman that, despite God's warning of death, eating from this tree will open their eyes, and they will know good and evil (Gen 3:5). Until now, Genesis has only and repeatedly declared creation as "good." The Man and the Woman, as the "supremely good" image of God in the midst of God's "good" creation, already know what is good. They have not yet, however, experienced evil. The only reference to evil so far has been in "the tree of the knowledge of good and evil." The serpent's promise to open their eyes, then, is only an offer to introduce the Man and the Woman to evil. When they eat the fruit of the tree their eyes are, indeed, opened, and they perceive their own nakedness. Aware of themselves for the first time, they hide from each other by making garments out of fig leaves, and later they hide from the God whose image they are. When God comes looking for the Man and the Woman and discovers what they've done, he expels them from the garden, the place of God's presence. Creation was good, even supremely good, but now the Man and the Woman know good *and evil*, and they—like their knowledge—can no longer be contained by or within God's good garden.

We then quickly read of the first murder (Gen 4:1-8). The story of Cain killing his brother Abel is told as a tragedy, in which Cain is punished for his actions and cries out to the LORD for mercy (Gen 4:9-16). A few verses later, however, we read of another murder, this time without any sense of tragedy or remorse: "I killed a man for wounding me, a boy for striking me," says Lamech, the great-grandson of Adam's great-grandson (see Gen 4:23-25). In merely seven narrative generations we've plummeted from "very good" to tragic murder to boasting of murder.

The fall is steep indeed, and within a few chapters the story takes a heart-rending turn: "The LORD regretted making human beings on the earth, and he was heartbroken" (Gen 6:6). Even after the destruction of nearly all life with the Flood (Gen 6–9), humanity—remember, the image of God on earth!—continues its efforts to assume the place of God in the order of creation. By Genesis 11, God has scattered humanity across the globe and divided them into disparate language groups.

Genesis 1–11 tells a dramatic story of reversal, from God's good creation secure in his garden to a wicked and self-centered humanity who are bound to experience death. Note the following contrasts:

> In Genesis 2, the LORD God breathes the breath of life into the Man he formed from the dirt (2:7), but in Genesis 6 he exclaims, "My breath will not remain in humans forever, because they are flesh" (6:3). The former gives the breath of life to the Man; the latter warns that that breath will not last forever.

> In Genesis 2, the LORD God plants a garden and places the Man in it, to work it and fill it with life (2:8, 15-25), but in Genesis 11 he scatters humanity "over all the earth" (11:9). The former roots the Man in the garden that is characterized by the presence of God; the latter scatters humanity away from the place of God's presence.

This is the Bible's Scene 2, which introduces conflict into the paradise of Scene 1. This conflict levels a fundamental threat against God's good creation, and this threat quickly unravels the fabric of creation and results in humanity turning away from God and turning against one another. "Conflict analysis names the overall goal in the narrative and then identifies the forces that help or hinder that goal."[18] Our analysis of the Bible's central conflict—that between God's good intention for his creation and the tragedy of brokenness in creation—will highlight the plot's movement toward reconciliation, restoration, and renewal rather than the threat of judgment, punishment, and destruction. This isn't a random or haphazard decision. "Conflict reveals the core values and beliefs of a narrative,"[19] and the Bible's core values and beliefs cluster around renewal rather than destruction. One purpose of the rest of this book is to substantiate this basic claim.

---

18. Rhoads, Dewey, and Michie, *Mark as Story*, 77.

19. Rhoads, Dewey, and Michie, *Mark as Story*, 77.

Scene 3: The King Chooses Israel: Redemption Initiated

If Scene 2 introduces the significant conflict that drives the story forward, Scene 3 presents the story's main action. "Here the initial conflict intensifies and grows ever more complicated."[20] The intensification of the biblical story's conflict begins when God calls a single man and his family and initiates the redemptive plan that will climax in the story of Jesus.

> The LORD said to Abram, "Leave your land, your family, and your father's household for the land that I will show you. I will make of you a great nation and will bless you. I will make your name respected, and you will be a blessing. I will bless those who bless you, those who curse you I will curse; all the families of the earth will be blessed because of you." (Gen 12:1-3)

The movement in this story is intriguing. After the Man and the Woman rebelled and introduced death into God's good creation, God expelled them from the garden and sent them away: "the LORD God *sent him out* of the garden of Eden to farm the fertile land from which he was taken" (Gen 3:23, emphasis added). Just in case that wasn't clear, the text immediately adds, "He *drove out* the human" (3:24, emphasis added). The story of brokenness begins with movement *away* from God. A few chapters later, the direction reverses from "away" to "toward": God calls Abram from his father's house and *toward* the place where he will experience the blessing of God (Gen 12:1-2). The story of restoration begins with movement *toward* the land God promises to show Abram.[21]

Abraham—God changes Abram's name to Abraham in Genesis 17—and his family are rather imperfect characters in the story of restoration. Abraham lies about his relationship to his wife, Sarah. Sarah gives Abraham her servant-girl, Hagar, to produce an heir, and then jealously banishes the girl and her son. Abraham's son, Isaac, also lies about his wife.

---

20. Bartholomew and Goheen, *Drama of Scripture*, 26.

21. The repeated use of the word *bless* in Genesis 12:1-3 is another link with Genesis 1–11: "The fivefold repetition of the word 'bless' is deliberately set in opposition to the fivefold occurrence of the word 'curse' in Genesis 1–11.…The repetition of 'bless' in Genesis 12:1–3 declares that through Abraham, God is at work to reverse the effect of judgment on his creation. Though sin has brought God's curse on creation, God is still at work to recover his purpose of blessing for all that he has made" (Bartholomew and Goheen, *Drama of Scripture*, 55). See also Wright, *New Testament*, 262–63.

Abraham's grandson has such a shaky relationship with integrity that his name means "cheat" (Gen 27:36). The fruit doesn't get any more appealing as you climb further down Abraham's family tree. Brothers sell brother into slavery. The people, discontent to be ruled by God, clamor for a king. One king takes a married woman as his own and conspires to have her husband killed in battle. Another marries a pagan woman and condones the murder of God's prophets. And so on. Abraham's family is no better than many of our own families. It may even be worse.

There is, however, one key difference. God decided that Abraham's family would be the vehicle of redemption and restoration, that Abraham's descendants would be the elect—or *chosen*—people of God, and that through Abraham's family "all the families of the earth will be blessed" (Gen 12:3). Whatever else Abraham's family is, it is God's chosen means for pouring out his blessing on humanity and the rest of creation.

This brings us back to *covenant*.[22] The relationship between Abraham and God is *covenantal*, that is, it establishes a familial relationship—or what Scott Hahn calls "a sacred kinship bond"[23]—between God and his people, not unlike how a marriage covenant establishes a relationship between a woman and a man. Like marriage, a covenant isn't simply an exchange of obligations, in which Party A promises to do X if/as long as Party B does Y. As Frank Moore Cross explains, covenant is "a widespread legal means by which the duties and privileges of kinship may be extended to another individual or group, including aliens."[24] The phrase "duties and privileges of kinship" aptly describes the relationship between Abraham's descendants and God. Notice that God calls Israel "my oldest son" (Ex 4:22), and the prophet Hosea expands on this relationship in a famous passage that begins, "When Israel was a child, I loved him, and out of Egypt I called my son" (Hos 11:1).[25] As God promises to provide

---

22. See Wright, *New Testament*, 260–62.

23. Scott Hahn, "Covenant," *The Lexham Bible Dictionary* (Bellingham, WA: Lexham Press, 2016).

24. Frank Moore Cross, *From Epic to Canon: History and Literature in Ancient Israel* (Baltimore: Johns Hopkins University Press, 1998), 8; cited in Hahn, "Covenant."

25. Famously, Matthew quotes this passage from Hosea as he forges links between Israel and Jesus; see Matt 2:13-15.

Abraham with children of his own, he also promises that Abraham and his descendants will be children to God.

The promise of many descendants may not be obvious in Genesis 12, where God says to Abraham, "I will make of you a great nation." Does making a great nation of someone involve the provision of offspring? Abraham apparently wondered the same thing, because he complains to God three chapters later: "'LORD God, what can you possibly give me, since I still have no children? The head of my household is Eliezer, a man from Damascus.' He continued, 'Since you haven't given me any children, the head of my household will be my heir'" (Gen 15:2-3). The context of Abraham's complaint is quite interesting. In Genesis 14, Abraham waged war against four kings who had kidnapped his nephew, Lot, and afterward was blessed by Melchizedek, the king of Salem and priest of God. Immediately after the encounter with Melchizedek, God says to Abraham, "Don't be afraid, Abram. I am your protector. Your reward will be very great" (Gen 15:1). Abraham's complaint, which I quoted above, is a response to God's offer of relationship ("I am your protector") and great reward.

I wouldn't have expected Abraham to react to a promise of relationship and reward in this way.

How can we make sense of Abraham's reply to God? Remember that God promised to make a great nation of Abraham, but it looks like his servant, Eliezer, will be the de facto father of the family. Apparently, Abraham valued the promise of progeny above God's other promises (land, blessing, protection, reward). What good is it, Abraham asks, to be reckoned a son of God if there is no grandson?

And so God repeats and clarifies his promise. "'This man will not be your heir. Your heir will definitely be your very own biological child.' Then he brought Abram outside and said, 'Look up at the sky and count the stars if you think you can count them.' He continued, 'This is how many children you will have'" (Gen 15:4-5). The covenant promise creates a kinship bond between God and Abraham; it also creates a kinship bond between Abraham and what will be, God promises, a great nation. In Genesis 15:6, Abraham accepts God's promise (the CEB translates this verse, "Abram trusted the LORD"), and God considers (or "reckons") that act of acceptance as a righteous response. That is, whatever else Abraham does—both the good and the bad—he has trusted God, and his covenant relationship with God is secure simply on the basis of that trust.

There isn't space to discuss the history of the covenant here, either in the five books of Moses or throughout the rest of the Hebrew Bible.[26] But we can quickly summarize the rest of the story. Abraham's promised "great nation" (recall Gen 12:2) eventually find themselves living as slaves in *the* great nation of the ancient world: Egypt. The people cry out to God, and God raises up for them a deliverer, Moses, who spearheads a showdown between YHWH and the Egyptian pharaoh, eventually leading the people out of Egypt and into the wilderness. As the people encamp in the Sinai desert at the base of a mountain, God enacts a covenant with the people, a covenant that reaffirms the relationship between YHWH and Abraham's descendants.

> Moses went up to God. The LORD called to him from the mountain, "This is what you should say to Jacob's household and declare to the Israelites: You saw what I did to the Egyptians, and how I lifted you up on eagles' wings and brought you to me. So now, if you faithfully obey me and stay true to my covenant, you will be my most precious possession out of all the peoples, since the whole earth belongs to me. You will be a kingdom of priests for me and a holy nation. These are the words you should say to the Israelites." (Exod 19:3-6)[27]

This passage is the paradigmatic expression of Israel's election, of Israel's having been *chosen* as the unique, peculiar people of God (= "my most precious possession out of all the peoples"). Note especially that this statement comes *before* any commandment or law is placed upon the people. Israel is the beneficiary of a divine act of grace and mercy. "The deeply relational nature of God's saving activity is beautifully captured in the phrase 'brought you to myself.' God's intention is to have a people

---

26. David Clines offers a helpful proposal: "The theme of the Pentateuch is the partial fulfilment—which implies also the partial non-fulfilment—of the promise to or blessing of the patriarchs. The promise or blessing is both the divine initiative in a world where human initiatives always lead to disaster, and are an affirmation of the primal divine intentions for humanity" (David J. A. Clines, *The Theme of the Pentateuch*, 2nd ed., JSOTSup 10 [Sheffield: Sheffield Academic Press, 1997], 30; original in italics).

27. We will discuss Exodus 19:4-6 in more detail when we get to 1 Peter (chapter 4).

with whom he is in relationship."[28] There is no hint here of having to earn or merit God's blessing; there is only the expectation that the people will respond to that blessing with faithful obedience and staying true to the covenant. This idea will recur in the next chapter of Exodus, at the start of the Ten Commandments: Before the people are told what they must or must not do, they are reminded of what God has already done: "Then God spoke all these words: I am the Lord your God who brought you out of Egypt, out of the house of slavery. You must have no other gods before me..." (Exod 20:1-21; vv. 1-3 quoted). Notice, then, that the Ten Commandments are not a list of rules to be followed (though God certainly demands obedience to them from his people). "The Ten Commandments are good news"; they are "keys to living fully human lives," not "horrible constraints to make life difficult."[29]

Perhaps the truest thing to recognize about "the Law"—that thing that Christian readers often chastise Jews for over-prizing—is that it embodies yhwh's offer of life to Abraham's descendants. As the people camp on the edge of the promised land, poised to cross the Jordan and take hold of what God offered their illustrious grandfather, Abraham, Moses summarizes the people's obligation under the Law:

> Look here! Today I've set before you life and what's good versus death and what's wrong. If you obey the Lord your God's commandments that I'm commanding you right now by loving the Lord your God, by walking in his ways, and by keeping his commandments, his regulations, and his case laws, then you will live and thrive, and the Lord your God will bless you in the land you are entering to possess. But if your heart turns away and you refuse to listen, and so are misled, worshipping other gods and serving them, I'm telling you right now that you will definitely die. (Deut 30:15-18)

We miss the point if we read the Law as God's instructions for how to earn, merit, or achieve the promise of life. The point, rather, is that God

---

28. Bartholomew and Goheen, *Drama of Scripture*, 64.

29. Bartholomew and Goheen, *Drama of Scripture*, 69. N. T. Wright describes the Torah as "the way of life by which [Abraham's descendants] should express their answering fidelity to him" (i.e., to God; Wright, *New Testament*, 261).

has already given life to Israel, and he calls his people to live out that life in faithful obedience to the terms God lays out in the covenant. Not "horrible constraints" but rather "keys to living fully human lives."[30]

Looking ahead to Scenes 4–6

Other covenantal moments are worth exploring in the Hebrew Bible, but we must leave behind Scenes 1–3 (the story of the Hebrew Bible) and move on to Scenes 4–6 (the story of the NT).[31] We will have occasion in the chapters that remain to return in some detail to these earlier scenes. As I mentioned at the start of this introduction, the consensus across the NT canon is that we can understand neither Scenes 1–3 nor Scenes 4–6 except in relation to each other. The Hebrew Bible—or the Old Testament—and the NT are inextricably related to each other, and their relationship isn't one of contrast or contradiction. If the point of this book is to remember Jesus with the NT, the goal of this introduction is to hammer home the claim that the memory of Jesus in the NT is embedded already in Israel's scriptures. As we will see, Israel's scriptures are also, simultaneously, embedded in the memory of Jesus.

---

30. Bartholomew and Goheen, *Drama of Scripture*, 69.

31. Of course, the whole point of referring to "Scenes 1–3" and "Scenes 4–6" is to stress that the Hebrew Bible and the New Testament are not two different stories but rather two parts of one larger story, the story of God putting his family back together.

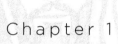

Chapter 1

Introducing Jesus, the Christ: Paul as Memorial Entrepreneur

The closest thing we have to a surviving author who was an eyewitness to the life of Jesus is the Apostle Paul, who, before engaging in his missionary work, met two of the apostles.... Still, one of the most striking features of Paul's surviving letters is just how little he actually tells us about Jesus's life prior to his death.[1]

"Thinking with" Jesus

I was born in the aftermath of the Watergate scandal, on the seventy-eighth day of Jimmy Carter's presidency. Five years earlier, on Saturday, June 17, 1972, my mother was not yet fifteen when five men were arrested attempting to fix a malfunctioning wiretap at the Democratic National Committee headquarters in the Watergate Hotel.[2] Watergate exerted a weight on American culture that may explain some features of my early experiences, for example why one popular sitcom from my childhood featured Alex Keaton, a Young Republican who toted a lunchbox with

---

1. Bart D. Ehrman, *Jesus before the Gospels: How the Earliest Christians Remembered, Changed, and Invented Their Stories of the Savior* (New York: HarperOne, 2016), 102, 103.

2. See the chronicle of events in Michael Schudson, *Watergate in American Memory: How We Remember, Forget, and Reconstruct the Past* (New York: Basic Books, 1992), 16–20.

Richard Nixon's likeness, and why so many political scandals during my lifetime tend to be known as This-or-That-Gate.

Watergate—and especially the memory of Watergate in late-twentieth-century American political discourse—offers an interesting way to think about Paul as Jesus's "memorial entrepreneur." On the twentieth anniversary of the Watergate break-in, Michael Schudson noted: "While Watergate may be a significant factor when people think back on their formative political experiences, it has regularly seemed to commentators all but invisible in daily American life."[3] Those two descriptors—"significant factor" and "all but invisible"—seem incompatible. But there they are, side-by-side in a relatively bland statement whose accuracy can hardly be challenged. Yes, Watergate shook American political institutions to the core, such that, as 1973 and the first half of 1974 unfolded, the future of American constitutional government seemed increasingly imperiled. But no, it has not had any lasting or fundamental effect on the American political institutions it threatened.[4]

The parallel, with Watergate and American politics on one hand and Jesus and Paul on the other intrigues me. It would be foolish to suggest that Jesus is "all but invisible" in Paul's letters. If anything, Jesus is conspicuously visible in Paul's writings. Paul uses Jesus's name, *Iēsous*, 213 times in the thirteen letters that bear his name. If we ignore the six letters whose authenticity Pauline scholars question,[5] that number drops to 142, which is still quite significant.[6] Not surprisingly, he uses the word *Christos* ("anointed one, Christ") even more often.[7]

---

3. Schudson, *Watergate in American Memory*, 13.

4. See Schudson, *Watergate in American Memory*, 10–14.

5. Of the thirteen letters that bear Paul's name, seven are universally accepted as authentic letters written by Paul (viz., Romans, 1–2 Corinthians, Galatians, Philippians, 1 Thessalonians, and Philemon). The other six letters, which are collectively referred to as the "deutero-Pauline" or "disputed Pauline" letters (viz., Ephesians, Colossians, 2 Thessalonians, 1–2 Timothy, and Titus), are variously suspected of having been written after Paul's death, perhaps by some of his disciples. Paul didn't write Hebrews; neither does Hebrews claim to have been written by Paul.

6. For example, Paul uses the word *Iēsous* at least once in every chapter of Galatians, Philippians, and 1 Thessalonians; at least once in every chapter of Romans except chapters 9, 11, and 12; and at least once in every chapter of 1 Corinthians except chapters 7, 10, 13, and 14. Paul does not use *Iēsous* in eight of 2 Corinthians' thirteen chapters (2 Cor 2, 3, 5, 6, 7, 9, 10, and 12); even so, he still uses *Iēsous* nineteen times in this letter. These patterns are not by themselves meaningful, but they nevertheless support my claim that Paul's use of the word *Iēsous* is significant.

7. The thirteen Pauline letters use *Christos* 382 times; the seven undisputed Pauline letters use *Christos* 269 times.

Even with all these references *to* Jesus, Paul is famously silent *about* Jesus. Very little of Jesus's teaching appears in Paul's letters, and when Paul does include something that sounds like Jesus's teaching, he doesn't usually bother to tell the reader, "Hey, this comes from Jesus." For example, when Paul instructs his readers in Rome, "Bless people who harass you—bless and don't curse them" (Rom 12:14), his words remind us of Jesus's teaching in Matthew's Sermon on the Mount and Luke's Sermon on the Plain:[8]

Matthew 5:44	Romans 12:14	Luke 6:27-28
But I say to you, love your enemies and pray for those **who harass you**.	Bless people **who harass you**—bless and don't <u>curse</u> them.	But I say to you who are willing to hear: Love your enemies. Do good to those who hate you. <u>Bless those who curse you</u>. Pray for those who mistreat you.

Despite the similarities between Paul's instruction in Romans and Jesus's in Matthew and Luke, nowhere does Paul give any hint that he's passing along teachings of Jesus. In fact, Romans 12 is one of those rare chapters where Paul doesn't mention Jesus's name,[9] even though echoes of Jesus's teaching are especially resonant in this chapter.[10] In other words, here in Romans 12, where it might have been easiest for Paul to point out for his readers that Jesus stands behind and authorizes his moral instructions, he doesn't. If Jesus is there, he is invisible, all but forgotten as the source of the profoundly difficult instruction, "Bless people who harass you—bless and don't curse them" (Rom 12:14).

---

8. I have put verbal similarities between Romans and Matthew (in Greek) in **bold typeface** and <u>underlined</u> similarities between Romans and Luke. Though both Paul and Luke use forms of the word *curse* (*kataraomai*), they do so in very different ways. We might also note that Matthew and Luke share words that Paul does not include, even though some of these would have been appropriate for Romans 12 (e.g., Matthew's and Luke's commands to love, their references to enemies, and their commands also to pray).

9. Paul does use *Christos* once, in Romans 12:5.

10. See Eric K. C. Wong, "The De-Radicalization of Jesus' Ethical Sayings in Romans," *NovT* 43 (2001): 245–63 (esp. pp. 247–55), though Wong severely over-interprets the Gospel texts and Romans in his desire to contrast Jesus and Paul. For a more balanced discussion, see Michael B. Thompson, *Clothed with Christ: The Example and Teaching of Jesus in Romans 12.1–15.13*, JSNTSup 59 (Sheffield: Sheffield Academic Press, 1991), 90–110.

Let's return to Watergate. Michael Schudson notes the deplorable state of Americans' knowledge of the details of the Watergate scandal and the resignation of the thirty-seventh president of the United States.[11] In the twenty-five years since Schudson's book, that knowledge has only further degraded. Watergate is a public event, and it offers "tools…for a society's thinking out loud about itself, not only at the time but in retrospect."[12] As a public event, Watergate is arguably a foundational component of American political memory. Even if the majority of Americans today can't remember when the Watergate burglars were arrested (17 June 1972), when Nixon resigned from office (8 August 1974),[13] or what, precisely, led to his resignation, they do understand comparisons of contemporary events to Watergate via the "-gate" suffix (e.g., "Bridgegate," or "Emailgate," or "Faceliftgate") or comparisons with Richard Nixon.[14] Watergate, as a public event, provides "cultural forms" for American political discourse and activity, and these forms "store and transmit information that individuals can make use of without themselves 'memorizing' it."[15] The memory of Watergate affects the way many people perceive, understand, and react to events in the present even if knowledge and discussion of Watergate itself is largely missing and inadequate.

The parallel with Paul and Jesus is instructive. Scholars disagree and debate whether Paul's knowledge of Jesus's life and teachings was inadequate, but no one can deny that such knowledge is almost completely missing from Paul's letters. Bart Ehrman calls the apostle Paul the "closest thing we have to a surviving author who was an eyewitness to the life of Jesus," and yet Paul, Ehrman notes, is almost useless as a source

---

11. "In a 1986 national survey of high school students, 35.5 percent didn't know that Watergate took place after 1950. More than one in five associated it with the resignation of a president other than Richard Nixon" (Schudson, *Watergate in American Memory*, 11–12).

12. Schudson, *Watergate in American Memory*, 14.

13. Full disclosure: Even after doing research on Watergate, I had to look up the date of Nixon's resignation.

14. A fulsome list of "-gate" scandals is available at https://en.wikipedia.org/wiki/List_of_scandals_with_%22-gate%22_suffix. During the summer of 2017, comparisons between Donald J. Trump and Richard M. Nixon in the media were ubiquitous.

15. Schudson, *Watergate in American Memory*, 51.

of knowledge about the historical Jesus.[16] He provides a list of things we learn about Jesus from Paul. I'll quote that list in full; it won't take long:

> Jesus was born of a woman (Gal. 4:4)....He was born as a Jew (Gal. 4:4). He was descended from the line of King David (Rom. 1:3). He had brothers (1 Cor. 9:5), one of whom was named James (Gal. 1:19). He had twelve disciples (1 Cor. 15:5). He conducted his ministry among Jews (Rom. 15:8). He had a last meal with his disciples on the night he was turned over to the authorities (1 Cor. 11:23). Paul knows two things Jesus said at his last supper (1 Cor. 11:23-25). Paul knows two other teachings of Jesus: that Christians should not get divorced (1 Cor. 7:10) and that they should pay their preacher (1 Cor. 9:14). Jesus appeared before Pontius Pilate (1 Tim. 6:13; this datum is found only in a letter Paul probably did not himself write). Jesus died of crucifixion (1 Cor. 2:2). Those responsible for his death were Judeans (1 Thess. 2:14-15).[17]

This comprehensive list is in complete contrast to the list of things Paul *doesn't* say about Jesus: "to make a complete list, all you would have to do is cite virtually any story in the Gospels, and it would be something Paul doesn't tell us."[18] It is difficult to know how much weight to put on Paul's silence regarding Jesus's life and teachings. It's possible to acknowledge Paul's silence about Jesus, but not infer—as some claim—that Paul was disinterested in the facts of Jesus's life. "If we had nothing but Paul's letters...we would know very little about him. Nevertheless, in letters not intended to provide biographical details, the number of allusions is probably enough to confirm both Paul's knowledge of and interest in Jesus prior to his death and resurrection."[19]

The question remains: How well (or: How *much*) does Paul remember Jesus? Paul was keenly interested and invested in knowledge of Jesus, despite the paucity of biographical details in Paul's letters. "His was a

---

16. Ehrman, *Jesus before the Gospels*, 102; see this chapter's epigram.

17. Ehrman, *Jesus before the Gospels*, 103–4; I have converted the format of this material from a bulleted list (in Ehrman) to paragraph form.

18. Ehrman, *Jesus before the Gospels*, 105.

19. James D. G. Dunn, *Jesus Remembered*, Christianity in the Making 1 (Grand Rapids: Eerdmans, 2003), 143; see also pp. 181–84; idem, "Jesus Tradition in Paul," in *Studying the Historical Jesus: Evaluations of the State of Current Research*, ed. Bruce D. Chilton and Craig A. Evans, NTTS 19 (Leiden: Brill, 1998), 155–78.

knowing of Jesus that . . . permeates the apostle's thinking and writing and that shines through his epistles."[20] Rather than the word *knowing*, I prefer the phrase "thinking with." Paul "thinks with" Jesus to understand and respond to the challenges facing his communities, including problematic notions about the future (1 Thess; 1 Cor 15), social divisions within his communities (1 Cor; Phil 4; Rom 14–15), the expression of spiritual gifts within the communities' worship gatherings (1 Cor 11–14; Rom 12), and so on. Indeed, hardly any aspect of the Pauline communities' life and thought escapes being filtered through the influence of Jesus's life and teachings.

Perhaps an example is in order. Early in his letter to the Thessalonians, as Paul offers prayers of thanksgiving for his readers, he says, "You became imitators of us and of the Lord when you accepted the message that came from the Holy Spirit with joy in spite of great suffering. As a result you became an example to all the believers in Macedonia and Achaia" (1 Thess 1:6-7). A scholar who emphasizes Paul's silence regarding Jesus would rightly observe that this verse teaches us nothing about Jesus as a historical figure. But notice how Paul describes his own pattern of behavior—his moral norms, expectations, and actions—in relation to Jesus, on one hand, and his readers, on the other. Joshua Jipp helpfully argues that Paul portrays Jesus as a royal, kingly figure who, among other things, "secures the internal harmony of the community through providing *a royal pattern for his subjects to imitate*. For Paul, the Torah is refracted through the lens of the Jesus-tradition and the narrative configuration of the king who embodied Lev. 19:18—'you shall love your neighbor as yourself.'"[21] Paul's and his gentile converts' daily, mundane ethical conduct reflected and transmitted the memory of Jesus. The memory of Jesus provided a template that shaped and a frame that interpreted Paul's early Christian

---

20. Georgia Masters Keightley, "Christian Collective Memory and Paul's Knowledge of Jesus," in *Memory, Tradition, and Text: Uses of the Past in Early Christianity*, ed. Alan Kirk and Tom Thatcher, SemeiaSt 52 (Atlanta: SBL Press, 2005), 129–50 (132).

21. Joshua W. Jipp, *Christ Is King: Paul's Royal Ideology* (Minneapolis: Fortress, 2015), 60–76 (p. 60 quoted); see also Gal 5:14; 6:2; Rom 13:8-10.

communities, even if the memory of Jesus was also a mirror in which the community saw itself.[22]

If we focus on the explicit references to and quotations of the Jesus tradition that would later be written down in the Gospels, we might conclude that Paul doesn't remember Jesus very much at all. But even a cursory reading of Paul's letters reveals this would be a limited and short-sighted conclusion. This chapter demonstrates that Paul, at every turn, exhibits a concern to root his readers' way of thinking and living in the memory of Jesus.

Paul, Jesus's First "Memorial Entrepreneur"

Why are we starting with Paul? Common sense tells us that the Christian story begins with Jesus. The apostle Paul may be an extremely early character in this story, but he is not its beginning. Paul's letters would seem to agree. Throughout Paul's letters, Jesus's life, death, and resurrection are in the past. Even so, Paul gives us our earliest evidence for Jesus. The first time Jesus of Nazareth is mentioned in a preserved document is in Paul's letter to the Thessalonians, written around the year 50 CE, followed quickly by his letter to the Galatians (c. 51 CE).[23] The first time the name "Jesus" (*Iēsous*), as a reference to the man from Nazareth, was written down in a text we still have today, was in the phrase, "To the Thessalonians' church that is in God the Father and the Lord Jesus Christ" (1 Thess 1:1). In other words, the first reference to Jesus already addresses him as "Lord" (*kyrios*) and as "Christ" (*christos*). *And this is the earliest extant reference to Jesus!*

First Thessalonians is woefully short on details about the life and teaching of the historical Jesus; throughout the entire letter we only learn

---

22. For the language of "mirror, template, and frame," see Barry Schwartz, "Where There's Smoke, There's Fire: Memory and History," in *Memory and Identity in Ancient Judaism and Early Christianity: A Conversation with Barry Schwartz*, ed. Tom Thatcher, SemeiaSt 78 (Atlanta: SBL, 2014), 7–37 (p. 16).

23. For a discussion of Pauline chronology and the dating of Paul's letters, see James D. G. Dunn, *Beginning from Jerusalem*, Christianity in the Making 2 (Grand Rapids: Eerdmans, 2008), 497–518 (Dunn provides dates for 1 Thessalonians and Galatians on pp. 509 and 512).

one thing about him (he was killed by the Jews, just like Israel's prophets; 1 Thess 2:15). Yet 1 Thessalonians offers us glimpses of Paul and his companions commemorating Jesus in their daily lives and their reading of Israel's scriptures. We learn that Jesus was killed and was raised from the dead (1:10; 4:14), that he embodies the appropriate way of living for his followers, both in Greece (1:6-7) and in Judea (2:14), that he is granted honorific titles ("Lord" and "Christ," but also "Son [of God]" and "Deliverer" [1:10]), and that his followers await the unveiling of his presence (*parousia*; 2:19; 3:13; 4:15; 5:23), in which he will march at the head of an army of saints (3:13; 4:16). Again, all of this describes *the very first appearance of Jesus of Nazareth in the literary record.*

In this earliest Christian text, Paul repeatedly refers to "the gospel" (*euangelion*).[24] Paul refers to both "the gospel of God" (1 Thess 2:2, 8, 9) and "the gospel of Christ" (3:2). This gospel—"of God" and "of Christ"— has now been "entrusted" to Paul and his companions (2:4), so that now it is also "our gospel" (1:5). Paul's internalization of the gospel of God/ Christ—again, which is now "our gospel"—draws Paul's identity into the mission and proclamation of Jesus's message. Paul isn't *a* preacher of the gospel; he is *the* preacher of the gospel to gentiles, the apostle to the gentiles, the one who has been entrusted and commissioned to take the message of Israel's messiah to the nations. Here Paul's second letter, which he wrote to the Galatians, becomes relevant:

> The influential leaders didn't add anything to what I was preaching— and whatever they were makes no difference to me, because God doesn't show favoritism. But on the contrary, they saw that I had been entrusted with the gospel for people who aren't circumcised [i.e., gentiles], just as Peter had been to the circumcised. The one who empowered Peter to the apostolic calling for the circumcised empowered me also to the Gentiles. James, Peter, and John, who are considered to be key leaders, shook hands with me and Barnabas as equals when they recognized the grace that was given to me. So it was agreed that we would go to the Gentiles, while they continue to go to the people who were circumcised. (Gal 2:6-9; CEB modified)

24. The CEB often translates *euangelion* as "gospel" (e.g., throughout Romans and Philippians). In 1 Thessalonians, however, it only uses "good news" (1:5; 2:2, 4, 8, 9; 3:2; see also 3:6).

This passage concludes in the first- and third-person plural: "*we* would go to the Gentiles, while *they* continue to go to the people who were circumcised." Despite this ending, the passage as a whole has a strong first-person *singular* tone: the influential leaders in Jerusalem didn't add anything to *Paul's* message (v. 6); *Paul* had been entrusted with the gospel for the uncircumcised (v. 7); he who empowered Peter to preach the gospel to Jews also empowered *Paul* to preach to gentiles (v. 8); the grace of the apostolic call to the gentiles was given to *Paul* (v. 9).

We see in Paul's language that he was protective—even territorial—about his status as the apostle to the gentiles. That Paul was protective of his apostolic status isn't controversial; Paul repeatedly insists on his divine credentials, in part because not everyone accepted them.[25] But his claim goes further: Paul doesn't claim simply to be *an* apostle; he insists he is *the* apostle to the gentiles, the one commissioned by Jesus himself to proclaim the gospel to the gentiles, to gather them as an offering to the Lord, and to present them to the Lord as a sacrifice, "acceptable and made holy by the Holy Spirit" (Rom 15:16). Paul's apostolic vocation extends to *all* the gentiles, to call them "to faithful obedience for his name's sake" (Rom 1:5), including the gentiles in Rome to whom Paul has not preached the gospel (1:13-15). This concern to spread the umbrella of his apostolic authority over the Roman gentiles "explains his concern for writing in the first place."[26]

Paul's self-understanding and self-presentation as *the* apostle to the gentiles provides a key to unlocking multiple facets of his ministry, including his preaching to gentiles, his letter-writing, as well as the contents of his letters.[27] From another angle of perception, however, we can describe Paul as Jesus's "memorial entrepreneur," as one who is invested in

---

25. For examples, see Gal 1:10–2:10; 1 Cor 9:1-23; 2 Cor 10–13.

26. Runar M. Thorsteinsson, *Paul's Interlocutor in Romans 2: Function and Identity in the Context of Ancient Epistolography*, ConBNT 40 (Stockholm: Almqvist & Wiksell, 2003), 105–6; see also Rafael Rodríguez, *If You Call Yourself a Jew: Reappraising Paul's Letter to the Romans* (Eugene, OR: Cascade, 2014), 10–11; A. Andrew Das, *Solving the Romans Debate* (Minneapolis: Fortress, 2007), 56–57.

27. In *If You Call Yourself a Jew*, I argue that Romans is Paul's proclamation of his gospel to the gentiles in Rome, "partly to remind you of what you already know," but then also "because of the grace that was given to me by God" (Rom 15:15). The grace given to him by God is his commission as *the* apostle to the gentiles, as he goes on to explain in Romans 15:16-24.

developing, proposing, and defending a particular reputation for Jesus. In this case, Paul is invested in advancing a reputation for Jesus as Israel's messiah. As apostle to the gentiles, Paul takes singular responsibility for how Jesus is presented to gentiles and how they respond to him.[28] In other words, Paul saw himself as the gatekeeper for Jesus's memory—his reputation—among gentiles. The role and responsibility of "reputational entrepreneurs" (or "memorial entrepreneurs") involves "two critical tasks: to propose early on a resonant reputation that is linked to the cultural logic of critical 'facts' and then to make that image stick, diverting other interpretations."[29] As we saw in the introduction, the authors of the NT—including Paul—fit the "critical 'facts'" of Jesus's life into a "cultural logic" defined by the story of Israel's scriptures. This isn't a controversial claim, even if the details of that fit remain matters of debate. More controversial is this: Paul proclaimed Jesus as the king of Israel, and he founded communities of gentile converts who pledged allegiance to Jesus as the vice-regent and representative of Israel's God.[30]

In the remainder of this chapter, we will very quickly trace Paul's presentation of Jesus in a thoroughly biblical (= Old Testament) framework. Our journey through the texts will be cursory; because of space constraints, we will only discuss Paul's earliest letter (1 Thessalonians) and his most significant letters (Galatians and Romans; 1–2 Corinthians). Even so, Paul's earliest and most significant letters will suffice to show that Paul only ever understands Jesus inasmuch as he aligns Jesus with Israel's scriptures. In other words, *alignment* rather than *replacement* characterizes how Paul relates Moses's Torah and Israel's messiah. Moreover, within this biblical alignment, Paul identifies Jesus as Israel's *king*, whose reign brings peace, first for the Jews and then for the gentiles.

---

28. Not everyone accepted Paul's claim to be *the* apostle to the gentiles, the sole apostolic authority charged with taking the gospel to the nations. Our point here is simply that *Paul* thought he was singularly invested with the responsibility and authority to preach the gospel to gentiles, and with rare exceptions he was not particularly open to others plowing in his field.

29. Gary Alan Fine, *Difficult Reputations: Collective Memories of the Evil, Inept, and Controversial* (Chicago: University of Chicago Press, 2001), 78.

30. This is an increasingly common theme in the scholarly discussion. For a recent, thoughtful example, see Matthew W. Bates, *Salvation by Allegiance Alone: Rethinking Faith, Works, and the Gospel of Jesus the King* (Grand Rapids: Baker Academic, 2017).

"Christ Is the Goal of Torah"

In the introduction I mentioned that Paul, at the start of his letter to non-Jewish Christians in Rome, describes the "gospel of God" as being "promised ahead of time through his prophets in the holy scriptures concerning his son, who was descended from David" (Rom 1:2-3; my translation). Translators and commentators, however, resist the implication that Paul says the scriptures are, somehow, about Jesus, the Son of God. At the beginning of verse 3, the phrase "concerning his son" is clear enough, and it follows immediately after the words "in the holy scriptures." Even so, some translations insert the phrase "the gospel" to clarify that Paul must *actually* have meant that the gospel—and not Israel's scriptures—is about God's Son. For example, here's the CEB's translation of Romans 1:2-3: "God promised *this good news* about his Son ahead of time through his prophets in the holy scriptures. His Son was descended from David" (italics added).[31]

Romans commentaries, like translations of Romans, take it as given that "concerning his son" in verse 3 describes "the gospel of God" in verse 1.[32] They seem uncomfortable with the possible implication that Paul refers to "the holy scriptures concerning his son." We can, however, say without any sense of exaggeration that, just as Paul portrays Jesus in scriptural/Jewish garb, so also he portrays Israel's scriptures as embodied in Jesus.[33]

But is this portrayal a fundamental, defining aspect of Paul's memory of Jesus, or are his appeals to the Hebrew Bible ad hoc, useful for the immediate occasion but not fundamental to his understanding of the gospel? This is actually a critical question for scholarship on Paul; it is a part of the question of Paul's "Jewishness" and the extent to which his "Christian faith" represented a break with his Jewish identity. The present discussion will demonstrate Paul's irreducibly biblical/Jewish memory of

---

31. See also the NRSV.

32. See, e.g., James D. G. Dunn, *Romans 1–8*, WBC 38A (Nashville: Thomas Nelson, 1988), 11; Richard N. Longenecker, *The Epistle to the Romans*, NIGTC (Grand Rapids: Eerdmans, 2016), 63.

33. Richard B. Hays, *Echoes of Scripture in the Letters of Paul* (New Haven: Yale University Press, 1989), 85.

Jesus, such that neither his "Christian faith" nor his commission as apostle to the gentiles justifies a claim that Paul "no longer identified himself as a Jew."[34]

The Thessalonian Correspondence

As the earliest surviving Christian documents,[35] Paul's letters to the Thessalonians are a logical place to begin. Those letters, however, never quote from and rarely echo or allude to Israel's scriptures. Commentaries on 1 Thessalonians, however, generally accept seven allusions to Hebrew biblical tradition.[36] In these allusive references Paul "thinks with" Israel's scriptures. That is, the texts of the Hebrew Bible provide the images and language with which he describes the God of Israel (to whom his gentile readers in Thessalonica have converted; 1 Thess 2:4; 3:13; 4:6), the people of God (i.e., his readers; 4:8; 5:8), and their opponents (2:16; 4:5). Some of these allusions deserve our attention.

The question of whether or not Paul wrote his letters to an audience of gentiles, Jews, or both is often important and somewhat difficult to discern. Not so for 1 Thessalonians. Paul describes his readers as having "turned to God from idols" and who now "serve the living and true God" (1 Thess 1:9).[37] Paul, therefore, writes to *gentile* Christians in Macedonia, off the northern edge of the Aegean Sea just west of the border between Asia and Europe. While the Christian community in Thessalonica included Jewish believers (Acts 17:1-4), Paul writes 1 Thessalonians to the believers that fell under his purview as the apostle to the gentiles.

---

34. Love L. Sechrest, *A Former Jew: Paul and the Dialectics of Race*, LNTS 410 (London: T&T Clark, 2009), 113–64 (p. 163 quoted). Sechrest argues that Paul "identified himself as an Israelite who was born a Jew but no longer was one" (164). The distinction between "Jew" and "Israelite" will need to be made with more care.

35. As I mentioned earlier (see note 5, above), Pauline scholars question whether 2 Thessalonians was written by Paul or by one of his followers.

36. See E. Springs Steele, "The Use of Jewish Scriptures in 1 Thessalonians," *BTB* 14 (1984): 12–17. Steele discusses the following as potential allusions: (i) Jer 11:20 (1 Thess 2:4); (ii) Gen 15:16; 2 Macc 6:13-15; Dan 8:23 (2:16); (iii) Zech 14:5 (3:13); (iv) Jer 10:25; Ps 79:6 (4:5); (v) Deut 32:35; Ps 94:1 (4:6); (vi) Ezek 36:27; 37:14 (4:8); and (vii) Isa 59:17 (5:8). Abraham Malherbe (*The Letters to the Thessalonians: A New Translation with Introduction and Commentary*, AB 32B [New York: Doubleday, 2000], 56) does not include 3:13 and he adds 5:22, which may allude to Job 1:1, 8; 2:3.

37. Malherbe, *Letters to the Thessalonians*, 56.

Paul alludes to Israel's scriptures to describe the God to whom the gentiles have converted. When Paul describes God as one "who continues to examine our hearts" (1 Thess 2:4), he employs "a well-known theme from the OT."[38] The prophet Jeremiah, for example, receives a message from the Lord revealing that Judah and Jerusalem have abandoned their covenant with YHWH and "are following other gods and serving them" (Jer 11:1-13; v. 10 quoted). As Jeremiah laments the people's wickedness, he calls upon the "LORD of heavenly forces, righteous judge, who tests the heart and mind" (11:20). The prophet repeats this idea a few verses later in 12:3 and again in 17:10, each time contrasting those who "turn their hearts from the LORD" (17:5) and "those who trust in the LORD" (17:7). The same contrast is visible in 1 Thessalonians 2, where Paul portrays himself and his companions, like the prophet Jeremiah, as those whose hearts have been tested and approved by God, while his opponents in Philippi, like Jeremiah's Judah and Jerusalem, turn from and oppose Israel's God (1 Thess 2:2). Paul's allusion is more than scriptural imagery adorning his letter to Thessalonian gentiles who may or may not have heard its echo. Paul here reveals the extent to which he "thinks with" Israel's scripture, framing himself and his efforts to preach the gospel to gentiles in Macedonia within the story of Israel. Significantly, his use of Jeremiah as a frame offers Paul the resources to understand and explain not just his ministry but also hostile reactions to it.

But if Paul thought of himself and his experiences in scriptural terms and images, how did the Hebrew Bible enable his thinking about Jesus? Perhaps the only example of a link between Jesus and the Hebrew Bible in this relatively short letter occurs in Paul's prayer for the Thessalonians in chapter 3:

> Now may our God and Father himself and our Lord Jesus guide us on our way back to you. May the Lord cause you to increase and enrich your love for each other and for everyone in the same way as we also love you. May the love cause your hearts to be strengthened, to be blameless

---

38. Charles A. Wanamaker, *The Epistles to the Thessalonians*, NIGTC (Grand Rapids: Eerdmans, 1990), 95; Wanamaker cites Pss 7:9; 17:3; Jer 11:20; 12:3; 17:9 [sic; v. 10].

in holiness before our God and Father *at the arrival of our Lord Jesus with all his holy ones.* Amen. (3:11-13, CEB; my translation in italic)

In the last phrase, Paul anticipates "our Lord Jesus" arriving or returning "with all his holy ones." Readers often ask who, specifically, Paul imagines accompanying Jesus at his parousia.[39] Does Paul imagine Jesus being accompanied by angels from heaven, the supernatural beings that attend God in his heavenly throne room? Or does he have in mind "the saints [i.e., Christians] who have departed this life"?[40]

The core question isn't "Who attends Jesus at the parousia?" but "Why does Paul portray Jesus with an entourage?" A simple—and perhaps not wrong—answer to this question is: because the Holy Spirit revealed to Paul the conditions or circumstances of Jesus's return at the end of the age. But the problem with this answer is that it only pushes the question back one level. The question remains, why does Jesus return with an entourage?

We can address the substance of the question when we appreciate that Paul is echoing the postexilic prophet Zechariah,[41] who looked forward to "a day...that belongs to the LORD," on which YHWH would summon Israel's enemies ("all the nations") to Jerusalem for battle. In a dramatic image, the LORD himself will stand upon the Mount of Olives, splitting the mountain in half and carving out a valley through which the residents of Jerusalem will escape their enemies: "You will flee through the valley of my mountain, because the valley of the mountains will reach to Azal. You will flee just as you fled from the earthquake in the days of Judah's King Uzziah. The LORD my God will come, and all the holy ones with him" (Zech 14:5).

---

39. The word *parousia* ("presence, coming, advent"), which Paul uses in 1 Thessalonians 3:13, denotes "arrival as the first stage in presence" (BDAG s.v.). Scholars disagree whether the term refers to Jesus's "coming" from somewhere else (and so his absence in the present time) or to the unveiling of Jesus's already-current "presence." I lean toward the latter of these options.

40. Leon Morris, *The First and Second Epistles to the Thessalonians*, rev. ed., NICNT (Grand Rapids: Eerdmans, 1991), 111. "The saints" is another translation of *tōn hagiōn*, which I translated as "holy ones." See also Wanamaker, *Thessalonians*, 145; Malherbe, *Letters to the Thessalonians*, 214.

41. "[Zechariah 14:5] may be the source of Paul's thought" (Wanamaker, *Thessalonians*, 145).

Zechariah announces that God himself, standing upon the Mount of Olives and defeating the enemies of Israel, will come to Zion accompanied by his royal entourage ("all the holy ones with him"). This entourage may be militaristic in nature and refer to the heavenly army that YHWH leads into battle, or it may serve to purify the people whom the Lord saves on that day.[42] "On that day," says the prophet (14:6, 8; compare v. 7), "the LORD will become king over all the earth. On that day the LORD will be one, and the LORD's name will be one" (14:9, CEB modified). "The very might that enables Yahweh to vanquish the nations and to bestow upon Jerusalem an exalted role in the universe must inevitably assume its rightful place as the supreme power in the created realm."[43] YHWH, the God of Israel, is this "supreme power in the created realm," and the prophet envisions him, on the day of the Lord, retaking his throne in Jerusalem to establish justice for his people, vengeance for their enemies, and peace throughout the world.

This is the language Paul echoes in 1 Thessalonians 3:13, though he introduces one significant change. When Paul imagines the apocalyptic scenario portrayed by Zechariah, he sees not YHWH ("our God and Father") but the Lord Jesus, standing astride Mount Zion, rescuing his people and defeating his enemies, accompanied by a heavenly entourage. Moreover, this vision of Jesus is nothing less than his enthronement as king. We saw that Zechariah, just a few verses after prophesying the return of YHWH and "all the holy ones with him," declares that "the LORD will become king over all the earth" (Zech 14:5, 9). For the last three decades scholars have come to appreciate a concept called *metalepsis*, in which an echo of one part of a text reverberates with other ideas found in that text.[44] In this instance, Paul echoes words from Zechariah 14:5, but that echo is meant to reverberate with Zechariah's broader prophetic vision, including verse 9. Paul goes on to describe Jesus's appearance as a returning king who

---

42. Carol L. Meyers and Eric M. Meyers, *Zechariah 9–14: A New Translation with Introduction and Commentary*, AB 25C (New York: Doubleday, 1998), 430.

43. Meyers and Meyers, *Zechariah 9–14*, 439.

44. So Hays (*Echoes of Scripture in the Letters of Paul*, 20–21): "When a literary echo links the text in which it occurs to an earlier text, the figurative effect of the echo can lie in the unstated or suppressed (transumed) points of resonance between the two texts" (p. 20 quoted); see also idem, *The Conversion of the Imagination: Paul as Interpreter of Israel's Scripture* (Grand Rapids: Eerdmans, 2005), 2.

is greeted and escorted by his subjects, heralded by "the signal of a shout by the head angel and a blast on God's trumpet" (1 Thess 4:16-17).[45] In other words, Paul isn't simply using words that appear also in Zechariah 14:5. Instead, he is thinking in terms and images he has learned from scripture (here, Zechariah), and those terms and images provide Paul the raw materials for his anticipation of how God will resolve the drama of history.

As we will see, Paul continues to think in scriptural terms and images in his later letters. In fact, his understanding of Jesus is *determined and defined* by Israel's scriptures.

Galatians and Romans

If we had to listen carefully for the echo of scripture in Paul's Thessalonian letters, our ears are blown out by the volume of the allusions to and quotations of scripture in Galatians and Romans. Once we've adjusted, these later letters continue and extend the pattern we saw in the earlier Thessalonian letters: namely, that Paul understands God, Jesus, and the people of God in terms and images provided by Israel's scriptures. This point is easily—and so also often—missed. Generations of Christians have learned to speak of "Paul's 'Law-free' gospel." That is, Paul proclaimed salvation in/by Jesus apart from the Jewish Law. In this understanding, Paul thought of the Law as impermanent, as something that would, at some point, come to an end. It came to an end with the advent of Jesus Christ. Here's a typical example: "if, as Paul says, the law was a *temporary provision*, the coming of Christ meant that the period of its validity was now at an end."[46]

This understanding of Paul finds its primary support in the letters of Galatians and Romans. Consider the following:

---

45. Richard Hays (Hays, *Echoes of Scripture in the Letters of Paul*, 29–32) offers seven criteria ("tests") for identifying echoes of scripture in Paul. His fourth criterion, "thematic coherence," asks, "How well does the alleged echo fit into the line of argument that Paul is developing?" My claim here is that the echo of Zechariah 14:5 and the resonance with verse 9 set up exactly Paul's portrayal of Christ's parousia in 1 Thessalonians 4. Surprisingly, neither Hays nor Joshua Jipp (*Christ Is King*) discuss Zechariah 14's echoic resonance in 1 Thessalonians 3:13; 4:16-17, despite its relevance for both discussions.

46. F. F. Bruce, *Paul, Apostle of the Heart Set Free* (Grand Rapids: Eerdmans, 1997), 191; my emphasis.

But since no one is made righteous by the Law as far as God is concerned, it is clear that the righteous one will live on the basis of faith. The Law isn't based on faith; rather, the one doing these things will live by them. (Gal 3:11-12)

So why was the Law given? It was added because of offenses, until the descendant would come to whom the promise had been made. It was put in place through angels by the hand of a mediator.... Before faith came, we were guarded under the Law, locked up until faith that was coming would be revealed, so that the Law became our custodian until Christ so that we might be made righteous by faith. (Gal 3:19, 23-24)

Sin will have no power over you, because you aren't under Law but under grace. (Rom 6:14)

When we were self-centered, the sinful passions aroused through the Law were at work in all the parts of our body, so that we bore fruit for death. But now we have been released from the Law. We have died with respect to the thing that controlled us, so that we can be slaves in the new life under the Spirit, not in the old life under the written Law. (Rom 7:5-6)

When Pauline scholars claim that, with the advent of Christ, the purpose and function of the Law in the drama of scripture has come to an end, they do so with strong support from Paul.

But is this really what Paul had to say about the Law? Are we sure that Paul envisions the *end* of the Law as a consequence of Christ's coming?

In fact, the answer to both questions is no.

Both Galatians and its younger-though-much-bigger sibling, Romans, attribute a significant and enduring function of the Law (or better, the Torah) of Moses.[47] For example:

---

47. The Hebrew word *torah* means "direction, instruction, law," and the LXX often translates *torah* with the Greek word *nomos* ("law, principle, custom"). The English word *law* (or even *Law*) conveys only one aspect of these words, so I translate *nomos* as "Torah" whenever it refers to the Mosaic covenant.

Galatians 5:13-14	Romans 13:8-10
You were called to freedom, brothers and sisters; only don't let this freedom be an opportunity to indulge your selfish impulses, but serve each other through love. *All the Torah has been fulfilled in a single statement*: "Love your neighbor as yourself" [Lev 19:18].	Don't be in debt to anyone, except for the obligation to love each other. Whoever loves another person *has fulfilled the Torah*. The commandments...are all summed up in one word: "You must love your neighbor as yourself" [Lev 19:18]. Love doesn't do anything wrong to a neighbor; therefore, *love is what fulfills the Torah*.

In both texts, Paul gives his readers a command to love one another, and he provides the justification for this commandment by quoting Leviticus 19:18, Torah's instruction to "love your neighbor as yourself."

And yet he goes even further. "Love of neighbor" is not, for Paul, simply *an* act of obedience to Torah. "Love of neighbor" is the *fulfillment* of Torah, and whoever loves their neighbor "has fulfilled the Torah" (Rom 13:8).[48] This is all the more surprising when we appreciate the echo of the Jesus tradition in these verses. That is, Paul could have said, "The *gospel* is summed up in one word: 'You must love your neighbor as yourself.'" Or he could have appealed to the example and teaching of Jesus, echoing the tradition in which Jesus sums up the Torah's commandments as "love of God" and "love of neighbor" (Mark 12:29-31 and parallels). But he doesn't. Instead, he tells his gentile readers that they, by loving one another, have fulfilled Torah. And all this in two letters that are famous for Paul's insistence that his gentile readers should *not* keep Torah!

This view of Torah—as something fulfilled by Paul's uncircumcised, gentile converts in Christ through love of neighbor—doesn't come like a bolt out of the blue. Paul exhibits this view of Torah throughout the letter to the Romans. As we've already seen, he describes "the holy scriptures" as being "concerning his son," that is, as being about Jesus. In the same chapter he declares, "God's righteousness is being revealed in the gospel," and

---

48. One of BDAG's definitions for *plēroō* ("fulfill") is "to bring to a designed end" (s.v., §4), adding; "depending on how one prefers to interpret the context, *plēroō* is understood here either as *fulfill* = do, carry out, or as *bring to full expression* = show it forth in its true [meaning], or as *fill up* = complete" (s.v., §4b). I interpret Paul's use of *plēroō* in Galatians 5:14 and Romans 13:8 in this second sense ("bring to full expression").

then he supports that declaration by quoting from "the holy scriptures": "as it is written, 'The Righteous One will live by faith'" (Rom 1:17, CEB modified [quoting Hab 2:4]). Two chapters later he returns to the revelation of God's righteousness. Paul tells his gentile readers that none of them "will be treated as righteous in his presence by doing what the Torah says," because that isn't what Torah does for gentiles. Instead, "the knowledge of sin comes through the Torah" (3:20). Anyone who's read the Hebrew Bible knows that God didn't give Torah to Israel in order to point out their sin. Torah was the offer of life to Israel (Deut 30:15-20). But Paul, writing to gentiles in Rome, notes that, *for gentiles*, Torah doesn't give life; instead, it only offers the gentile "the knowledge of [their own] sin." A few chapters later Paul will assume the voice of a gentile and ask, "So did something good [i.e., Torah] bring death to me? Absolutely not!...We know that the Torah is spiritual, but I'm made of flesh and blood, and I'm sold as a slave to sin" (Rom 7:13-14). God offered Israel life when he gave them the Torah. For the gentiles, however, Torah only produces knowledge of sin. What hope remains, then, for a gentile who would worship Israel's God?

Paul immediately gives an answer: "But now God's righteousness has been revealed apart from the Torah...God's righteousness is revealed through the faithfulness of Jesus Christ for all who have faith in him" (Rom 3:21-22, CEB modified). This seems to confirm the traditional Christian view that Torah is obsolete, that now the covenantal basis for the relationship between God and his people is "the faithfulness of Jesus Christ." But notice the ellipsis between "the Torah" and "God's righteousness"; notice that we left out a part of verse 21. The entire verse reads: "But now God's righteousness has been revealed apart from the Torah, *to which Torah and the Prophets serve as witnesses*" (3:21, my translation). While Torah brings the knowledge of sin to gentile converts, it also testifies to God's righteousness toward them: his offer of life and blessing, as he had promised to Abraham that "all the families of the earth will be blessed because of you" (Gen 12:3).

Even in Romans 7, where the impossibility of finding life in Torah is portrayed in the starkest of terms, Paul describes the Torah as "spiritual" (Rom 7:14), and he describes the commandment as being "intended to give life" (7:10). And in the next chapter, in Romans 8, Paul continues to talk about Torah (vv. 2-4), where he uses the word *nomos* four times. The CEB translates these verses as follows:

> The law [*nomos*] of the Spirit of life in Christ Jesus has set you free from the law [*nomos*] of sin and death. God has done what was impossible for the Law [*nomos*], since it was weak because of selfishness. God condemned sin in the body by sending his own Son to deal with sin in the same body as humans, who are controlled by sin. He did this so that the righteous requirement of the Law [*nomos*] might be fulfilled in us. Now the way we live is based on the Spirit, not based on selfishness. (Rom 8:2-4)

Notice how the CEB translates *nomos* as "law," with a lowercase *l*, twice in verse 2 and as "Law," with a capital *L*, in verses 3 and 4. The implication is that, in verse 2, *nomos* means "principle" or even, perhaps, "power" or "authority." James Dunn, however, has argued that Paul is describing a single *nomos*—the Torah—from two different angles. We'll quote him at length:

> Paul tries to squeeze so much into two compact phrases that he runs some risk of confusing his readers. Does he still mean the law [= Torah] here, the law given to Israel? How could the Paul who warned his Galatian converts so passionately against submitting to the slavery of the law (Gal 4:1-11; 5:1-4) speak of the same law as liberating? Yet readers who had time to reflect on the course of the argument would probably soon find themselves driven to the surprising conclusion that Paul must mean the same law in both phrases, the law given to Israel. "The law of sin and death" could hardly be other than "the law of sin which is in my constituent parts (7:23), the very law which sin used so deceitfully to bring man [*sic*] to death (7:11–13). "The law of the Spirit of life" is more surprising, but it is in fact only an extreme expression of the defense of the law already made in describing it as "the commandment which was for life" (7:10) and as "spiritual" (7:14).[49]

It may indeed be surprising to us that Paul speaks of the Torah as liberating, but perhaps it shouldn't be. After all, love for one's neighbor is, for Paul, the fulfillment of Torah (Rom 13:8-10; Gal 5:14). The Torah may

---

49. Dunn, *Romans 1–8*, 436; see also Rom 3:27; 7:22-25, and Dunn's commentary on these verses.

have been unable to empower gentiles to love their neighbor, but God has stepped in and made this possible (Rom 8:3). As a result, "the righteous requirement of the Torah" is now "fulfilled in us" (8:4).

Far from having come to an end, the Torah in Galatians and Romans is active in the gospel, both negatively (making sin known; Gal 3:22; Rom 3:20) and positively (finding fulfillment among Paul's gentile converts; Gal 5:13-14; Rom 8:4). When Paul says, "Christ is the goal of the Torah, which leads to righteousness for all who have faith in God" (Rom 10:4), he isn't claiming that Torah, having attained its goal, is now obsolete and invalidated. After all, this is the same Paul who asked back in Romans 3, "Do we then cancel the Torah through this faith?" He answers with the "emotionally charged and highly negative response,"[50] *mē genoito*, which the CEB renders, "Absolutely not!" He then adds—and this is the point— "Instead, we *confirm* the Torah" (Rom 3:31, emphasis added). If Paul argues in Romans 3 that faith confirms Torah, why should that faith render Torah obsolete in Romans 10? Instead, for Paul, Christ's faithfulness to God is the truest expression of obedience to Torah, and loving one's neighbor the truest means of fulfilling Torah and of imitating Christ.

The Corinthian Correspondence

There are other ways in which Paul remembers Jesus in images and themes that he received from his scriptural heritage. These images and themes not only enabled Paul to communicate to others the significance of Jesus's life, death, and resurrection; they defined his own understanding of Jesus. Without scripture, in other words, Paul's memory of Jesus vanishes, not unlike the way Alzheimer's erases a person's recent memories. One of the most famous examples of Paul's appeal to Israel's scripture occurs in his first letter to the Christians in Corinth. (Paul wrote the Corinthian letters after Galatians but before Romans.[51]) In 1 Corinthians 15, as he did in Galatians and as he will do in Romans, Paul draws strong and direct links between the gospel of Jesus Christ and the Torah, the scriptures of Israel. Perhaps just as importantly, he reveals that these links are

---

50. Longenecker, *Romans*, 344.

51. Dunn, *Beginning from Jerusalem*, 512.

not his own creation; he received them from others and now hands them on to his converts in Corinth:[52]

> Brothers and sisters, I want to call your attention to the good news that I preached to you, which you also received and in which you stand. You are being saved through it if you hold on to the message I preached to you, unless somehow you believed it for nothing. I passed on to you as most important what I also received: Christ died for our sins in line with the scriptures, he was buried, and he rose on the third day in line with the scriptures. He appeared to Cephas, then to the Twelve. (1 Cor 15:1-5)

The good news Paul proclaimed to the Corinthians is wholly taken up with the death, burial, resurrection, and appearances of Jesus. But these events are themselves put into a context defined by their alignment with "the scriptures" (*kata tas graphas*).[53] The gospel doesn't replace Israel's Torah; it complements (or, perhaps better, supplements) it.

But the central events of the gospel are not, for Paul, the only things "in line with the scriptures." His role as apostle to the gentiles is itself a scriptural role that performs a fundamental function in Jesus's fulfillment of Torah and its promises. In 2 Corinthians 3, Paul defends the legitimacy of his apostolic calling, and his defense resonates with the language of scripture and echoes divine promises from Jeremiah and Ezekiel. In Jeremiah, God declares his intention to "make a new covenant with the people of Israel and Judah" and to "put my Instructions within them and engrave them on their hearts" (see Jer 31:31-34). Ezekiel also mentions the people's "heart": "I will remove your stony heart from your body and replace it with a living one, and I will give you my spirit so that you may walk according to my regulations and carefully observe my case laws"

---

52. For a very helpful discussion, see Jerry L. Sumney, "'Christ Died for Us': Interpretation of Jesus' Death as a Central Element of the Identity of the Earliest Church," in *Reading Paul in Context: Explorations in Identity Formation. Essays in Honour of William S. Campbell*, ed. Kathy Ehrensperger and J. Brian Tucker, LNTS 428 (London: T&T Clark, 2010), 147–72 (see pp. 157–59 for a discussion of 1 Cor 15:3-5).

53. Anthony Thiselton (*The First Epistle to the Corinthians*, NIGTC [Grand Rapids: Eerdmans, 2000], 1190–91, 1195–96) rightly rejects attempts to identify the specific scriptural referents of verses 3 and 4: "it would amount to *unintended reductionism and constraint if we seek to isolate some specific individual text* rather than understanding the resurrection of Christ as the witness to a climactic fulfillment of a cumulative tradition of God's promised eschatological act of sovereignty and vindication in grace" (p. 1195; italics in the original).

(Ezek 36:26-27; see also 11:19). Paul claims the Corinthian Christians are "a letter written by Christ and transcribed by us."[54] He tells them, "You weren't written with ink but with the Spirit of the living God. You weren't written on tablets of stone but on tablets of human hearts.... He has qualified us as ministers of a new covenant, not based on what is written but on the Spirit, because what is written kills, but the Spirit gives life" (2 Cor 3:3, 6).

Understandably, Paul's language is frequently read as a critique of the Mosaic covenant, as Christianity *replacing* Judaism.[55] Such a reading, however, makes no sense of Paul as an interpreter of Israel's prophets. Neither Jeremiah nor Ezekiel envisages the end of YHWH's covenant with Israel; both describe a renewal and reestablishment of YHWH's relation with Abraham's descendants as his chosen people.[56] The "new covenant" passage from Jeremiah 31 begins, "The time is coming, declares the LORD, when I will make a new covenant *with the people of Israel and Judah*" (31:31, emphasis added). Jeremiah anticipates the inscription of "my Instructions" on the hearts of the people of Israel and Judah. The Hebrew word Jeremiah uses for "Instructions" is *torah* (LXX = *nomous*). This is the same word found in Exodus 24:12: "The LORD said to Moses, 'Come up to me on the mountain and wait there. I'll give you the stone tablets with the instructions [Heb.: *torah*; LXX = *nomon*] and the commandments that I've written in order to teach them.'"

Ezekiel's prophecy, like Jeremiah's, is an oracle of the restoration *of Israel*, who has been "scattered... to the nations and dispersed... into other lands" (Ezek 36:19). Here God promises that he "will take you

---

54. In the CEB, 2 Corinthians 3:3a reads, "You show that you are Christ's letter, delivered by us." Murray Harris (*The Second Epistle to the Corinthians*, NIGTC [Grand Rapids: Eerdmans, 2013], 263) argues convincingly that *phaneroumenoi* is probably a passive participle ("you are shown to be") rather than middle ("you show that you are"). He also argues that *Christou* is not a possessive genitive ("Christ's letter"): "the letter was 'from Christ' (genitive of source or subjective genitive)." The passive participle *diakonētheisa* probably portrays Paul as the amanuensis (or secretary) who recorded the letter Christ wrote/dictated rather than the person who delivered it.

55. See, e.g., Hays, *Echoes of Scripture in the Letters of Paul*, 122–53; Margaret Thrall, *The Second Epistle to the Corinthians*, 2 vols., ICC (Edinburgh: T&T Clark, 1994–2000), 226–27, 234–37.

56. *Pace* Richard Hays (*Echoes of Scripture in the Letters of Paul*, 128), who claims, wrongly, that in Jeremiah "God claims *a new people* for himself" (my emphasis), citing Jer 38:33c [LXX; ET = 31:33c]. In this exact verse Jeremiah identifies YHWH's covenantal people as "the house of Israel" (*tō oikō Israēl*).

[Israel] from the nations," and "gather you from all the countries" and bring them, in a new enactment of the exodus, to the land promised to Abraham (36:24). Jeremiah and Ezekiel didn't anticipate a day when God would abandon his people Israel, erase the Torah from the stone tablets that had been inscribed by the finger of God (Exod 31:18; Deut 9:10), and begin again, with a *new* covenant offered to a *new* people. They looked forward to a day when YHWH would *renew* his covenant *with his chosen people*! If Paul wanted to denigrate the Mosaic covenant, he would find neither Jeremiah nor Ezekiel helpful. If 2 Corinthians 3 seems to denigrate the Mosaic covenant, Paul has either misread the Prophets or we have misread Paul.

Another option, however, is available to us. Perhaps Paul isn't twisting Jeremiah and Ezekiel into critiques of the Mosaic covenant. Perhaps, instead, he is keying his ministry among the gentiles—including the gentiles' response to his gospel, their turn toward Israel's God and allegiance to Jesus as Israel's king—to the prophets' anticipation of that day when YHWH would renew his covenant with the descendants of Abraham and, in so doing, fulfill his promise to bless all the families of the world through Abraham (Gen 12:1-3). In 2 Corinthians 3:6 Paul describes the Mosaic covenant ("what is written"; lit. "the letter, the written document") in stark terms,[57] which he contrasts with the Spirit of God: "what is written kills, but the Spirit gives life." But we should not generalize his claim that Torah kills, written as it is on stone tablets and scrolls rather than fleshy heart-tablets. God explicitly and repeatedly presents Torah as life-producing (e.g., Deut 30:15-20), a presentation Paul himself reflects (e.g., Rom 7:13). When he says the written Torah kills or, as elsewhere, that "the knowledge of sin comes through Torah" (Rom 3:20), Paul is describing Torah's effect *on gentiles*. He dramatically enacts this effect of Torah on gentiles in Romans 7, where he vividly portrays a Judaizing gentile's experience of "coming under the law at some point, learning about his desire and sin, and being unable to do

---

57. Murray Harris (*The Second Epistle to the Corinthians*, 272) rightly argues that *to gramma* refers "not to writing in general but to the Mosaic Law (especially the Decalogue) in particular."

what he wants to do because of enslavement to sin and flesh."[58] Here in 2 Corinthians 3, as in Romans 7, he refers to Torah's effect on gentiles, and—as he will do in Romans 8—he posits the Spirit as the solution to the "gentile problem."[59]

This will help us avoid a stark problem in 2 Corinthians 3:11: "If the glory that fades away was glorious, how much more glorious is the one that lasts!" The CEB's phrase "the glory that fades" translates the Greek *to katargoumenon*, which the NRSV renders "what was set aside." The common understanding of 2 Corinthians 3:11 is that Paul contrasts the Mosaic Law, as that which fades, with the new covenant of the gospel, "the one that lasts" (*to menon*).[60] The problem with this reading, however, is that Paul will emphatically deny that the gospel "sets aside" or "abolishes" the Mosaic Torah using exactly the same word he uses here in 2 Corinthians 3:11: "Do we then cancel [*katargoumen*] the Torah through this faith? Absolutely not! Instead, we confirm the Torah" (Rom 3:31). If Paul insists that faith confirms rather than cancels (or sets aside) Torah in Romans 3:31, then what was "set aside" in 2 Corinthians 3:11?

The answer is found in Paul's reference to "the ministry that brought death" in 2 Corinthians 3:7. We have already explained that Torah portrayed itself as YHWH's offer of life to Israel, a portrayal Paul himself reflects. Torah was God's covenant with Abraham's descendants, through whom he would bless "all the families of the earth" (Gen 12:3). Many gentiles in the Roman Empire were attracted to Judaism and exhibited interest in observing Jewish practices during the first two centuries CE.[61] Their exposure to Jewish practices and customs resulted largely from interpersonal

---

58. Stanley K. Stowers, "Romans 7:7-25 as a Speech-in-Character (Προσωποποιία)," in *Paul in His Hellenistic Context*, ed. Troels Engberg-Pedersen (Minneapolis: Fortress, 1995), 180–202 (191–92). I argue that Paul speaks in the voice of a gentile proselyte to Judaism in Rodríguez, *If You Call Yourself a Jew*, 137–46; see also idem, "Romans 5–8 in Light of Paul's Dialogue with a Gentile Who 'Calls Himself a Jew,'" in *The So-Called Jew in Paul's Letter to the Romans*, ed. Rafael Rodríguez and Matthew Thiessen (Minneapolis: Fortress, 2016), 101–31 (esp. pp. 120–26).

59. I have taken this phrase from Matthew Thiessen's excellent book, *Paul and the Gentile Problem* (Oxford: Oxford University Press, 2016).

60. Thrall, *The Second Epistle to the Corinthians 1-7*, 252–54; Harris, *The Second Epistle to the Corinthians*, 290–91.

61. See Michele Murray, *Playing a Jewish Game: Gentile Christian Judaizing in the First and Second Centuries CE*, Studies in Christianity and Judaism 13 (Waterloo, ON: Wilfrid Laurier University Press, 2004), 11–27.

interactions in cities across the Roman Empire, and people from every social class seem to have been susceptible to finding Judaism attractive.

Not all Jews, however, were open to gentiles adopting Jewish practices and/or seeking to become Jews.[62] Paul himself describes gentiles who "call themselves Jews" and attempt to persuade other gentiles to adopt Jewish practices as "shaming God by breaking Torah" (Rom 2:23); they are "guilty of transgression in the very act of trying to keep the Jewish law."[63] As a result, Torah produces "the knowledge of sin" for the judaizing gentile (Rom 3:20); for the judaizing gentile, "the commandment that was intended to give life brought death" (Rom 7:10). All of this suggests that, in Paul's view, gentiles who attempt to take on Torah as their own find that it brings them death. Torah is, for them, a "ministry of death." The "ministry of the Spirit" (which is "more glorious" and "brings righteousness"), comes through Jesus, whom Paul calls "the Lord" and, surprisingly, whom he identifies with "the Spirit" (2 Cor 3:8, 14-18). Rather than Torah's *replacement*, Paul remembers Jesus as the *key* to a proper understanding of Torah, the fulfillment of God's promise (given to Abraham and recounted in the Torah) and the solution to the gentile problem. Torah brings this gentile problem into focus but doesn't solve it apart from the faithfulness of Christ and the transforming work of the Spirit.

Paul's Vivid Memory of Jesus Christ

Space prevents us from considering two of Paul's shorter (and later) letters, Philippians and Philemon, not to mention the disputed Pauline letters and Luke's portrayal of Paul in the Acts of the Apostles. But we have enough here to begin drawing together some observations.

First, while it is certainly true that we could never put together a biography of Jesus or a digest of his teaching from what we learn about him in Paul's letters, we should not let that blind us to the enormous presence and significance of Jesus in Paul's writings. Paul "thinks with" Jesus, and

---

62. See Matthew Thiessen, *Contesting Conversion: Genealogy, Circumcision, and Identity in Ancient Judaism and Christianity* (Oxford: Oxford University Press, 2011).

63. Matthew Thiessen, "Paul's So-Called Jew and Lawless Lawkeeping," in *The So-Called Jew in Paul's Letter to the Romans*, ed. Rafael Rodríguez and Matthew Thiessen (Minneapolis: Fortress, 2016), 59–83 (78).

as such Jesus is interwoven into every aspect of Paul's apostolic activities, from his interpretation of scripture to his moral judgments to his expectations for the future. As such, Paul is Jesus's "moral entrepreneur," a herald (and even an architect) of Jesus's reputation, especially among communities of gentile converts who respond in faith to the message that Jesus is Israel's messiah, her king.

Second, and perhaps less obviously, Jesus is for Paul not so much the harbinger of something new ("Christianity") so much as the catalyst for the fulfillment of ancient promises. Long ago YHWH had appeared to Abraham and inaugurated a covenant with him, that the whole world would be blessed through the great nation that God would bring forth from Abraham's line. That covenant continued through the Sinai revelation, in which Abraham's descendants gathered in the wilderness and were constituted as the people of God, "a kingdom of priests" and "a holy nation" (Exod 19:6). Though Israel would exhibit what Eugene Peterson calls "a saw-toothed history," moving back and forth between highs and lows, "they were always God's people."[64] As God's people, their destiny was always entangled with the nations of the world (e.g., Isa 49:6); their fortunes were bound up with their neighbors'. "If their failure brings riches to the world, and their defeat brings riches to the Gentiles, how much more will come from the completion of their number!" (Rom 11:12). We can, however, read this relationship backward: the blessing of the gentiles doesn't signal YHWH's abandonment of his people but rather Israel's blessing. The new covenant, in other words, isn't the obsolescence of the old covenant but rather its re*new*al, its fulfillment, its establishment (Rom 3:31; 10:4). We saw in the introduction that "covenant" and "kingdom of God" are related concepts. When Paul presents himself as an ambassador of Christ (2 Cor 5:20) and of his kingdom,[65] he isn't replacing the

---

64. Eugene H. Peterson, *A Long Obedience in the Same Direction: Discipleship in an Instant Society* (Downers Grove: IVP Books, 2000), 86–87 (p. 87 quoted).

65. Scholars often claim that Paul shows little interest in "the kingdom of God," which would be surprising given that the Synoptic Gospels present the kingdom of God as the central theme of Jesus's teaching. In point of fact, however, Paul *does* refer to the kingdom of God often enough (e.g., see 1 Thess 2:12; Gal 5:21; 1 Cor 4:20; 6:9-10; 15:24-25, 50; Rom 14:17). For a helpful discussion of "Paul's royal ideology" that corrects significant scholarly misconceptions, see Joshua W. Jipp, *Christ Is King: Paul's Royal Ideology* (Minneapolis: Fortress, 2015).

covenants of the Hebrew Bible with the kingdom of God. Instead, the kingdom of God is God's faithful execution of his covenantal promises to Abraham and his descendants.

Because of this, and third, we should observe the ways that Paul brings his gentiles' life and faith in line with Torah, the Law of Moses. Paul vehemently rejected any notion or claim that his gentile converts should perform or be expected to perform "works of Torah," especially works such as circumcision and Sabbath-observance, that marked out gentile proselytes as having abandoned their ethnic and national identity in order to become Jews. He even goes so far as to wish that people who are pressuring his gentile converts to be circumcised would bring the knife a little closer to home: "I wish that the ones who are upsetting you would castrate themselves!" (Gal 5:12). Even so, Paul urges his gentile readers to love their neighbors, and he does so not simply out of obedience to a specific command (e.g., Lev 19:18) but in order to "fulfill Torah" (Rom 13:8-10; see also Gal 5:14). In this sense he can refer to gentiles who "don't have the Law" [= Torah] but who nevertheless "instinctively do what the Law requires" (Rom 2:14), and he can even claim that, thanks to Jesus, "the righteous requirement of the Law [is] fulfilled in us" (Rom 8:4). Christ, as Joshua Jipp argues, "fulfills the Torah, incarnates it in his paradigmatic exemplification of Lev. 19:18, and secures the transformation of his subjects through empowering them to love another and 'so fulfill the law of Christ' (Gal. 6:2)."[66]

Paul's memory of Jesus didn't consist of facts about Jesus (what he did, what he said, what was done to him). This isn't to deny that Paul knew facts about Jesus; I'm not sure how we would prove what Paul *didn't* know. The memory of Jesus in Paul's letters isn't so much a memory *of* but rather a memory *through*, as Paul "thinks with" Jesus in order to address all manner of questions facing his gentile converts throughout the eastern Mediterranean basin. Paul rarely took the time in his letters to narrate the facts of Jesus's life, and when he does mention something we might identify as a datum about or teaching of Jesus, he rarely identifies it as such.[67] Like Watergate in American memory, Jesus is never explained in Paul's letters;

---

66. Jipp, *Christ Is King*, 70.

67. See our discussion of Rom 12:14, above.

his specter, however, is ever-present, serving as the context in which the present is perceived, interpreted, and responded to.

Within a generation of Paul's death, the early church would produce documents that turned from "thinking with" Jesus to "thinking about" Jesus. We shouldn't push the distinction too sharply. The authors of our Gospels "think with" Jesus no less than does Paul, though they also introduce an element of "thinking about" Jesus that has no real counterpart in Paul's letters. The earliest of these is the Gospel according to Mark, a forerunner to and literary source of the longer and later Gospels according to Matthew and Luke. In addition to these three texts—known collectively as the "Synoptic Gospels"—the author of Luke's Gospel wrote a second volume, the Acts of the Apostles, which continues the story begun in Luke and connects it with the spread of the gospel from Jerusalem to Rome and the ends of the earth (Acts 1:8). We will turn our attention to these texts in chapter 2.

Chapter 2
Jesus as Subject:
The First Gospels and Acts

Oh, Mac. What did you do?[1]

Distortions and Truth

In May 1995, Mayor Richard Arrington Jr. dedicated a statue in Kelly Ingram Park in Birmingham, Alabama. The park sits across the street from the landmark 16th Street Baptist Church. Both the church and the park served as a staging ground for many of the pivotal events of the mid-twentieth-century Civil Rights Movement. Today, the park boasts a number of statues commemorating those heady and turbulent days. Arrington, the first African American mayor of Birmingham, commissioned a statue by Ronald "Mac" McDowell that would memorialize the iconic photograph of police officer Richard Middleton and his German shepherd, Leo, attacking Walter Gadsden, a seventeen-year-old high school student. That photograph, taken by photojournalist Bill Hudson, appeared in newspapers across the country (including on the front page of *The New York Times*) and is credited with helping to galvanize public support for civil rights protesters nation- and worldwide.

---

1. Malcolm Gladwell, *The Foot Soldier of Birmingham*, Revisionist History, 2017, http://revisionist history.com/episodes/14-the-foot-soldier-of-birmingham; see the transcript of Gladwell's podcast at https://medium.com/@emaina1/the-foot-soldier-of-birmingham-with-malcolm-gladwell-revisionist -history-podcast-transcript-82cbd4e628a3.

If we compare Hudson's photograph with McDowell's statue, we quickly encounter the difference between disinterested representation and commemorative expression of a historic moment. McDowell, an artist and sculptor, freely acknowledges that he altered details of Hudson's photograph in order to draw out the meaning of the encounter between White officer and Black teen. "Well," explains McDowell, "I saw that the boy was maybe 6'4". The officer is maybe 5'10", 5'9", and I said, 'This is a movement about power,' so I made the little boy younger and smaller, and the officer taller and stronger."[2] When Malcolm Gladwell asks McDowell about the boy's posture ("In the photograph I noticed the boy is leaning in, and in your sculpture he's leaning back. Tell me about that"), McDowell explains:

> He's leaning back because I wanted to depict him showing that, "I'm not going to fight you, I'm not leaving, I'm not moving, I'm standing, but I'm not gonna fight you. This is a non-violent protest." That's why his hands are open and he's going back, like, "Do whatever you're gonna do. Put the dog on me, beat me with the club, whatever you wanna do." And I saw all of that when I saw the photograph.

McDowell makes Officer Middleton's sunglasses larger and more unseeing in order to portray him as blind to the injustice he polices, and his representation of the dog Leo becomes less German shepherd and more vicious wolf.

---

2. Gladwell, *The Foot Soldier of Birmingham*. All quotations come from Gladwell's podcast.

McDowell's interpretive and artistic changes are not the isolated products of an active imagination. We all see what McDowell sees. For example, the Associated Press article announcing Bill Hudson's death in June 2010 offers the following description of Hudson's photograph: "His most enduring photograph of the [Civil Rights] era, taken on May 3, 1963, shows an officer in dark sunglasses in Birmingham grabbing a young black man by his sweater and letting a police dog lunge at the man's stomach. The man, Walter Gadsden, with his eyes lowered, has a passive look."[3] "Grabbing." "Letting." "Lunge." "Passive." Bill Hudson's Wikipedia page prominently features his photo of Gadsden and Middleton, with the caption, "Bill Hudson's image of Parker High School student Walter Gadsden being attacked by dogs was published in *The New York Times* on May 4, 1963."[4] The Associated Press and Wikipedia interpret Hudson's picture along the same lines as McDowell's artistic recreation of that encounter, even if they do so less dramatically. I suspect we all see what McDowell sees: a vicious dog-almost-wolf, a dispassionate police officer blind to injustice, and a child caught in the teeth of an oppressive system.

---

3. The Associated Press, "Bill Hudson, a Photojournalist During the Civil Rights Era, Dies at 77," *The New York Times*, 26 June 2010, https://www.nytimes.com/2010/06/27/us/27hudson.html.

4. https://en.wikipedia.org/wiki/Bill_Hudson_(photographer).

McDowell's statue tells a story that is much larger than the single event Bill Hudson recorded in his photograph. First, we need to acknowledge that McDowell's commemorative statue distorts the encounter between Officer Middleton and the young Walter Gadsden. For one thing, Walter Gadsden never participated in the Civil Rights Movement. A year after the unveiling of McDowell's statue, Gadsden gave an interview about his memory of the events of May 3, 1963. When asked how he got involved in the movement, Gadsden says, "Now that's, that's one thing that, uh...I always had a problem with. I never did get involved with the Civil Rights Movement." This is a bombshell! Walter Gadsden, the boy at the heart of one of the most iconic images of the Civil Rights Movement, claims never to have been a part of or involved with that movement!

But there are other surprises. In addition to Gadsden's disassociation with the most important domestic social movement in twentieth-century America, Officer Middleton wasn't the cold, unseeing instrument of injustice we see in Hudson's photo. Middleton wasn't *unleashing* his dog on Gadsden; he was *protecting* Gadsden, who had ducked behind some barricades in order to avoid the approaching protestors.[5] Malcolm Gladwell summarizes the entire scenario: "The most famous photograph of the Civil Rights Movement is of a startled cop trying desperately to hold his dog back from biting a bystander who wasn't that much of a fan of the Civil Rights Movement."

The commemorative statue in Kelly Ingram Park certainly doesn't tell *this* story. Not even a little bit.

In light of these surprising details, there's no denying that McDowell's sculpture misrepresents a specific moment in Birmingham, Alabama, on May 3, 1963. We could even argue, somewhat counterintuitively, that the photograph behind the commemorative sculpture also fails to tell the actual story of the encounter between Gadsden and Officer Middleton. This should seem impossible; after all, unaltered film photographs don't lie. How could anyone possibly claim that a photograph misrepresents

---

5. Officer Middleton's colleague, Bobby Hayes, explains: "If you look at the picture, you can tell he's holding the dog back. But that, that line's taut, the dog's feet are in the air, the best I recall, and Dick's got him here. He's holding that line. He's not gonna let him bite that guy" (Gladwell, *The Foot Soldier of Birmingham*).

the events it captures? And yet, what we see in the photograph and in the sculpture simply didn't happen, and what actually happened isn't what we see, whether in the photograph or in the sculpture.[6]

The problem isn't the image in the photograph. The problem is our *interpretation* of the photograph.

Let's return to McDowell's sculpture. Even after we acknowledge the problematic representation of Walter Gadsden's encounter with Officer Middleton, we still can't escape the fact that the Foot Soldier of Birmingham statue is a powerful—and powerfully authentic—commemoration of the struggle for civil rights reform in the American South during the Jim Crow era. How should we explain McDowell's sculpture, especially the tension between its acknowledged distortions and its undeniable ability to express the realities of racial injustice? This question is bigger than simply, "Why did the artist change the details of the photograph?" McDowell has already explained why he changed what he did, and his explanation clarifies the motivations behind the *production* of the commemorative statue.

But we also need to understand the sculpture's *reception*, its interpretation. We've already observed how viewers of Bill Hudson's photograph already mis-see the confrontation between Gadsden and Officer Middleton. On one hand, McDowell's sculpture is simply another example of this "mis-seeing." On the other hand, when we look at McDowell's commemorative representation of Bill Hudson's photograph, we see our own interpretive angles confirmed and incorporated into the image itself. When we look at Hudson's photograph of a White police officer trying to protect a Black teen from his lunging police dog, we see an act of racial oppression and brutality.

But why do we misread, or "mis-see," Hudson's photograph so dramatically? Why do McDowell's vicious near-wolf, his unfeeling cop, and his self-sacrificing victim—all of whom unquestionably misrepresent the figures in Hudson's picture—authentically express our own interpretations of the photograph?

---

6. "Bill Hudson's editor says later that he picked that particular photo out of the many taken that day because he was riveted by the saintly calm of the young man and the snarling jaws of the German shepherd" (Gladwell, *The Foot Soldier of Birmingham*).

Part of the answer must be that McDowell's sculpture doesn't simply commemorate a moment caught on film. It also expresses the values and struggles of the Civil Rights Movement. Walter Gadsden and Officer Middleton were characters in a riveting drama. Even if we have misunderstood the parts played by these two men, we have not misunderstood the larger drama in which they appear. Birmingham in 1963 was ground zero of the confrontation between a racialized system of government and the men and women who suffered injustice under that system. Black people in the American South—and not just in the South—had been the objects of abuse, oppression, and terror. Less than four months after Hudson photographed Gadsden and Officer Middleton, four members of the Ku Klux Klan bombed the 16th Street Baptist Church, killing four young girls who are themselves commemorated by a statue in Kelly Ingram Park.

In this context, reading Hudson's picture as documentation of racial violence makes sense. The subject of Bill Hudson's photograph isn't Walter Gadsden and Officer Middleton. Hudson's photograph chronicled what Diane McWhorter called "the Big Truth about segregation, evil in black and white." This "Big Truth" survives even if Hudson's photograph, under the influence of our interpretive prejudices, is "as much a fiction as Harriet Beecher Stowe's novel [Uncle Tom's Cabin]."[7] The photograph was useful to the Civil Rights Movement not because it showed the world how one White police officer treated one Black teen. Hudson's photograph was useful because it was able to "grasp and communicate present realities that the language of history cannot express."[8] McDowell's statue, which effaced the "particulars" of the encounter between Officer Middleton and Walter Gadsden, brought out the "present realities" of Birmingham in 1963.

McDowell's artistic distortions of Hudson's photograph are actually the vehicles through which the "present realities" of the Jim Crow South

7. Diane McWhorter, "The Moment That Made a Movement," *Washington Post*, 2 May 1993, https://www.washingtonpost.com/archive/opinions/1993/05/02/the-moment-that-made-a-movement/20eef454-daa6-45f3-a29a-4b03b9d16097 (accessed 10 October 2017).

8. Barry Schwartz, *Abraham Lincoln and the Forge of National Memory* (Chicago: University of Chicago Press, 2000), 231.

are brought to expression. The broader social and moral truths are conveyed through the distortion of details. This isn't uncommon.[9]

In chapter 1 we saw that Paul "thinks with" Jesus, even if his letters don't give us many examples of him "thinking about" Jesus. As we move on to the Gospels of Matthew and Mark and the two-volume narrative, Luke-Acts, we come to the earliest examples of extended "thinking about" Jesus. The Gospels and Acts are extended commemorative accounts of Jesus's life and teaching. They offer representations of Jesus not unlike a figure sitting for a portrait in oil on canvas. The authors offer us an image—a portrait—of Jesus, here teaching his followers, there healing the crowds; here clearing the temple courts, there sharing a meal with the disciples. The Gospels and Acts are about Jesus in a way Paul's letters were not.

Before we turn to the Gospels and Acts, we need to put them into historical context. These texts may be about Jesus and—in the case of Acts—the experiences of his earliest followers, but they were written years after the events they narrate. As such, they bear signs of later contexts (later, that is, than Jesus's ministry in the 20s–30s CE). For example, in Mark's account of Jesus's debate about handwashing before meals, the Markan narrator breaks in to explain to his readers (in the second half of the first century CE) the significance of what Jesus did (in the first half of the century). Whereas Jesus says, "Don't you know that nothing from the outside that enters a person has the power to contaminate? That's because it doesn't enter into the heart but into the stomach, and it goes out into the sewer," the author of Mark adds, "By saying this, Jesus declared that no food could contaminate a person in God's sight" (Mark 7:18-19). Understanding the Gospels, then, requires us to know something about when and under what circumstances they were written. This is the task of the next section.

Approaching the Gospels and Acts

The NT includes four Gospels, each of which is named for the individual whom the church credits with writing them. Ecclesial tradition

---

9. Barry Schwartz begins his discussion of Abraham Lincoln in American memory with US Representative Fred Schwengel's distortion of Lincoln into a "civil rights champion" (see *Forge of National Memory*, 1–5).

attributes two of the Gospels to Jesus's disciples (Matthew and John) and the other two to associates of the apostles (Mark and Luke, who are linked with Peter and Paul, respectively).

The Gospels themselves, however, don't identify who wrote them. Though none of the original copies of our Gospels still exists, we think those original copies didn't have the titles we associate with them ("According to Matthew," "According to Mark," and so forth). At some point in the second century CE, the church gave the Gospels their names. Compare this situation with the thirteen letters that claim Paul as their author. All thirteen begin, "From Paul."[10] None of the Gospels begin this way. The closest we get to a claim of authorship is the preface to Luke's Gospel:

> Many people have already applied themselves to the task of compiling an account of the events that have been fulfilled among us. They used what the original eyewitnesses and servants of the word handed down to us. Now, after having investigated everything carefully from the beginning, I have also decided to write a carefully ordered account for you, most honorable Theophilus. I want you to have confidence in the soundness of the instruction you have received. (Luke 1:1-4)

The author specifically addresses one of his readers, Theophilus (perhaps his patron, or sponsor, who assisted in the publication and dissemination of the text), and he explains the reason he is writing another "account of the events that have been fulfilled among us." The author never identifies himself, beyond referring to himself as "I" and, importantly, making a distinction between himself and "the original eyewitnesses and servants of the word."[11] We get no indication that the author's name is "Luke," and we get explicit confirmation that the author was not an actual eyewitness to the ministry of Jesus.

None of the Gospels appear to have been written by Jesus's eyewitnesses, though perhaps our authors, called "evangelists," had access to some of those eyewitnesses and included stories and information they

---

10. In Greek, the texts begin simply by identifying their author: *Paulos* (lit., just "Paul"). The CEB translation clarifies that this is the standard Hellenistic way letter-writers would identify themselves.

11. For a technical treatment of Luke's preface, see Loveday Alexander, *The Preface to Luke's Gospel: Literary Convention and Social Context in Luke 1.1–4 and Acts 1.1*, SNTSMS 78 (Cambridge: Cambridge University Press, 1993).

learned from them.[12] Luke's Gospel, as we have seen, plainly says it isn't written by an eyewitness to Jesus's life and teaching. Neither Matthew nor Mark claim they were written by one of Jesus's disciples, though Christians in the second century CE would identify the author of Matthew as the disciple of the same name (see Mark 3:18 parr.). The Gospel of John makes two references to eyewitness testimony. First, after he recounts how Jesus died, the narrator says, "The one who saw this has testified, and his testimony is true. He knows that he speaks the truth, and he has testified so that you also can believe" (John 19:35). Then, after Jesus tells Peter to feed his sheep,[13] he sees "the disciple whom Jesus loved" and asks about him. The narrator says, "This is the disciple who testifies concerning these things and who wrote them down. We know that his testimony is true" (21:24). It isn't clear whether either of these verses intends to claim that the so-called beloved disciple (= "the disciple whom Jesus loved"; see John 13:23; 19:26; 21:7, 20) wrote the Fourth Gospel, or whether the author is claiming to have recorded the beloved disciple's testimony. In my view, the author is claiming that he knows the beloved disciple and is writing down his testimony; he isn't claiming to *be* the beloved disciple.

Whether or not the Gospels preserve eyewitness testimony to Jesus's life and teachings, they are anonymous texts (i.e., their authors don't identify themselves within the texts). Even if their traditional names—Matthew, Mark, Luke, and John—preserve accurate information about their actual authors, the texts themselves don't emphasize their authors' identity. Their anonymity, in fact, serves to focus the readers' attention not on their respective evangelist but rather on their subject: "Jesus Christ, God's Son" (Mark 1:1).[14] If, however, none of the Gospels were written by Jesus's closest associates, that would not erode the confidence we put in their

---

12. For a clear and succinct expression of the standard scholarly view, see Paula Fredriksen, *From Jesus to Christ: The Origins of the New Testament Images of Christ*, 2nd ed. (New Haven: Yale University Press, 2000), 3–4. Perhaps the strongest scholarly argument for a connection between eyewitness memory and the Gospels is put forward by Richard Bauckham (*Jesus and the Eyewitnesses: The Gospels as Eyewitness Testimony*, 2nd ed. [Eerdmans, 2017]), though his work been subject to considerable criticism (e.g., see Judith C. S. Redman, "How Accurate Are Eyewitnesses? Bauckham and the Eyewitnesses in the Light of Psychological Research," *JBL* [2010]: 177–97).

13. We will discuss this passage in more detail in chapter 3.

14. I am grateful to Joel Green for this way of assessing the Gospels' anonymity.

representations of Jesus. The church didn't canonize the four NT Gospels because of their judgments about who wrote them. The church attributed these Gospels to apostolic figures or their associates because they were already valued as inspired texts. In other words, the conclusion that the eyewitnesses to Jesus's ministry didn't write the Gospels isn't a theological conclusion but a historical conclusion, one that doesn't affect the question of their accuracy or their inspiration.

Another historical conclusion: Mark's Gospel is the oldest of the four NT Gospels; it was written before Matthew, Luke-Acts, and John, and the authors of the later Gospels (at least Matthew and Luke, but perhaps also John) were well acquainted with Mark. This conclusion, known as "Markan priority," is broadly accepted among scholars for reasons we don't have time to get into here.[15] Briefly stated, those reasons include: (i) almost all of Mark's material appears in Luke and, especially, Matthew, (ii) Mark's Greek as well as his portrayal of Jesus and the disciples seem rougher and less refined than Matthew's and, especially, Luke's, (iii) it is easier to explain Matthew's and Luke's additions to Mark than to explain Mark's curious decision, if he were familiar with Matthew and/or Luke, to omit so much material in the longer Gospels, and (iv) though Mark is the shortest Gospel, his stories are longer and more detailed than the parallel versions in the other Gospels.[16] For these and other reasons, NT scholars are convinced that Mark was written before its longer and more famous companions.

None of the Gospels say when they were written, so scholars piece together clues from the texts to make educated guesses. Mark's Gospel is usually dated around the Jewish war with Rome (66–70 CE), which ended with the catastrophic destruction of the Jerusalem temple. The majority of scholars date Mark to the buildup to the war (c. 65–70 CE),

---

15. See Arthur J. Bellinzoni Jr., ed., *The Two-Source Hypothesis: A Critical Appraisal* (Macon, GA: Mercer University Press, 1985), which includes essays that make "the case for the priority of Mark" (pp. 21–93) as well as essays that argue "against the priority of Mark" (pp. 95–217). See also Mark Goodacre's argument for Markan priority in *The Case Against Q: Studies in Markan Priority and the Synoptic Problem* (Harrisburg, PA: Trinity Press International, 2002), 19–45.

16. Compare Mark's version of the story of the Gadarene demoniac, which takes about 325 words in the Greek text and spans twenty verses (5:1-20), with the shorter versions in Matthew 8:28-34 (135 words; seven verses) and Luke 8:26-39 (293 words, fourteen verses).

though a strong plurality of scholars date Mark to the immediate aftermath of the war (c. 71–75 CE).[17] If Matthew and Luke (and Acts) were written after Mark and were familiar with the written Gospel of Mark, then they may have been written c. 80–95 CE, though no compelling reason exists why Matthew and/or Luke could not have been written even in the 70s.[18] The first three Gospels (and Acts), then, were likely written sometime during the years 65–95 CE, a full generation or two after the events they narrate.

We should take seriously that the Gospels, as stories *about* Jesus, do in fact reflect the conditions *in which* they were written (in addition to reflecting the conditions *of which* they speak). Research on social memory helps explain this situation, in which the Gospels maintain their quality as stories about Jesus even as they also bear the marks of being texts from later in the first century. The early Christians could not but remember Jesus with the questions, concerns, and cares of their own present in mind, and their memory of Jesus could not but bear the marks of their present in its portrayals and representations of Jesus.[19] As Mark narrated the story of Jesus in the 60s or 70s of the first century, his narration was shaped by and addressed the uncertainties of life in those later decades even as he told stories of the 20s and 30s. The same is true of the later Gospels.

Sometimes, however, Gospels scholarship misses the fact that narrations of the past *in* the present are, nevertheless, narrations *of* the past. Social memory theory refuses "to authorize any sharp distinction between memory and tradition."[20] Memory fuses past and present. That is,

---

17. James Crossley (*The Date of Mark's Gospel: Insight from the Law in Earliest Christianity,* JSNTSup 266 [London: T&T Clark, 2004]) dates Mark very early, c. 41 CE, on the basis of Mark's treatment of Jewish Law. His discussion of the Law in "earliest Christianity" is very good, though his proposal for dating Mark has not convinced many others.

18. Scholars typically want to leave enough time for Mark to have circulated throughout the Roman Empire in order for the authors of Matthew and Luke to become familiar with it, but we have no idea if "enough time," in this instance, means one year or ten. These are, in other words, little more than guesses.

19. See Alan Kirk and Tom Thatcher, "Jesus Tradition as Social Memory," in *Memory, Tradition, and Text: Uses of the Past in Early Christianity,* ed. Alan Kirk and Tom Thatcher, SemeiaSt 52 (Atlanta: SBL Press, 2005), 25–42.

20. Kirk and Thatcher, "Jesus Tradition," 32. In this context, the word *memory* refers to recollection of events in the past. The word *tradition,* as distinct from memory, refers to changes, expansions, and developments in how memory is recalled and expressed. The point here, then, is that memory and tradition are not two distinct concepts.

memory makes the challenges and questions of the present understandable and gives them meaning by aligning them with the perspectives and values of the past. The challenges and questions of the present undoubtedly affect how people remember and understand the past, but past perspectives and values also affect how people understand and live in the present. The present is rendered manageable because of its connection to the past, a past that already defines a society's identity, their values, their hopes and fears.

At the same time, memory and commemoration make the past relevant to the present by selectively and creatively shaping the past to speak to present concerns. These are distorting dynamics; memory dis-figures or re-figures both the present and the past even as it preserves and interprets them both. Recall the distortion—the preservation and interpretation—of the past and the present that we saw in Ronald McDowell's *Foot Soldier* statue. Without the larger social injustices of the Jim Crow South, Bill Hudson's photograph of a White police officer keeping his dog off a young Black teen may not have caught anyone's eye. But within the context of those injustices, Hudson's photograph became meaningful and would eventually inspire McDowell's commemorative sculpture in Kelly Ingram Park.

Jesus as Subject: Commemorating Jesus in Narrative

For the remainder of this chapter, we will briefly discuss each of the Synoptic Gospels (Matthew, Mark, and Luke), as well as the Acts of the Apostles.[21] We will consider each Gospel in the order they were written: first, the Gospel of Mark, then the Gospel of Matthew, and then finally the two-volume Luke-Acts.[22] If Jesus was the *vehicle* of early Christian

---

21. The Gospel of John has substantial differences from the Synoptic Gospels; its language, theology, and even order and dating of events differ markedly from the other canonical narratives. Therefore, we will consider the Fourth Gospel in the next chapter.

22. The encoded author of Luke-Acts was an eyewitness of and participant in some of the events or stories of Paul's career; note the so-called "we passages," which begin in Acts 16:10 and continue, with a few interruptions, to the end of the narrative.

memory in Paul's letters, he is the *object* of early Christian memory in the Gospels and Acts. Our goal will be to glimpse something of Jesus as the object of memory, to see the Gospels as portraits of Jesus painted three to five decades after his life. Why did Mark, Matthew, and Luke expend the effort to commemorate Jesus in written texts, especially in light of the difficulties obtaining writing materials and compiling such lengthy written narratives, as well as the relative scarcity of individuals who could read them? What did they accomplish by commemorating Jesus as they did? And what do they have to say to us today?

In the Gospel of Mark, we will pay close attention to the two figures called "king" in the earliest Gospel. Mark's narrative is surprising here, not just because of *whom* Mark calls king but also because of *how*. As we will see, in Mark's story no one is seriously or genuinely called king. In the story, the title "king" is only given ironically, even sarcastically. Even so, Mark shows us what happens when a wannabe king pretends his way to power (spoiler: the result is gruesome). He tells the story of Jesus's enemies mocking him for any aspirations he may have harbored to be king. Despite their scorn, they unwittingly elevate him to the throne and exalt him in the very act of mocking and crucifying him. We will then turn to the Gospel of Matthew, where we will trace how the evangelist expands, deepens, and strengthens the connections between the life of Jesus, king of the Jews, and Israel's biblical traditions. Everything from Jesus's birth to his death happened in order to fulfill the scriptures; this included his teaching in parables and his healings and exorcisms. The Gospel of Luke, however, goes even further than Matthew; the Third Evangelist goes to special lengths to show how Jesus's resurrection from the dead also fulfills the scriptures. Finally, in the second half of Luke's narrative, we will see how Jesus the king continues to be active in the advance of his kingdom despite his surprising departure off the stage in Acts 1. (That is, in addition to being the main character in Scene 4 ["The Coming of the King: Redemption Accomplished"], Jesus continues to be an active character in Scene 5 ["Spreading the News of the King: The Mission of the Church"].)

Are You the King of the Jews? Mark's Gospel

We don't know much about how the early Christians remembered Jesus before the Gospel of Mark was written, sometime around the year 70 CE.[23] As we saw in chapter 1, Paul doesn't offer very many biographical details about Jesus. He does, however, attest Jesus's enormous influence on how his followers understood the past and perceived the present.

Suddenly, with Mark's Gospel, the remembered life of Jesus comes into glorious display, complete with accounts of his activities, snapshots of his teaching, hints at his emotional reactions to those around him, and especially a presentation of his execution by crucifixion "to liberate many people" (Mark 10:45). Some have suggested that Mark's account of the Jesus tradition is revolutionary, a corrective to previous ways of remembering Jesus.[24] The theory here is that Mark wrote his Gospel in order to correct other prominent ways of remembering Jesus in the mid-first century CE. I prefer to approach Mark's Gospel as an *instance* of the Jesus tradition, a commemorative portrayal of Jesus that takes advantage of potentials already latent within the Jesus tradition even as he does something innovative: he *writes* the first enduring extended narrative of Jesus's life.[25] In other words, Mark is representative of first-generation memories of Jesus rather than being an exact replication of or a corrective response to those memories.

One of the more pervasive aspects of Mark's portrait of Jesus is his royal status. From beginning to end, Jesus announces the coming and

---

23. Scholars often refer to a document, which they call "Q," that they suppose existed and offered Matthew and Luke a source for Jesus's teachings in addition to Mark's Gospel. If Q ever existed, it doesn't any longer, though it has often been reconstructed on the basis of the material in Matthew and Luke but not Mark. Q is usually thought to have been written before Mark; if this is right, Q would offer us an example of Jesus's memory before Mark. Since everything about Q is hypothetical, we will not pay any attention to it here. For a reconstruction of Q, see James M. Robinson, Paul Hoffmann, and John S. Kloppenborg, eds., *The Critical Edition of Q*, Hermeneia (Minneapolis: Fortress, 2000).

24. See, for example, Werner H. Kelber, *The Oral and the Written Gospel: The Hermeneutics of Speaking and Writing in the Synoptic Tradition, Mark, Paul, and Q* (Philadelphia: Fortress, 1983); Kelber reiterated this thesis in Werner H. Kelber and Tom Thatcher, "'It's Not Easy to Take a Fresh Approach': Reflections on *The Oral and the Written Gospel*, Twenty-Five Years Later," in *Jesus, the Voice, and the Text: Beyond* The Oral and the Written Gospel, ed. Tom Thatcher (Waco, TX: Baylor University Press, 2008), 27–44.

25. See my discussion of the Jesus tradition in Rafael Rodríguez, *Structuring Early Christian Memory: Jesus in Tradition, Performance, and Text*, European Studies on Christian Origins, LNTS 407 (London: T&T Clark, 2010).

arrival of the kingdom of God. At one time it was fashionable among NT scholars to note that the phrase "kingdom of God" is lacking from the Hebrew Bible. As a result, Jesus's emphasis on the kingdom of God was seen as a departure from biblical Jewish ideas, an innovation of the new faith that would become Christianity. More recently, however, scholarship acknowledges that the reign of YHWH, the relationship of Israel's (and/or Judah's) king to YHWH, and the eschatological hope for YHWH to assume his rightful place as king in relation to all other nations and their gods are all pervasive ideas in biblical and postbiblical Judaism. In addition, the idea of God's reign and his kingdom is related to other key biblical themes. We already said in the introduction that "covenant" and "kingdom of God" are related ideas. We will give an example of the relationship between them here.

Toward the end of his life, David, the king of Israel, surveyed his situation and was disturbed that he lived in a cedar palace while the chest containing the tablets of the covenant, the site of God's presence, dwelt in a tent (2 Sam 7:1-2). David intends to address this asymmetry, but God sends the prophet Nathan to tell him, "You are not the one to build the temple for me to live in" (7:5). In fact, 2 Samuel 7 makes clear David has not been and will not be building anything at all. Throughout David's illustrious reign, God has been building up David's kingdom and his dynasty. "I took you from the pasture," says the Lord, "from following the flock, to be leader over my people Israel" (7:8). Just as he had promised he would make Abraham a great nation (Gen 12:1-3), YHWH promises to make David's name great (2 Sam 7:9). Then he adds:

> And the LORD declares to you that the LORD will make a house for you. When the time comes for you to die and you lie down with your ancestors, I will raise up your descendant—one of your very own children—to succeed you, and I will establish his kingdom. He will build a house for my name, and I will establish his royal throne forever. I will be a father to him, and he will be a son to me. Whenever he does wrong, I will discipline him with a human rod, with blows from human beings. But I will never take my faithful love away from him like I took it away from Saul, whom I set aside in favor of you. Your house and your king-

45

dom will be secured forever before me. Your throne will be established forever. (2 Sam 7:11-16; CEB modified)[26]

The word *house* (Heb.: *bayit*; Grk: *oikos*) can take on a range of meanings. The word *house* is used in 2 Samuel 7 to refer to David's palace (vv. 1, 2), to the planned temple of YHWH (vv. 5, 6, 7, 13), and to the promised Davidic dynasty (vv. 11, 16). In this passage, then, YHWH rejects David's plan to build a "house" (= temple) for him, announces that David's heir will actually build a "house" (= temple) for God's name, and finally promises that he himself will build David's "house" (= dynasty).

This is the Davidic covenant, and it is directly related to the Davidic kingdom, in which the son of David is reckoned the son of God (see 7:14) as he rules over the people of God.[27] The son of David rules on YHWH's behalf, and so his kingdom is also God's kingdom. After the destruction of Jerusalem in 586 BCE and the end of the Davidic monarchy, the promise of an eternal Davidic dynasty gave rise to eschatological hopes for a future restoration of the kingdom of Israel. Jews could turn to the Davidic covenant to express their hope that, someday, God would drive out sinners (both foreign and Jewish) and raise up a new son of David to sit on Israel's throne.

Fifty years before the birth of Jesus, a Jewish text called the Psalms of Solomon implored God, saying: "See, O LORD, and raise up for them their king, the son of David, at the time which you foresaw, O God, to rule over Israel your servant" (Pss. Sol. 17:21).[28] At the same time—and this is a very important point—the reign of the son of David was also the reign of YHWH. Consider again Psalms of Solomon 17, which begins, "O LORD, you are our king forever and ever" (17:1) and which prays for the

---

26. See the discussion in Adela Yarbro Collins and John J. Collins, *King and Messiah as Son of God: Divine, Human, and Angelic Messianic Figures in Biblical and Related Literature* (Grand Rapids: Eerdmans, 2008), 25–30; see also John J. Collins, "Pre-Christian Jewish Messianism: An Overview," in *The Messiah in Early Judaism and Christianity*, ed. Magnus Zetterholm (Minneapolis: Fortress, 2007), 1–20 (esp. p. 3); Matthias Henze, *Mind the Gap: How the Jewish Writings between the Old and New Testament Help Us Understand Jesus* (Minneapolis: Fortress, 2017), 59–67.

27. David's voice applies the language of "covenant" to YHWH's promise in 2 Samuel 23:5: "He has made an eternal covenant [Heb.: *berit olam*; Grk. *diathēkē aiōnion*] with me, laid out and secure in every detail. Yes, he provides every one of my victories and brings my every desire to pass."

28. Translation taken from Kenneth Atkinson, "Psalms of Solomon," in *Outside the Bible: Ancient Jewish Writings Related to Scripture*, ed. Louis H. Feldman, James L. Kugel, and Lawrence H. Schiffman, 3 vols. (Philadelphia: Jewish Publication Society, 2013), 2:1903–23.

rise of a new son of David to be king. This text spends considerable time anticipating the just actions and reign of the new Davidic king (17:26-33) before declaring that this Davidic king is himself ruled by YHWH. "The LORD himself is his king" (17:34), says the psalmist, and the power he wields is the power of God.[29] The bulk of Psalms of Solomon 17 is a reflection on the utopian reign of the godly son of David, but its final words declare that God himself is Israel's true king: "The LORD himself is our king forever and ever" (17:46).

Recall the synopsis of the Bible's drama in six scenes, which we discussed in the introduction.[30] In Scene 3, "The King Chooses Israel: Redemption Initiated," we discussed the related concepts "covenant" and "kingdom of God." "The King" who "chooses Israel" can only be YHWH, the creator God of Israel, who rules the whole earth but who has chosen a nation of slaves to be his people, the vehicle through which "all the families of the earth will be blessed" (Gen 12:3). Scene 4, then, was called "The Coming of the King: Redemption Accomplished." Consider the question: Who is "the King" in the title of Scene 4?

The most reasonable answer must be: YHWH, the same figure who was the King of Scene 3. The covenant between Israel and God was a promise of presence: the people would dwell in YHWH's presence, and he would dwell in theirs. As Israel violated that covenant, God sent prophets to the people to declare to them their sinfulness, to invite them to change their hearts and ways, and to warn them of God's wrath if they persisted in their unfaithfulness. The wrath of God included a number of punishments, including defeat by Israel's enemies and exile to other lands.[31]

---

29. Consider the following, which sounds very much like some of the more exalted NT language used to describe the reign of Jesus: "he shall strike the earth with the word of his mouth forever, he shall bless the people of the LORD in wisdom with joy. And he himself shall be pure from sin, so that he may rule a great people, that he may rebuke rulers and remove sinners by the strength of his word.... God has made him strong in the holy spirit, and wise in the counsel of understanding, with strength and righteousness" (Pss. Sol. 17:35-37).

30. Recall that this discussion drew on Bartholomew and Goheen's book, *Drama of Scripture*.

31. The northern kingdom of Israel was defeated by the Assyrian Empire in 722 BCE, and the Israelites were exiled to other lands while other peoples were resettled in the land of the northern kingdom. The southern kingdom of Judah was defeated by the Babylonian Empire in 586 BCE. The Judahites were exiled to Babylon and, to a lesser extent, Egypt, though the land was not repopulated by non-Judahite peoples. In the late sixth century BCE, the Persian Empire conquered the Babylonians, and the exiled Judahites were permitted to return to their land, to rebuild Jerusalem and her walls, and to build a second temple of YHWH.

But another aspect of Israel's punishment, which is noted less often in Christian contexts, was YHWH's departure from the people. The prophet Ezekiel, writing from Babylon before the destruction of Jerusalem in 586 BCE, sees a vision of the throne of God in the Jerusalem temple, with God sitting on his throne. Then, in a threatening gesture, God stands up and moves toward the threshold of the temple (that is, he moves toward the door): "Then the LORD's glory rose from above the winged creatures and moved toward the temple's threshold. The temple was filled with the cloud, and the courtyard was filled with the brightness of the LORD's glory" (Ezek 10:4). The risen, standing LORD declares his judgment against the people, and then he leaves the city: "the winged creatures raised their wings. The wheels were next to them, and the glory of Israel's God was above them. The LORD's glory ascended from the middle of the city, and it stopped at the mountain east of the city" (11:22–23). Israel's God no longer dwells in his temple; he has been driven out by the sins of his people.

But he will not be gone forever. He will return. So the prophet Isaiah proclaims the end of God's wrath and the restoration of the covenantal relationship between YHWH and Israel:

> Comfort, comfort my people!
>   says your God.
> Speak compassionately to Jerusalem,
>   and proclaim to her that her compulsory service has ended,
>   that her penalty has been paid,
>   that she has received from the LORD's hand double for all her sins!
> A voice is crying out:
> "Clear the LORD's way in the desert!
>   Make a level highway in the wilderness for our God!
> Every valley will be raised up,
>   and every mountain and hill will be flattened.
>   Uneven ground will become level,
>   and rough terrain a valley plain.
> The LORD's glory will appear,

and all humanity will see it together;
the LORD's mouth has commanded it." (Isa 40:1-5)[32]

Isaiah announces that the LORD, YHWH, Israel's God, will return to his people. The penalty for their sins will come to an end, and the people will make preparations for the King's return to Zion. They will prepare his way in the desert, filling in the valleys and leveling the mountains. When the King returns, the nation will be restored, and "all humanity will see it together." And the King who returns is Israel's God, YHWH.

The Gospel of Mark doesn't reject any of this. Nevertheless, Mark's answer to our question is more complicated. Who is the King in the title of scene 4, the King who comes and accomplishes redemption? Mark's Gospel, from its very first line, declares that Jesus Christ, the Son of God, is the coming King, the king of Israel who shepherds the people. In other words, in the earliest sustained commemorative portrayal of Jesus we have available to us today, *this teacher and exorcist is already elevated to the status of king.* Mark's Gospel already shows signs of appreciating how surprising—we might even say unbelievable—it is to put forward a crucified teacher and healer from Galilee as Israel's king. As we will see, it wasn't easy to be called king in Roman-controlled Galilee and Judea.

We start, first, with a couple of facts. Mark uses the word *basileus* ("king") twelve times. Those twelve uses, however, are not evenly distributed throughout the Gospel. With one exception,[33] Mark uses the word *basileus* in only two chapters: Mark 6 and Mark 15. Or, to say the same thing a different way, Mark calls only two men "king": Herod Antipas, the son of Herod the Great, in Mark 6, and Jesus, who was publicly mocked and crucified, in Mark 15. Let's consider these in narrative order: first Herod Antipas, then Jesus.

---

32. Isaiah 40–55 is usually attributed to "deutero-Isaiah," perhaps a sixth-century BCE prophet in Babylon whose oracles were appended onto prophecies of the eighth-century BCE prophet Isaiah, from Judah. However, the Jews of the late Second Temple era, including the early Christians, were not aware of or interested in theories of Isaianic composition and redaction, so distinctions between Isaiah, deutero-Isaiah, and trito-Isaiah (Isa 56–66) hardly matter here.

33. The one exception is in Mark 13:9: "Watch out for yourselves. People will hand you over to the councils. You will be beaten in the synagogues. You will stand before governors and kings [*basileōn*] because of me so that you can testify before them."

In Mark 6, the author calls Herod Antipas "king Herod" (6:14).[34] After verse 14, he repeatedly calls Antipas "the king" in his account of John the Baptist's execution.[35] This is something of a problem, for historians as well as for Antipas. Rome never gave Antipas the title "king." Antipas's father, Herod the Great, had been granted the title "king of Judea" by the Roman senate, and in 37 BCE he returned to Judea and assumed his now-infamous rule over the Jews.[36] Herod's sons, however, were not called "kings"; they were called "tetrarchs," literally "rulers of one-fourth" or "one of four rulers." (Herod's grandson, Herod Agrippa, would be granted the title "king" by the emperors Caligula and Claudius in 41–44 CE.) In other words, *Antipas, the Herod of Mark 6, was never called "king," whether of Judea or of Galilee.*

Not that Antipas didn't want to be called "king." According to the Jewish historian Josephus, Antipas sailed to Rome, encouraged by his wife Herodias, to ask the emperor to grant him the title "king."[37] Josephus correctly refers to Antipas as a "tetrarch" (*Ant.* 18.240). So also do Matthew and Luke; when they tell the story of Antipas and his execution of John the Baptist, they both call Antipas a "tetrarch."[38] Antipas,

---

34. It can be difficult to keep straight all the various men named "Herod" in this period. Herod the Great was the patriarch of the Herodian dynasty; this is the Herod who reigned as "king of the Jews" when Jesus was born. When he died (4 BCE), his kingdom was divided between three of his sons (who were given the title "tetrarchs"): Archelaus, Philip, and Herod Antipas. This last (viz., Herod Antipas) is the Herod who appears in Mark 6. Though Mark calls him "Herod," we will call him "Antipas" in order to avoid confusion. One of Herod the Great's grandsons, Herod Agrippa, will be granted the title "king" just like his grandfather; again, to avoid confusion we will call this figure "Agrippa." (This is the "Herod" who appears in Acts 12. Agrippa's son, also known as Herod Agrippa, is often called "Agrippa II" and appears in Acts 25–26 as "King Agrippa.")

35. Mark 6:22, 25, 26, and 27. Also, notice Antipas's promise to give "even as much as half my *kingdom*" (*heōs hēmisous tēs* basileias *mou*) in verse 23. The CEB translates *basileus* as "the ruler" in verse 25 and simply as "he" in verse 27; this obscures Mark's repeated and rapid-fire references to Herod Antipas as "king."

36. Notice Matthew's portrayal of Herod and his subjects when the magi come to Jerusalem from the East, asking about "the newborn king of the Jews" (Matt 2:1-12; v. 2 quoted). Herod and all the citizens of Jerusalem are troubled, presumably at least in part because Herod was not *born* "king of the Jews" but was appointed to that status by a foreign, pagan body. As we already saw in Psalms of Solomon 17, this could be widely seen as a problematic, even illegitimate method of enthronement.

37. See Josephus, *Antiquities of the Jews*, 18.240–56.

38. See Matt 14:1; Luke 3:19; 9:7; Acts 13:1. Matthew refers to Herod Antipas as "king" in Matthew 14:9, which Mark Goodacre explains as an example of "editorial fatigue" (see *Case Against Q*, 42; see also idem, "Fatigue in the Synoptics," *NTS* [1998]: 45–58).

in other words, was a petty prince rather than a king. In fact, his bid to become king ends badly. When he arrives in Rome, his nephew—Herodias's brother—accuses him of plotting against the emperor, and Caesar sends Antipas and Herodias into exile.[39] Antipas never does become king.

Why, then, does Mark repeatedly call Antipas "king" when he very conspicuously never was a king? One explanation is that Mark is reflecting local usage.[40] Or perhaps "such constitutional niceties" didn't really matter in Galilee.[41] Or perhaps Mark simply made a mistake.[42] These are all popular explanations for Mark's repeated references to this Herod, Herod Antipas, as "king."

None of these explanations, however, consider the possibility that Mark intentionally calls Antipas a "king" in a passage where Antipas fails to live up to regal expectations. Mark's repeated references to Antipas as "king"—he calls Antipas "king" not once or twice but *five times!*—is sarcastic, even derogatory.[43] Mark places the reality of Antipas's power, which is weak and pathetic and manipulated by his wife and (her) daughter, in stark juxtaposition with the consequences of that power: the execution of John the Baptist by beheading. We should recognize that this is certainly an interpretive presentation; from other, even more typical perspectives

---

39. For an introductory discussion of Herod the Great and his confusing family (including a helpful family tree), see Steve Mason, *Josephus and the New Testament*, 2nd ed. (Peabody, MA: Hendrickson, 2003), 147–64.

40. Harold W. Hoehner, *Herod Antipas*, SNTSMS 17 (Cambridge: Cambridge University Press, 1972), 149–50; Adela Yarbro Collins, *Mark: A Commentary*, Hermeneia (Minneapolis: Fortress, 2007), 303.

41. R. T. France, *The Gospel of Mark: A Commentary on the Greek Text*, NIGTC (Grand Rapids: Eerdmans, 2002), 252.

42. Francis J. Moloney, *The Gospel of Mark: A Commentary* (Grand Rapids: Baker Academic, 2002), 126 (in addition to the main text, see n. 47); see also Helen Bond, "Herodian Dynasty," *DJG2* 379–82 (381).

43. See Joel Marcus, *Mark: A New Translation with Introduction and Commentary*, 2 vols., AB 27 (New Haven: Yale University Press, 1999–2009), 1:398: "[The title 'king' is] an example of the evangelist's irony, for it is prominent in a passage in which Herod is outwitted and manipulated by two women and hamstrung by his own oath and his fear of losing face before his courtiers. Throughout the passage, moreover, we see that this supposed 'king' is not even in control of himself, much less of his subjects; he is, rather, overmastered by his emotions, which swing wildly from superstitious dread (6:14, 16) to awe, fascination, and confusion (6:20), to a sexual arousal that seems to border on insanity (6:22-23), to extreme depression (6:26). In this context his pretensions to royal authority (6:16, 27) appear almost farcical; Herod is one who merely *appears* to rule (cf. 10:42), whereas actually his strings are pulled by others."

(e.g., economics, politics, and so on), it is possible to characterize Antipas's forty-three-year rule—his *tetrarchy*—over Galilee and Perea as "good and prosperous."[44] Mark, however, was characterizing Antipas's Galilee prophetically, not economically or politically.

Mark brings the story of Antipas's birthday banquet and the beheading of John the Baptist (Mark 6:14-29) together with the story of Jesus feeding the crowd in the wilderness (6:30-44). The effect is to contrast two "royal feasts." Antipas's feast ends with John's head on a platter; Jesus's ends with baskets-full of leftovers, even after everyone has eaten their fill. Though Mark never calls Jesus "king" in Mark 6, Jesus's compassion on the crowd, "because they were like sheep without a shepherd," clearly if implicitly establishes Jesus as an alternative to Antipas's Roman-sponsored rule.[45] The feeding of the five thousand reverberates with echoes of the exodus: after death in the court of a "king" (or a pharaoh), a large multitude goes out into the wilderness and experiences a miraculous provision of bread.[46] In this context, with the exodus ringing in our ears, the description of the crowds as "sheep without a shepherd" and Mark's account of Jesus stepping into the role of shepherd signal Jesus's function as leader of the people, as king.[47]

Beyond the story of Antipas's birthday in Mark 6, the only other place where Mark uses *basileus* (other than Mark 13:9) is in his account of Jesus's trial and crucifixion (Mark 15). "[T]he central irony in the passion narratives of the Gospels is that Jesus's crucifixion turns out to be his elevation

---

44. Bond, "Herodian Dynasty," 381.

45. The Fourth Gospel brings the royal implications of the feeding of the five thousand out into the open. After the miraculous feeding, John says, "Jesus understood that they were about to come and force him to be their king, so he took refuge again, alone on a mountain" (John 6:15). We will pay closer attention to the sheep and shepherding imagery in chapter 3.

46. The Fourth Gospel explicitly links the miraculous provision of bread in the feeding of the five thousand with the exodus: "Our ancestors ate manna in the wilderness, just as it is written, 'He gave them bread from heaven to eat'" (John 6:30-60; v. 31 quoted).

47. "As a metaphor, the shepherd of sheep was a common figure of speech in Israel for a leader of Israel like Moses (Isa 63:11), or more often of a Joshua-like military hero who would muster Israel's forces for war" (James R. Edwards, *The Gospel According to Mark*, Pillar New Testament Commentary [Grand Rapids: Eerdmans, 2002], 191; see also Rikki E. Watts, *Isaiah's New Exodus and Mark*, WUNT 2/88 [Tübingen: Mohr Siebeck, 1997], 80, 179). Joel Marcus (*The Way of the Lord: Christological Exegesis of the Old Testament in the Gospel of Mark* [Louisville: Westminster John Knox, 1992], 159–64) discusses the royal shepherd imagery in Mark 14:27 as a resonance of Zechariah 9–14.

to kingship."[48] Unlike the title "king" in Mark 6, the use of "king" in Mark 15 is obviously sarcastic. All six references to Jesus as "king" in Mark 15 are "heavy with irony, since none of the characters—neither Pilate, nor the soldiers... nor the taunting passersby at Golgotha—really believes that Jesus is a king."[49] Crucifixion, as the act of "lifting up" victims above their peers, was an intentionally ironic means of execution, "designed to mimic, parody, and puncture the pretensions of insubordinate transgressors by displaying a deliberately horrible mirror of their self-elevation."[50]

Mark was not the first person to recognize the parodic, sarcastic intentions of crucifixion as a mocking "exaltation." Those intentions were already woven into the fabric of crucifixion as a public, symbolic event. If a person got above himself, Rome was happy to exalt and elevate him further, by lifting him up onto a cross. Such an exaltation, such an elevation was a mocking, macabre enthronement that lampooned even the *idea* of any alternative to Roman power as surely as it fixed its victim's body with iron and wood.[51]

If Mark was not the first person to recognize crucifixion's sarcastic intentions, he nevertheless turned those intentions against Jesus's crucifiers, both the Romans who affixed him to the cross and the Jews who called for them to do so. With each reference to Jesus as "king of the Jews," Mark winks to his audience, acknowledging a truth shared between him and his readers but hidden from the characters in the narrative. Every time Pilate ironically calls Jesus "king of the Jews" (Mark 15:2, 9, 12), every time the soldiers mock Jesus as "king of the Jews (15:18), every time lookers-on read the charge against him—"the king of the Jews"—or taunt him with jeers of "the Christ, the king of Israel" (15:26, 32), they speak a truth they don't understand. In the climactic act of their failure to recognize the king of Israel, they themselves enthrone him.

These two scenes—"King" Antipas's birthday banquet and Jesus's parodic coronation via crucifixion—make up Mark's use of the word *basileus*

---

48. Joel Marcus, "Crucifixion as Parodic Exaltation," *JBL* 125 (2006): 73–87 (73).

49. Marcus, "Parodic Exaltation," 73.

50. Marcus, "Parodic Exaltation," 78.

51. "Since... there was an overlap between the imagery of elevation and that of enthronement, it should come as no surprise that not only crucifixion and exaltation but also crucifixion and kingship were sometimes conflated by the guardians of punishment" (Marcus, "Parodic Exaltation," 83).

("king"). We should appreciate what Mark accomplishes in calling Antipas and Jesus "king." Jesus had been mocked for his pretentions to be "king of the Jews" in the most public way imaginable. No one in the narrative of Mark 15 *actually* thought Jesus was king, but Mark and his audience—including us—know better. Within the span of a single generation, Mark turns the parodic sneer of crucifixion against Rome's appointed representative in Galilee. In an exact photographic negative of Mark 15, Mark 6 recounts a pretense to power, but Mark, like Pilate, lampoons that pretension in order to expose it as false. In both chapters, only Mark and his audience are in on the truth. Only Mark and his audience are properly positioned to see that Jesus *and not Antipas*, Jesus *and not Rome*, reigns as king.

The King who comes in Scene 4 to accomplish the redemption of his people is Jesus Christ, the Son of God.

This Fulfilled the Word Spoken through the Prophet: Matthew's Gospel

At some point after Mark's Gospel was written, Matthew took up stylus and parchment to write his account of Jesus's life and teachings. Like Mark—but unlike Luke and John—Matthew doesn't provide much reflection on his role as an author.[52] Matthew includes an astonishing amount of material he would've found in Mark, so much so that it's possible to read Matthew as "an enlarged edition of Mark," because "Matthew reproduces 90% of the subject matter of Mark in language very largely identical with that of Mark."[53] Yet Matthew does more than simply "enlarge" Mark's account; he *retells* the story of Jesus, taking up many of Mark's features and much of his content and employing them for his own narrative representation.

---

52. Compare Luke's prefaces (Luke 1:1-4; Acts 1:1) and John's explicit statements of purpose (John 20:30-31; 21:24-25).

53. B. H. Streeter, *The Four Gospels: A Study of Origins, Treating of the Manuscript Tradition, Sources, Authorship, and Dates* (London: Macmillan, 1924), 151. Richard Beaton ("How Matthew Writes," in *The Written Gospel*, ed. Markus Bockmuehl and Donald A. Hagner [Cambridge: Cambridge University Press, 2005], 116–34 [120]) lowers the estimate to "roughly 80 per cent," though this is still an astounding number.

At the beginning of the Gospel of Mark, Jesus responds to the arrest of John the Baptist by returning to Galilee and proclaiming the gospel: "The time *is fulfilled*! Here comes God's kingdom! Change your hearts and lives, and trust this good news!" (Mark 1:15, CEB modified). Toward the end of Mark, Jesus tells the mob who came out to arrest him, "Have you come with swords and clubs to arrest me, like an outlaw? Day after day, I was with you, teaching in the temple, but you didn't arrest me. But let the scriptures *be fulfilled*" (14:48-49, emphasis added). These are the only two times Mark uses the word *fulfill* (*plēroō*), and both are concerned with the fulfillment—the completion—of God's plan for his people.[54] This idea functions as a sort of bookends, or frame, for Mark's portrait of Jesus.

Matthew takes Mark's framing idea of fulfillment, expands it, and weaves it throughout his Gospel. Both of these actions—expanding and weaving—are significant. Perhaps few things are as peculiarly and uniquely Matthean as the so-called fulfillment formulas, by which Matthew claims that this or that event in Jesus's life happened in order to "fulfill what the prophet said."[55] Surprisingly, although Mark 1:15 does use the word *fulfill* (Grk.: *plēroō*), Matthew's account of this same moment in Jesus's life does not.

Mark 1:14–15 (CEB modified)	Matthew 4:17
After John was arrested, Jesus came into Galilee announcing God's good news, saying, "The time is fulfilled! Here comes God's kingdom! Change your hearts and lives, and trust this good news!"	From that time Jesus began to announce, "Change your hearts and lives! Here comes the kingdom of heaven!"

The fact that Matthew avoids the word *fulfill* in Matthew 4:17 might suggest he is less interested in the concept of fulfillment than was Mark.

---

54. Adela Yarbro Collins (*Mark*, 686–87) rightly says of Mark: "It is certainly the case that Mark does not develop the idea of the fulfillment of scripture to the extent that Matthew does, but he does seem to express the notion here."

55. Jeannine K. Brown, "Matthew, Gospel Of," in *DJG2* 570–84 (573, 578). See Matt 1:22-23; 2:15, 17-18, 23; 4:14-16; 8:17; 12:15-21; 13:34-35; 21:4-5; 27:9. Brown also cites Matthew 2:5; 3:3; and 13:14-15. Neither Brown nor Richard Beaton ("How Matthew Writes," 128) include Matthew 26:54, 56 in their list of "fulfillment quotations," though Beaton does discuss these latter verses as "perhaps the best summary of Matthew's orientation" to the Old Testament.

On closer inspection, however, Matthew has expanded Mark's idea, with no less than five references to Jesus's fulfillment of scripture before Jesus's first public word.[56] First, Mary's pregnancy fulfilled the Isaianic prophecy in Isaiah 7:14 (Matt 1:22-23). Second, Jesus's family's flight to Egypt and their return to Judea and Galilee fulfilled Hosea 11:1 (Matt 2:15). Third, Herod's slaughter of the baby boys in Bethlehem fulfilled Jeremiah 31:15 (Matt 2:17-18). Fourth, Jesus's family's move to Nazareth fulfilled the word of "the prophets," though we're not sure which specific prophetic text Matthew has in mind (Matt 2:23). Finally, Jesus's return to Galilee and settlement in Capernaum fulfilled Isaiah 9:1-2 (Matt 4:14-16).

In Mark, Jesus declares, "the time is fulfilled." Matthew goes further than Mark and explains to his audience precisely *how* Jesus brings fulfillment.[57]

Matthew does more than expand the theme of fulfillment that opens and closes Mark's portrait of Jesus. He also weaves it throughout his own portrait. For example, Mark concludes the series of Jesus's parables with a narrative aside to his audience: "With many such parables he continued to give them the word, as much as they were able to hear. He spoke to them only in parables, then explained everything to his disciples when he was alone with them" (Mark 4:33-34). Mark has already explained Jesus's practice of teaching through parables in terms of Isaiah's complaint against Israel's sluggishness and failure to understand (Mark 4:10-12, echoing Isa 6:9-10). Matthew, hearing Mark's echo, specifies the prophetic referent of Jesus's words by mentioning Isaiah by name:

This is why I speak to the crowds in parables: although they see, they don't really see; and although they hear, they don't really hear or understand. What Isaiah prophesied about them is fulfilled [*anaplēroutai*; CEB

---

56. Jesus speaks to John the Baptist in Matthew 3:15 and to the devil in Matthew 4:4, 7, and 10. His first words to the public occur in Matthew 4:17.

57. Just as he expanded on Mark's opening reference to fulfillment, Matthew also expands Mark's closing reference to fulfillment. The Markan Jesus declares to everyone gathered in the garden, "But let the scriptures be fulfilled" (Mark 14:49). In Matthew, however, Jesus first turns to the disciples, armed and ready for battle, and asks them: "Do you think that I'm not able to ask my Father and he will send to me more than twelve battle groups of angels right away? But if I did that, how would the scriptures be fulfilled that say this must happen?" (Matt 26:53-54). Then he turns to the crowds and repeats, "All this has happened so that what the prophets said in the scriptures might be fulfilled" (26:56).

"has become completely true"]:[58] "You will hear, to be sure, but never understand; and you will certainly see but never recognize what you are seeing. For this people's senses have become calloused, and they've become hard of hearing, and they've shut their eyes so that they won't see with their eyes or hear with their ears or understand with their minds, and change their hearts and lives that I may heal them." (Matt 13:13-15)

Up to this point in chapter 13, Matthew has only repeated Mark's account of Jesus's teaching, though he makes explicit what Mark only implied: Jesus teaches the crowds in parables in order to fulfill (*anapleroō*) Isaiah's oracle about Israel.

Matthew will, however, integrate his interest in the fulfillment of scripture even more tightly into Jesus's teaching in parables. At the end of Jesus's parabolic teaching in Mark 4, the Markan narrator doesn't explicitly link Jesus's parables with Israel's scriptures.[59] Matthew, however, provides a prophetic warrant for Jesus's parabolic teaching: "Jesus said all these things to the crowds in parables, and he spoke to them only in parables. This was to fulfill what the prophet spoke: 'I'll speak in parables; I'll declare what has been hidden since the beginning of the world'" (Matt 13:34-35, citing Ps 78:2). Matthew portrays Jesus as the voice that speaks through the psalms in declaring God's mysterious purposes. The psalm proclaims the "riddles" (or "parables": *parabolē*; Heb.: *mashal*) of the exodus, of Israel's deliverance from Egypt and wandering in the wilderness (where "they forgot God's deeds as well as the wondrous works he showed them"; Ps 78:11), and YHWH's subsequent favor on Judah. The psalm says, "God rejected the tent of Joseph and didn't choose the tribe of Ephraim. Instead, he chose the tribe of Judah, the mountain of Zion, which he loves" (Ps 78:67-68). Like the psalmist, Matthew also follows up Jesus's fulfillment of "what the prophet spoke"[60] with an account of election and rejection,

---

58. Matthew 13:13 stands out for two reasons. First, it is Matthew's only use of a compound form of *plēroō*, here *anaplēroō*. Second, it is the only fulfillment quotation spoken by Jesus. All the other fulfillment quotations in Matthew are spoken by the narrator.

59. "With many such parables he continued to give them the word, as much as they were able to hear. He spoke to them only in parables, then explained everything to his disciples when he was alone with them" (Mark 4:33-34).

60. For a discussion of the psalms as prophecy in the Synoptic Gospels, see J. Samuel Subramanian, *The Synoptic Gospels and the Psalms as Prophecy*, LNTS 351 (London: T&T Clark, 2008).

first with an explanation of the parable of the weeds (Matt 13:24-30; see also 13:36-43), and second with the parable of the net (13:47-50). Matthew, in other words, integrates his interest in Jesus and the fulfillment of scripture with Mark's portrayal of Jesus's parabolic teaching. Jesus, as Matthew presents him, continues and extends the drama already begun in Israel's history and scriptures, and Matthew goes to significant lengths to draw out the connections between that drama's various scenes.

We've already seen that Matthew knits his account of Jesus's birth, as well as Jesus's return to Galilee, with Israel's scriptural tradition, noting multiple points of connection in which Jesus embodies Israel's story. Some people claim that Jesus thought he was "Israel-in-person, Israel's representative, the one in whom Israel's destiny was reaching its climax."[61] Whether or not this is right, we're making a more modest point, namely that *Matthew* thought Jesus was Israel-in-person and that, *for Matthew*, the whole nation of Israel was represented in the person of Jesus. Jesus, *according to Matthew*, picked up the strands of Israel's story, drawing them together and bringing that story to its fulfillment (or, to use Wright's word, its "climax"). In other words, Matthew is "the controlling synthetic imagination" that forges the connections in his Gospel between the Jesus tradition and Israel's scriptural tradition, giving the latter "a focused christological interpretation."[62] Matthew provides interpretive comments in order to guide his readers' interpretation of Jesus toward Israel's scriptures, even as he also guides his readers' interpretation of the scriptures toward Jesus. Of course, Matthew isn't the first to bring Jesus and Israel's scriptures together. The apostle Paul, as we saw in the previous chapter, does something similar, as does the author of Mark. But Matthew's fulfillment quotations certainly "belong to the editorial level of Matthew's Gospel";[63] that is, they are a distinctively Matthean means of aligning Israel's venerable biblical tradition with the emerging Jesus tradition.

---

61. N. T. Wright, *Jesus and the Victory of God*, Christian Origins and the Question of God 2 (Minneapolis: Fortress, 1996), 477–539 (p. 538 quoted). Richard Hays (*Echoes of Scripture in the Gospels* [Waco, TX: Baylor University Press, 2016], 113), refers to Matthew's "typological identification of Jesus with Israel."

62. Hays, *Echoes of Scripture in the Gospels*, 108.

63. Maarten J. J. Menken, *Matthew's Bible: The Old Testament Text of the Evangelist*, BETL 173 (Leuven: Peeters, 2004), 2.

The Matthean theme of fulfillment weaves thickly through the early stages of Matthew's narrative, through the birth of Jesus and his return to Galilee. It appears again at select moments later in the narrative, in connection with his healings and exorcisms (8:17; 12:17-21) and, as we have seen, with his teaching in parables (13:34-35; see also 13:13-15). Matthew also weaves the fulfillment theme into his Passion narrative, his account of Jesus's suffering (= "passion") and death. After Peter identifies Jesus as "the Christ, the Son of the living God," Jesus goes on to warn the disciples that "he had to go to Jerusalem and suffer many things from the elders, chief priests, and legal experts, and that he had to be killed and raised on the third day" (16:21; see also 17:22-23; 20:18-19). When Matthew says Jesus "had to go to Jerusalem and suffer," the clear implication is that these events must be fulfilled.

In Matthew 21, Jesus enters Jerusalem amidst considerable celebration and shouts of "Hosanna!" and praise for "the one who comes in the name of the Lord." Even amidst the joyous ruckus of Jesus's entry into Jerusalem, we hear the low, ominous tones of impending suffering. As the shouts of "Hosanna!" echo through the hills, the shadow of the cross falls over the city. Jesus has already said he must go to Jerusalem, suffer at the hands of the Jewish leaders, and be killed. We might be tempted to forget that Jesus expects to encounter the opposition of his people. After all, here we see Jesus riding into Jerusalem as king, reenacting Solomon's contested claim on David's throne.[64] The prophet Zechariah remembered Solomon's ride on David's mule and looked forward to a day when a new king would enter the city and "the LORD their God will deliver" the people of Jerusalem from their enemies (Zech 9:9-17). Nearly twenty chapters earlier the magi came to Jerusalem and asked, "Where is the newborn king of the Jews?" (Matt 2:1-2). Now, on the eve of the Passover, a large crowd ushers Jesus into the city, announcing the arrival of Jesus and his kingdom.

This was always going to create problems. By definition, the arrival of a new king poses a challenge to the current leadership. Jerusalem was the site of Israel's most powerful and significant figures: the chief priest and his associates in the temple, as well as representatives of Roman power.

---

64. See 1 Kings 1:32-40.

Though the Roman governor was usually seventy miles away in Caesarea Maritima, on the eve of the Passover he and his soldiers had made the journey to the Jewish capital to take a more active role in maintaining political stability. Once Jesus was in the city, the tension and opposition mounted as he began to disrupt the temple, speak a parable of judgment against the temple leadership, and engage a riddling contest with Pharisees, Sadducees, and at least one legal expert (Matt 21:12–22:46).[65]

These actions lead to Jesus's arrest in Gethsemane and, significantly for Matthew, are a key example of the theme of fulfillment. The Gospel of Mark had already forged a connection between Jesus's arrest and the fulfillment of the scriptures. When Jesus rebukes the disciples for trying to defend him, he declares, "But let the scriptures be fulfilled" (Mark 14:49). Matthew expands the connection between Jesus's arrest and the scriptures. First, Jesus rebukes his disciples, who seem to have overlooked that Jesus could summon angelic armies from his Father if he wanted to. "But if I did that, how would the scriptures be fulfilled that say this must happen?" (Matt 26:54). Then, Jesus turns to the mob that has come out to arrest him, pointing out that their treacherous conduct fulfills the scriptures: "Have you come with swords and clubs to arrest me, like a thief? Day after day, I sat in the temple teaching, but you didn't arrest me. But all this has happened so that what the prophets said in the scriptures might be fulfilled" (26:55-56). In neither of these statements does Jesus or the narrator explain which particular scripture is being fulfilled in Jesus's arrest. Jesus's arrest fulfills "the scriptures" as a whole rather than a particular chapter and verse. (Careful readers of Matthew might recall Matthew 5:17, where Jesus declares, "Don't even begin to think that I have come to do away with the Law and the Prophets. I haven't come to do away with them but to fulfill them.") Matthew aligns Jesus with the entirety of Israel's scriptural heritage rather than a specific moment within that heritage.[66] Jesus's arrest doesn't fulfill this-or-that scripture; Jesus's arrest fulfills *the scriptures*.

---

65. See Tom Thatcher et al., eds., *The Dictionary of the Bible and Ancient Media* (London: Bloomsbury T&T Clark, 2017), esp. Thatcher's discussion of the role of riddles in contesting identity, including a marginalized identity in opposition to dominant social forces. See also Tom Thatcher, *The Riddles of Jesus in John: A Study in Tradition and Folklore*, SBLMS 53 (Atlanta: Society of Biblical Literature, 2000).

66. For a similar phenomenon in Luke's Gospel, see Rodríguez, "Textual Orientations."

Finally, the last time Matthew signals that the events of Jesus's suffering fulfill a prophetic oracle occurs in conjunction with Judas's remorse and the priests' purchase of a potter's field with the money he returned to them: "This fulfilled the words of Jeremiah the prophet: 'And I took the thirty pieces of silver, the price for the one whose price had been set by some of the Israelites, and I gave them for the potter's field, as the Lord commanded me'" (Matt 27:9-10). From birth to death, Jesus brings "the words of the prophets" to fulfillment.

Intriguingly, Matthew doesn't produce a fulfillment quotation formula in the resurrection appearances. Indeed, Matthew 28 is surprisingly devoid of any references to scripture.[67] We saw in the previous chapter that Paul explicitly links both Jesus's burial and his resurrection on the third day to "the scriptures" (1 Cor 15:3-4). Despite the fact that Matthew was happy to drop a "this fulfilled the word spoken through the prophet" into his narrative at least ten times, he didn't apparently feel the need to align the resurrection of Jesus with Israel's scriptures.[68] Perhaps this should surprise us.

The Events That Have Been Fulfilled among Us: Luke–Acts

While Matthew refrained from explicitly noting the connection between Jesus's resurrection and Israel's scriptures, Luke didn't. Luke, like Matthew, frames his narrative as an account of "the events that have been fulfilled among us" (Luke 1:1), events that have a strong connection with Israel's scriptural tradition (Luke 4:21).[69] Luke "is concerned to show that this 'new' story, the story of Jesus, joins the 'old,' scriptural story as its

---

67. Biblical imagery (or "echoes") may be present in the description of the angelic appearance or, more significantly, in Jesus' promise, "Look, I myself will be with you every day until the end of this present age" (Matt 28:20). For discussion, see Hays, *Echoes of Scripture in the Gospels*, 171–74; R. T. France, *The Gospel of Matthew*, NICNT (Grand Rapids: Eerdmans, 2007), 1112–19. The point here isn't that Matthew 28 lacks allusions to scriptural tradition. The point is that Matthew nowhere draws attention to any biblical context within which to understand Jesus's resurrection."

68. Matthew uses "writing" words fifteen times (*graphō* ["I write"; 10x], *graphē* ["writing, scripture"; 4x], and *epigraphē* ["inscription"; 1x]). He never connects any of these words with Jesus's resurrection, whether to provide scriptural warrant for the resurrection (*gegraptai;* "it is written") or to link Jesus's resurrection to Israel's *graphai* ("scriptures").

69. See Rodríguez, *Structuring Early Christian Memory*, 213–73; idem, "Textual Orientations," 200–205.

ongoing manifestation and, indeed, as the realization of God's ancient plan."[70] Four moments in the Third Gospel are especially relevant for Luke's alignment of Israel's scriptures with Jesus's resurrection.

First, in Jesus's parable of Lazarus and the rich man (Luke 16:19-31), the rich man pleads with Abraham to send Lazarus to his father's house in order to warn his brothers (presumably against the kind of life that enjoys considerable wealth while overlooking the needs of the poor). Abraham rejects the rich man's request, saying, "They have Moses and the Prophets. They must listen to them" (16:29). The rich man objects. He already knows, apparently, that his brothers don't listen to Moses and the Prophets, but he imagines that a visit from a dead beggar would change their hearts. Abraham, however, persists: "If they don't listen to Moses and the Prophets, then neither will they be persuaded if someone rises from the dead" (16:31). Scholars regularly (and rightly) note the connection that Luke's Abraham makes between Moses, on one hand, and "radical neighborliness," on the other.[71] I would point out, however, that Luke's Abraham also links Moses with resurrection.

Unfortunately, the link between Moses and resurrection has often been missed because verses 27-31 have been interpreted as a request for a sign.[72] But the point of Luke's parable isn't that God and/or Jesus won't give a sign; the point is that God has already given his people the Torah and the Prophets. The revelation of God's covenant with Israel in Torah and the Prophets is adequate for guiding God's people in the ways of mercy and justice.[73] Luke brings the idea of resurrection together with Torah and the Prophets: "if someone rises from the dead" (Luke 16:31), that

---

70. Joel B. Green, *The Theology of the Gospel of Luke*, New Testament Theology (Cambridge; New York: Cambridge University Press, 1995), 30.

71. See Paul Borgman, *The Way According to Luke: Hearing the Whole Story of Luke-Acts* (Grand Rapids: Eerdmans, 2006), 166–68.

72. Compare the Pharisees' request in Mark 8:11-12. Luke has an expression of this tradition at Luke 11:16, which he has incorporated into his account of the Beelzebul Controversy (11:14-23).

73. We might ask which chapter and verse of the Hebrew Bible would be sufficient for the rich man's brothers to know how to treat the poor and hungry. Richard Hays (*Echoes of Scripture in the Gospels*, 205–7) points to Deuteronomy 15:7-8; William Herzog (*Parables as Subversive Speech: Jesus as Pedagogue of the Oppressed* [Louisville: Westminster John Knox, 1994], 125) mentions Micah 6:8. The specific passage(s) from Torah and the Prophets that Luke's Abraham has in mind is probably not the point; the point is that Torah and the Prophets, had the rich man listened to them, would have prevented his current pathetic situation.

person would offer no advance on the will of God beyond Moses and the Prophets. Or, to say the same thing another way, Torah and the Prophets already speak the same message and with equal clarity as a messenger from beyond the grave. As we will see, the Third Evangelist will underscore this idea in Luke 24.

Second, shortly after the parable of Lazarus and the rich man, Jesus warns his disciples for the third time about events that will come to pass in Jerusalem. In this respect Luke reflects earlier accounts of the Jesus tradition. Both Mark and Matthew also narrate three "passion-resurrection predictions."[74] Luke goes even further than Mark and Matthew, however, and casts the third passion-resurrection prediction as a fulfillment of the Prophets. Jesus says, "Look, we're going up to Jerusalem, *and everything written about the Son of Man by the prophets will be accomplished.* He will be handed over to the Gentiles. He will be ridiculed, mistreated, and spit on. After torturing him, they will kill him. On the third day, he will rise up" (Luke 18:31-33, CEB modified). Neither Mark nor Matthew mentions the scriptures and/or the Prophets in any of their accounts of Jesus's passion-resurrection predictions. Similarly, the first two passion-resurrection predictions in Luke don't mention scripture. But here, in the fullest and most explicit anticipation of Jesus's suffering and vindication, Luke sees fit to make the point explicitly: the necessary events in Jerusalem— from Jesus's arrest to his trial and execution and on through his resurrection on the third day—bring to completion "everything written by the prophets."[75]

Third, one of the most direct connections between the scriptures and Jesus's suffering and resurrection occurs in Jesus's only encounter with Sadducees in Luke-Acts (Luke 20:27-38).[76] The Sadducees, "who deny that there's a resurrection" (20:27), present Jesus with a conundrum about marriage and resurrection. In his response, Jesus rejects the terms

---

74. See (i) Mark 8:31//Matt 16:21//Luke 9:22; (ii) Mark 9:31//Matt 17:22-23//Luke 9:44; and (iii) Mark 10:33-34//Matt 20:18-19//Luke 18:31-33. For the language of "passion-*resurrection* prediction," see Holly J. Carey, *Jesus' Cry from the Cross: Towards a First-Century Understanding of the Intertextual Relationship between Psalm 22 and the Narrative of Mark's Gospel*, LNTS 398 (London: T&T Clark, 2009), 46–48.

75. In 18:31, Luke doesn't use *plēroō* ("fulfill"); instead, he uses *teleō* ("complete, accomplish"). This use of *teleō*, however, is clearly synonymous with *plēroō*.

76. Both Mark and Matthew have parallels to this story; see Mark 12:18-27//Matt 22:23-33.

of their conundrum; the Sadducees, unfortunately, don't understand that "those who are considered worthy to participate in that age, that is, in the age of the resurrection from the dead, won't marry nor will they be given in marriage" (20:35). This response should have been sufficient to silence the Sadducees, to bring the contest between Jesus and his opponents to an end. But Jesus goes on to offer a scriptural basis for the widespread belief in the resurrection: "Even Moses demonstrated that the dead are raised—in the passage about the burning bush, when he speaks of the Lord as 'the God of Abraham, the God of Isaac, and the God of Jacob.' He isn't the God of the dead but of the living. To him they are all alive" (20:37-38). The Lukan Jesus alludes to Exodus 3, where the LORD calls to Moses from the burning bush and introduces himself, saying, "I am the God of your father, Abraham's God, Isaac's God, and Jacob's God" (Exod 3:6).[77] Modern readers might not find the hermeneutical principle at work in Jesus's interpretation compelling. Even so, it at least reveals that early Christians and other Jews of the Second Temple period understood the biblical texts to teach that God would raise the dead and reward the righteous.[78]

The fourth and final connection between resurrection and scripture occurs in the account of Jesus's resurrection appearances in Luke 24. In Luke's account of the empty tomb (Luke 24:1-12), the angelic messengers ("two men...in gleaming bright clothing") appeared to the women who had come to tend to Jesus's body and reminded them of Jesus's words: "Remember what he told you while he was still in Galilee, that the Human One [or "Son of Man"] must be handed over to sinners, be crucified, and on the third day rise again" (Luke 24:6-7). Jesus, according to Luke's angels, said three things "must" happen: Jesus must "be handed over," he must "be crucified," and he must "rise again." The word *must* translates the

---

77. The scriptural warrant for the resurrection is not unique to Luke. Both Mark 12:26-27 and Matthew 22:31-32 appeal to Exodus 3:6 as justification for the resurrection. The point of the present discussion, however, is that Luke enlarges the connection between the scriptures and Jesus's resurrection vis-à-vis what he found in his sources (Mark, and perhaps also Matthew), and in light of this enlarging the scriptural basis for resurrection in Luke 20:37-38 takes on additional meaning.

78. This is in contrast to a more modern hermeneutic that argues no Hebrew biblical text speaks of the resurrection before—or indeed other than—Daniel (see, e.g., Matthias Henze, *Mind the Gap: How the Jewish Writings Between the Old and New Testament Help Us Understand Jesus* [Minneapolis: Fortress, 2017], 147–79 [158]).

impersonal verb, *dei*, a verb Luke uses to make the point that "the will of God, as manifested and recorded in the OT, attained its complete fulfillment and exposition in Christ."[79] The threefold action of betrayal, crucifixion, and resurrection are "divine necessities," inevitable and ordained beforehand and, therefore, announced in Israel's prophetic scriptures.[80] The angels at the empty tomb don't explicitly mention the scriptures in connection with Jesus's resurrection, even if they do clearly imply a link between them.

The risen Jesus, however, does mention the scriptures in this connection. Twice. In the Emmaus episode, the risen Jesus is walking and speaking with two disciples who don't recognize him and don't understand the recent reports of the empty tomb. Jesus says to the disciples, "You foolish people! Your dull minds keep you from believing all that the prophets talked about. Wasn't it necessary [*edei*] for the Christ to suffer these things and then enter into his glory?" (24:25-26). The phrase "enter into his glory" refers to Christ's vindication in resurrection, since in the larger narrative of Luke-Acts Jesus has not yet ascended into heaven (Acts 1:9-11) and taken his seat at the right hand of God (Acts 7:56). After rebuking the disciples for their dull minds, Jesus "interpreted for them the things written about himself in all the scriptures, starting with Moses and going through all the Prophets" (Luke 24:27).[81] A few verses later, this time in the presence of a larger group of disciples, Jesus says:

> "These are my words that I spoke to you while I was still with you—
> that everything written about me in the Torah from Moses, the Prophets, and the Psalms must be fulfilled [*dei plērōthēnai*]." Then he opened
> their minds to understand the scriptures. He said to them, "This is what
> is written: the Christ will suffer and rise from the dead on the third
> day, and a change of heart and life for the forgiveness of sins must be
> preached in his name to all nations, beginning from Jerusalem. You are
> witnesses of these things." (Luke 24:44-48)

---

79. Moisés Silva, "δεῖ," *NIDNTTE* 1:636–38.

80. See Charles H. Cosgrove, "The Divine Δεῖ in Luke-Acts: Investigations into the Lukan Understanding of God's Providence," *NovT* 26 (1984): 168–90 (esp. 173–76).

81. See Rodríguez, "Textual Orientations," esp. pp. 205–8.

So, for Luke, the scriptures announced beforehand that the messiah would be raised from the dead, and Jesus fulfills this announcement. This is the climax of a development we can trace from Mark to Matthew to Luke. In the oldest Gospel, Mark declares that both Jesus's advent (Mark 1:15) and his arrest and suffering (14:49) fulfill the scriptures. The second Gospel amplifies this idea, incorporating it into the Matthean account of Jesus's birth and highlighting it in Jesus's parabolic teaching, his healing and exorcistic activities, his entrance into Jerusalem, and of course his arrest in the Garden of Gethsemane. Finally, the Third Gospel goes even further than Matthew and anchors Jesus's resurrection with Israel's scriptures. From birth to resurrection, the story of Jesus is, for Luke, the story of the fulfillment of Israel's prophetic scriptures.[82]

The Synoptic Gospels, then, present Jesus as Israel's king, a point that Mark makes by accepting the parodic enthronement of crucifixion, taking it seriously (i.e., the crucified Jesus *actually is* the king of the Jews, even if every affirmation of this claim in Mark 15 is sarcastic and mocking) and reflecting that parody back against Herod Antipas, Rome's appointed client-"king." While Mark roots Jesus's royal status in Israel's scriptural tradition, Matthew expands the connection, highlighting Jesus's fulfillment of scripture from birth to death. Luke reflects both of these same ideas: Jesus is Israel's king, and he fulfills Israel's scriptures. He goes even further, however, and explicitly connects Jesus's resurrection with Moses and the Prophets.

Luke's second volume, the Acts of the Apostles, continues the story that began in the Gospel of Luke. Acts opens with a statement to Luke's sponsor: "Theophilus, the first scroll I wrote concerned everything Jesus did and taught from the beginning, right up to the day when he was taken up into heaven" (Acts 1:1-2).[83] Luke describes the contents of his "first scroll" (i.e., the Gospel of Luke) in terms of "everything Jesus did and taught from the beginning," with the implication that this second scroll

---

82. See Richard Hays's essay, "Reading Scripture in Light of the Resurrection," in *The Art of Reading Scripture*, ed. Ellen F. Davis and Richard B. Hays (Grand Rapids: Erdmans, 2003), 216–38. Hays discusses the Markan account of Jesus's debate with the Pharisees [Mark 12:18-27] on pages 224–29, and he considers the Emmaus episode [Luke 24:13-35] on pages 229–32. I would like to thank Joel Green for bringing this essay to my attention.

83. For more on Theophilus, see Alexander, *Preface*, 187–200.

(i.e., the Acts of the Apostles) will cover everything Jesus continued to do and teach through his followers.

But we immediately run into some problems. Anyone who's read Acts knows the narrative scarcely gets started when Jesus flies off stage. There are twenty-eight chapters in Acts, and by the end of chapter 1 Jesus has left the building. In the opening scene, the risen Jesus reminds the disciples of John's baptism: "John baptized with water, but in only a few days you will be baptized with the Holy Spirit" (Acts 1:5; see Luke 3:1-20). The disciples ask if the restoration of Israel is next on the agenda, to which Jesus responds, "It isn't for you to know the times or seasons that the Father has set by his own authority. Rather, you will receive power when the Holy Spirit has come upon you, and you will be my witnesses in Jerusalem, in all Judea and Samaria, and to the end of the earth" (1:7-8). Jesus then, like Dr. Seuss's Lorax, "was lifted up," and he disappears into the heavens. Two angels appear and promise the disciples who are standing there, mouths agape, that Jesus will return "in the same way that you saw him go into heaven" (1:9-11). Less than half a chapter into his second volume, and Jesus—*the main character!*—is gone. How, then, could anyone think Acts is the story of *Jesus's* ongoing doings and teachings?

Despite his rapid withdrawal from center stage, Jesus remains active in the narrative of Acts in at least three ways. First, we should not overlook that Jesus makes a number of significant cameos, especially in connection with Saul/Paul.[84] In the aftermath of Stephen's murder (Acts 7:54-60), a persecution breaks out against the Jerusalem church (8:1-3), and the gospel spreads beyond Judea to Samaria and even to the ends of the earth (i.e., Ethiopia; 8:4-40). Luke then circles back around to a young man named Saul, who had witnessed and approved of Stephen's murder (7:58; 8:1) and initiated persecution of the church (8:3). Now, in Acts 9, Saul pursues Jesus's followers even beyond the borders of Judea, "still spewing murderous threats" against them but now journeying to Damascus, in

---

84. Contrary to popular opinion, "Saul" is not Paul's pre-conversion, Jewish name; neither Jesus nor Paul changed his name after his encounter with the risen Jesus. Luke continues to call him Saul until Acts 13 (four chapters after Saul's encounter with Jesus on the road to Damascus). When he narrates Barnabas and Saul's confrontation with a Jewish false prophet and sorcerer named Bar-Jesus/Elymas on the island of Cyprus (Acts 13:4-12), Luke adds a casual comment that Saul was "also known as Paul" (13:9). For the remainder of Acts Luke "only calls him 'Paul.' "

Syria, to apprehend anyone "who belonged to the Way" and remand them "as prisoners to Jerusalem" (9:1-2).

Suddenly, Saul finds himself surrounded by a light from heaven. He falls to the ground and hears a voice from heaven: "Saul, Saul, why are you harassing [= 'persecuting'] me?" (9:4). The narrator has not yet identified the mysterious person who speaks to Saul from the blinding light, though readers are likely to know what Saul doesn't: Just as YHWH spoke to Moses from the strange specter of a burning bush that didn't burn, so Jesus now speaks to Saul in a light from heaven. When Saul asks, "Who are you, Lord?" the voice replies, "I am Jesus, whom you are harassing [= persecuting]" (9:5). Jesus proceeds to instruct Saul, who will lose his sight because of his encounter with Jesus, on what he's to do. Jesus also appears to a Jew in Damascus, "a certain disciple named Ananias," whom Jesus sends to meet Saul, to lay hands on him and restore his sight, and (presumably) to proclaim the gospel to him.

This isn't the only place Jesus appears in Acts as a character on stage, an active agent in his own right. On two separate occasions Luke narrates visions in which the risen Jesus appears to Paul and encourages him on his course. First, in the Greek city of Corinth, Paul spent a number of Sabbaths in the Jewish synagogue, instructing both Jews and gentiles in the synagogue that Jesus is the messiah (Acts 18:1-8). When his companions, Silas and Timothy, came to Corinth from Macedonia, Paul stopped working his trade—he was a leatherworker (18:3)—and "devoted himself fully to the word, testifying to the Jews that Jesus was the Christ" (18:5). Luke says that at this point opposition from the Jews increased, and Paul publicly left the synagogue and began teaching from a private residence, which was right next door to the synagogue! The scene ends with a significant indication of success not just among gentiles but also among Corinthian Jews: "Crispus, the synagogue leader, and his entire household came to believe in the Lord. Many Corinthians believed and were baptized after listening to Paul" (18:8).

So far, the Paul-in-Corinth story has been a typical scene in Acts, in which Jesus is a topic within the story but not one of its active characters. That changes in the following verses. Immediately after he indicated some significant success for Paul's ministry in Corinth, Luke narrates the following visionary experience: "One night the Lord said to Paul in a vision, 'Don't be afraid. Continue speaking. Don't be silent. I'm with you and no one who attacks you will harm you, for I have many people in this city.' So he stayed there for eighteen months, teaching God's word among them" (Acts 18:9-11). "The Lord" who appears to Paul is certainly the risen Jesus.[85]

But the *timing* of Jesus's appearance to Paul is surprising. To this point in Acts, we've seen opposition to Paul rise to such fever pitch that he has been stoned and left for dead (Acts 14:19), beaten and thrown into prison (16:22-24), and secreted out of Thessalonica under threat of mob-riot (17:5-10). On more than one occasion, we might've expected Jesus to appear to Paul and encourage him to steadfast faithfulness. But in none of those scenes does Luke tell us Jesus appears to Paul. Not until Corinth, and Paul's relatively successful—and nonviolent!—experiences proclaiming the gospel does the risen Lord visit Paul and encourage him to continue on. Significantly, Paul is about to experience some potentially violent opposition in Corinth, when he's dragged before the Roman governor of Corinth (18:12-17), but even this comes to naught. Paul, in the midst of what Luke portrays as a comparatively peaceful and safe ministry in Corinth, experiences a vision in which the risen Jesus reemerges onto center stage and encourages Paul to continue confidently.[86]

I already mentioned that Jesus appears to Paul after his encounter on the road to Damascus on *two* separate occasions. The first, as we have seen, is in Corinth; the second is in Jerusalem, in Acts 23. If Jesus's appearance in Corinth is peculiar for occurring at a time when Paul was experiencing no significant opposition, his appearance in Jerusalem comes at a time of great uncertainty. Once again, Paul is at the center of a riot, this time in the Jerusalem temple where he was accused of defiling the temple by

---

85. Luke Timothy Johnson, *The Acts of the Apostles*, SP 5 (Collegeville, MN: Liturgical Press, 1992), 324; Ben Witherington III, *The Acts of the Apostles: A Socio-Rhetorical Commentary* (Grand Rapids: Eerdmans, 1997), 550.

86. *Pace* Witherington, *Acts of the Apostles*, 550, who describes Corinth as a "volatile atmosphere where danger loomed for Paul," even though Paul's experiences in Corinth seem much less volatile than in other cities around the Mediterranean. I would like to thank James A. Smith, of Cincinnati Christian University, for drawing my attention to the peculiarity of Luke's narrative arrangement.

bringing in gentiles, and the Roman commander had to intervene (Acts 21:27-40). Paul addresses the Jews in the temple in Acts 22, narrating his encounter with Jesus near Damascus and even revealing an as-yet-unknown vision in which Jesus appeared to Paul in the temple, sending him "far away to the Gentiles" (22:21).[87] When the Jews once again riot in response to Paul, the Roman commander brings Paul before the Jewish religious and political leadership in an attempt to find out why this guy provokes such an unruly response. When Paul appeared before "the entire Jewish Council" (Acts 22:30–23:10), he exploited a difference between the Pharisees and the Sadducees, and once again a riot ensued. And the Roman commander still had no idea what to make of Paul (or what to do with him).

In the midst of this opposition, in which Paul faced mob violence from his fellow Jews and tortuous examination from Roman soldiers, Luke tells us that Jesus once again appears to Paul: "The following night the Lord stood near Paul and said, 'Be encouraged! Just as you have testified about me in Jerusalem, so too you must testify in Rome'" (Acts 23:11). This appearance of Jesus strikes the reader as much less odd than the vision in Corinth. More importantly, it establishes the program for the rest of Luke's narrative, which will see Paul remain in prison and transported from Jerusalem to Caesarea and, ultimately, to Rome. Acts will end with Paul in Rome, under house arrest, receiving guests. "Unhindered and with complete confidence, he continued to preach God's kingdom and to teach about the Lord Jesus Christ" (28:31). Jesus, therefore, remains an active character in the Acts of the Apostles. Despite being lifted up and away in Acts 1, he continues to direct events toward his own desired aims.

Jesus's ongoing presence with his people (especially Paul) is one way Acts can be understood as all that Jesus continued to do and teach after the resurrection. A second way, no less important than the first, is through the intervention and working of his Spirit. The function and significance

---

87. Paul's vision of Jesus in the Jerusalem temple is not the second appearance we will discuss presently. Technically, Jesus doesn't appear in the narrative in Acts 22:17-21; rather, Paul narrates an encounter he had with Jesus. If we were to include this vision in our discussion of Jesus's appearances in Acts after his ascension, this would be the first of his appearances to Paul after the encounter on the Damascus road.

of God's Spirit in Luke-Acts is a common topic of discussion.[88] In Acts, Luke's favorite term for the Spirit by far is "Holy Spirit" (*pneuma hagion*), which he uses over forty times, though he also refers to "the Spirit," without any modifiers, a dozen times. In his Pentecost sermon, Peter quotes Joel's prophecy that God would "pour out my Spirit on all people," that "even upon my servants, men and women, I will pour out my Spirit in those days, and they will prophesy" (Acts 2:17, 18; citing Joel 2:28, 29). These are the only times Luke refers to "my Spirit," and in both he is quoting a prophetic oracle in which God (i.e., YHWH) is the speaker. Luke also refers to the "Spirit of the Lord" (*pneuma kyriou*) twice, once in Peter's rebuke of Sapphira (Acts 5:9) and once in his account of Philip's sudden disappearance following the baptism of the Ethiopian eunuch (8:39).

These are nearly all of the references to the Spirit of God in Acts. There is, however, one more, one that draws a strong connection between Jesus and the Spirit and that coincides with what we saw of Jesus's appearances to Paul. In Acts 16, Paul is moving westward overland through Asia Minor (modern-day Turkey) on what is known as his second missionary journey. Paul is traveling with Silas, a companion he picked up in Jerusalem after the Jerusalem council decided the question of the inclusion of gentiles (Acts 15). As he revisits some of the communities from the first missionary journey, he meets Timothy, who joins Paul and Silas on their travels west. At this point, Luke narrates a curious situation, in which Paul is actually *prevented* from preaching the gospel in Asia and Bithynia (modern-day western and northern Turkey):

> Paul and his companions traveled throughout the regions of Phrygia and Galatia because the Holy Spirit kept them from speaking the word in the province of Asia. When they approached the province of Mysia, they tried to enter the province of Bithynia, but the Spirit of Jesus wouldn't let them. Passing by Mysia, they went down to Troas instead. A vision of a man from Macedonia came to Paul during the night. He stood urging Paul, "Come over to Macedonia and help us!" Immediately after he saw the vision, we prepared to leave for the province of

88. See, e.g., Ju Hur, *A Dynamic Reading of the Holy Spirit in Luke-Acts*, JSNTSup 211 (Sheffield: Sheffield Academic Press, 2001).

Macedonia, concluding that God had called us to proclaim the good news to them. (Acts 16:6-10)

This is the only time in Luke-Acts that our author refers to the Spirit as "the Spirit of Jesus" (*to pneuma Iēsou*[89]). Our author is clearly referring to the Holy Spirit; in verse 6 Luke says "the Holy Spirit kept them from speaking the word in the province of Asia," and then immediately in verse 7 explains that the "Spirit of Jesus wouldn't let them" enter Bithynia. The Holy Spirit *is* the "Spirit of Jesus." Like Jesus's direct interventions in Saul's/Paul's life on the road to Damascus, in Corinth, and again in Jerusalem, the Spirit takes a direct role in positioning the characters where Jesus wants them, to do what Jesus wants them to do.[90] Moreover—and this is the truly significant point here—Luke's reference to the Holy Spirit as "the Spirit of Jesus" in 16:7 suggests that we might read all that the Spirit does in Acts as the work and will of Jesus. In other words, readers of the Acts of the Apostles should interpret Acts' nearly five dozen references to the Spirit of God as references to what Jesus continued to do and teach, even after the resurrection and ascension. Where the Spirit is at work, Jesus is at work.

We've identified two ways that Luke presents the Acts of the Apostles as all that Jesus continued to do and teach after the resurrection: through his continued presence and appearance, and through the agency of the Spirit of God. Now we add a third: Jesus is present and active in the actions and teaching of his followers. We have already quoted the most important text: "you will receive power when the Holy Spirit has come upon you, and you will be my witnesses in Jerusalem, in all Judea and Samaria, and to the end of the earth" (Acts 1:8). Here we see a blurring of sorts of the boundaries between the Holy Spirit and the actions of Jesus's followers, that when Jesus's followers bear witness to the life and teaching of Jesus, they are the embodiment of the Holy Spirit who is at work

---

89. A small number of witnesses (Codex Ephraemi Rescriptus [fifth century], an Old Latin manuscript [Gigas; thirteenth century], and some Coptic manuscripts) replace "the Spirit of Jesus" with "the Spirit of the Lord." The preponderance of Greek manuscripts, however, read *to pneuma Iēsou* in Acts 16:7.

90. Compare the actions of the "Spirit of Jesus" in Acts 16:7 with those of the "Spirit of the Lord" in Acts 8:39: in both texts, the Spirit moves the apostolic witness through geographical space, directing the locations in which the gospel is preached.

in them. So, for example, Luke repeatedly says things like, "then Peter, filled with the Holy Spirit" (4:8 NRSV; CEB "inspired by"),[91] in order to highlight that Jesus's followers' words and actions are divinely inspired and motivated. When they act, when they teach, they do so not just on the authority of Jesus but also, significantly, at the motivation and imposition of Jesus. The women and men who are filled with the Holy Spirit and advance the gospel are Jesus's witnesses, from Jerusalem to Judea and Samaria all the way through to the end of the earth. Where we see Jesus's followers at work, we see also Jesus at work.

Jesus Interpreted

The present chapter summarized briefly the earliest texts that commemorate the life and teaching of Jesus as their subject: Mark, Matthew, and Luke-Acts. We've seen how Mark takes the mocking, parodic intentions of crucifixion, embraces the parody, and turns it against Rome's client-ruler, Herod Antipas. Matthew extends the portrayal of Jesus as "the newborn king of the Jews" (Matt 2:2), repeatedly and explicitly tying Jesus's royal status to Israel's prophetic traditions, from birth to death. Luke goes even further, linking not just Jesus's life and death to the scriptures but also and especially his resurrection. These—Jesus's life, death, and resurrection—are "the events that have been fulfilled among us" (Luke 1:1), and despite Jesus's early departure from the stage in Luke's second volume, Acts, Jesus continues to act and teach throughout this second narrative, whether directly, through the Spirit, or through his followers. In all three texts (Mark, Matthew, and Luke-Acts), Jesus is the subject remembered in the commemorative activity at the heart of these texts. This contrasts sharply with the situation in the earlier letters of Paul, where we saw that Paul consistently "thought with" Jesus—especially in his reading and interpretation of Israel's scriptural traditions—but he didn't explicitly "think about" Jesus very much.

The Gospels and Acts are by analogy like Ronald McDowell's sculpture of Bill Hudson's photograph of Walter Gadsden and Officer Middleton.

---

91. In addition to Acts 4:8, see 2:4; 4:31; 6:3, 5; 7:55; 9:17; 11:24; 13:9, 52.

The Evangelists offer us interpretations of Jesus, interpretations that enable us not just to see Jesus but to understand him, much like McDowell's sculpture forces us to not only see a Black teen and a White police officer but also interpret the two figures within the broader realities of racial injustice in Jim Crow Alabama. Counterintuitively, the sculpture's details have been changed in order to reflect reality more authentically. The artist's interpretive work is the very link forging the connections between past and present.

In the same way, the Evangelists' interpretive work—whether one of them inaccurately refers to Herod Antipas as "king," or another goes to considerable lengths to point out connections between the events of Jesus's biography and prophetic anticipations in Israel's scriptures, or a third brings those scriptures in line with the expectation that God would raise his faithful Servant—forge the connections between the past and the present. Whereas historians of Jesus separate the historical wheat from the interpretive chaff, this chapter has shown how the Evangelists' interpretive work is the very means connecting us to the history of Jesus so that we can know anything about him at all.

There is, however, one key difference between the Gospels' commemoration of Jesus and Ronald McDowell's commemoration of Bill Hudson's photograph. We can compare the details of Hudson's original photograph against the details of McDowell's sculpture in order to see the artist's interpretive work. In the case of the Gospels, however, we can't compare the texts with "the original" that they commemorate. This difference underscores the importance of the claim we are making here: that the Evangelists' interpretive work is the very thing that preserves our connection with "the Jesus of history" (a standard but problematic term among historians of Jesus). Imagine for a moment that every copy of Bill Hudson's photograph were to vanish—print as well as digital copies—and all we had left to reconstruct the scene of Walter Gadsden's encounter with Officer Middleton were written references to the picture and, serendipitously, McDowell's sculpture. In this situation, we would be hard-pressed to reconstruct the original picture unless one of those written descriptions intentionally explained the changes McDowell inserted into his depiction.

In light of the photograph's role in galvanizing sympathy and support for the Civil Rights Movement, any reconstruction of the photograph would likely share McDowell's interpretive perspective. In fact, as we've already hinted, that interpretive perspective already conditions our viewing of the actual photograph! It is difficult to imagine that anyone would reconstruct Hudson's photograph more faithfully to its details than did McDowell.

And yet, in our hypothetical situation, if we couldn't see Hudson's picture but wanted to inquire into events in Birmingham, Alabama, on May 3, 1963, McDowell's commemorative sculpture would preserve for us a genuine connection between those events and today. We could see and experience, in other words, the reality of mid–twentieth-century racial injustice—*the very thing that motivated Hudson to take pictures in Birmingham in 1963 in the first place*—not just in spite of but because of McDowell's interpretive work. No, McDowell's sculpture isn't an exact replication of Hudson's photograph. But yes, that sculpture does document the same event and context depicted in that photograph. Similarly, rather than erasing the Evangelists' interpretive work, we should better appreciate how their interpretations bring us into contact with the Jesus who lived and breathed in first-century Galilee. No, the Gospels are not exact replicas of Jesus's life and teaching. But yes, they do document that life and teaching.

That interpretive work will go into overdrive when we turn to the Johannine literature. Even here, however, we will see that John's creative memory of Jesus isn't completely severed from the other commemorative patterns of the early Christians. The so-called Johannine Community was not an isolated phenomenon whose memory of Jesus would be unrecognizable to other Christians.

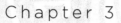

Chapter 3

Jesus Anew: Johannine Innovations as Memory

*It must be stated in no uncertain terms that **memory is distortion**. This is so regardless of any claims to veracity. If the criteria for veracity were defined by a given memory's **lack of distortion**, all discussion about the past would be rendered futile.*[1]

Remembering Is Remaking

We explored in the previous chapter the ways that distortions of reality can, sometimes and paradoxically, provide authentic access to reality. This is a disquieting, uncomfortable claim. Distortions are, by definition, degradations in the quality of the thing being distorted. Synonyms for *distortion* include "exaggeration," "misrepresentation," even "perversion"! Distortions present obstacles to, *not opportunities for*, understanding the world around us (and the past before us). Surely the task of the historian or the teacher is to remove distortions from our view of the past and to restore a clearer, *un*distorted vision of what actually happened!

Distortion, as a word, has thoroughly negative connotations. In popular usage, these negative connotations stem, at least in part, from an

---

1. Anthony Le Donne, "Theological Memory Distortion in the Jesus Tradition: A Study in Social Memory Theory," in *Memory in the Bible and Antiquity: The Fifth Durham-Tübingen Research Symposium*, ed. Stephen C. Barton, Loren T. Stuckenbruck, and Benjamin G. Wold, WUNT 212 (Tübingen: Mohr Siebeck, 2007), 163–77 (168; emphasis in the original).

unexamined assumption that what existed before the distortion was better than what existed after it. Consider the story of Elías García Martínez's fresco *Ecce Homo* ("Behold the Man"), which was painted on the wall

of a church in Borja, Spain, early in the twentieth century. This little-remarked painting came to international attention in 2012, when a local octogenarian, Cecilia Giménez, set herself to the loving task of restoring García Martínez's

painting, which had begun to deteriorate due to moisture on the church wall.[2] The "restoration" was disastrous. Jesus ends up looking like a forlorn monkey. As a result, some have taken to calling the fresco *Ecce Mono*, "Behold the Monkey." Giménez's work was certainly a distortion, a degradation of García Martínez's painting that made it more, not less, difficult to perceive what the original artist was trying to accomplish. The original fresco was, from most perspectives (but not all!), better than its distortion. The distortion diminished the value contained in the original.

We often, however, distort things in order to *clarify* or *improve* them. As Anthony Le Donne notes: "memory distortion is not necessarily malevolent"; distortion can simplify and clarify just as easily as it can obfuscate and obscure, which suggests we ought "to shake the negative connotations from the word 'distortion' in order to understand its necessary and beneficial function."[3]

Perhaps the most familiar example for everyday life is the use of corrective lenses (prescription glasses, contact lenses), which distort (bend, refract) light as it passes into our eyes in order to correct problems with the biological mechanisms involved in sight. Lenses don't simply correct

---

2. Raphael Minder, "Despite Good Intentions, A Fresco in Spain Is Ruined," *The New York Times*, 24 August 2012, https://www.nytimes.com/2012/08/24/world/europe/botched-restoration-of-ecce-homo-fresco-shocks-spain.html. For a follow-up on this story (with a somewhat happy ending), see Jorge Sainz, "Disfigured Spanish Fresco Is Hit for Artist, Town," Associated Press, 13 August 2013, http://news.yahoo.com/disfigured-spanish-fresco-hit-artist-town-151848237.html.

3. Le Donne, "Theological Memory Distortion," 167; italics in the original have been removed.

faulty sight, however; they also *enable* vision of things otherwise out of focus or invisible.[4]

Distortion, in instances such as these, doesn't *degrade* perception and understanding; it *enables* it! Perhaps we need a nonnegative word for this kind of distortion. We're not talking about distortion-as-corruption; we're talking about distortion as processes of organizing, sorting, explaining, focusing, clarifying, or in other ways making intelligible a mass of confusing, overwhelming, or incomprehensible data. We have used the word *interpretation*, or the phrase *interpretive work*, as a non-pejorative substitute for *distortion*. In both cases, however, we are pointing to the space between reality, on one hand, and the perception and apprehension of reality on the other.

We have already considered one especially powerful example of this "space between" in Bill Hudson's photograph and Ronald McDowell's sculpture. Racial injustice was not more severe, more shocking, more oppressive in 1963 than it was in, say, 1953. Why, then, did national and even international support for the Civil Rights Movement galvanize in 1963 in a way it hadn't done before? Part of the answer is Bill Hudson's iconic photograph that, although it didn't actually document a moment of racial brutality, focused viewers' gaze upon a single scene and made the oppressive systems of the Jim Crow South visible. Both Hudson's photograph and Ronald McDowell's commemorative sculpture enable viewers to perceive and identify with the struggles, sacrifices, and victories of the Civil Rights Movement by distorting the realities of a specific encounter between a young Black teen and a White police officer. This distortion, however, isn't degradation; it's clarification. Examples could be multiplied.[5] In fact, examples are ubiquitous, because memory isn't the act of

---

4. "When performing its proper function, a telescope lens distorts an imaged object in order to magnify it. Depending on the quality of the lens, the viewer is able to perceive an approximate distortion of distant objects not visible to the naked eye. The fact that the lens does not 'report' the object's image exactly how it was received is exactly its value" (Le Donne, "Theological Memory Distortion," 167).

5. For an example of distortion of images of George Washington in American memory before and after the Civil War, see Barry Schwartz, "Social Change and Collective Memory: The Democratization of George Washington," *American Sociological Review* 56 (1991): 221–36. Schwartz has also traced distortions in the memory of Abraham Lincoln from his assassination to the end of the twentieth century in idem, *Forge of National Memory*; idem, *Abraham Lincoln in the Post-Heroic Era: History and Memory in Late Twentieth-Century America* (Chicago: University of Chicago Press, 2008); idem, *Abraham Lincoln in the Post-Heroic Era: History and Memory in Late Twentieth-Century America* (Chicago: University of Chicago Press, 2008).

reproducing some idea or event from the past but of *remaking* it in the present; "memory distorts the past to render it intelligible to the present."[6]

The consequences for how we understand the task of the historian, known as historiography, are significant. In some quarters, the task of the historian is understood as separating interpretations of historical facts from those facts themselves. The interpretations are distortions (= degradations) of history, so the historian attempts to peel back, dig through, or otherwise compensate for those interpretations in order to restore the original historical saying or deed. One important example of this approach is John Meier's ongoing project, *A Marginal Jew*.[7] Meier is well aware of the impossibility of purely detached, objective historical research, and he comments at length on this impossibility.[8] Yet he approaches the job as a historian in impersonal terms. He pursues historical knowledge by "purely scientific means: empirical data from ancient documents, sifted by human minds operating by inference, analogy, and certain specific criteria."[9] He explicitly differentiates and separates "what comes from Jesus" (= the historical facts) from "what was created by the oral tradition of the early Church…and what was produced by the editorial work (redaction) of the evangelists" (= the interpretations of those facts).[10] Many historians of Jesus aim for the impossible: to isolate the facts as they existed prior to any interpretive operations being worked upon those facts.[11]

Memory studies, however, have emphasized the inescapable influence of interpretation and interpretive frames not merely on the reconstruction of the past in memorial and commemorative "texts" (written biographies,

---

6. Le Donne, "Theological Memory Distortion," 167.

7. John P. Meier, *A Marginal Jew: Rethinking the Historical Jesus*, 5 vols. (New Haven: Yale University Press, 1991–2016).

8. Meier, *A Marginal Jew*, 1:21–31.

9. Meier, *A Marginal Jew*, 1:31. Meier explains which criteria he employs, and how, in chapter 6 (1:167–95).

10. Meier, *A Marginal Jew*, 1:167. Meier critiques other historians for failing to meticulously isolate and eliminate Jesus's followers' interpretations of Jesus from the data. For example, he complains of Ben Meyer (*The Aims of Jesus* [London: SCM, 1979]): "The first part of the book (pp. 23–113) spells out method and 'indices' of judgment with great care; but, as the book proceeds, more and more of the redactional theology of the evangelists is declared to come from the historical Jesus, leaving one wondering how useful the indices really are" (Meier, *A Marginal Jew*, 1:185n3).

11. See, e.g., Meier, *A Marginal Jew*, 2:14n6.

songs, artist representations, historical analyses, ritual observances, and so on) but even in the initial perception of events that form the objects of later recall.[12] Human brains are not capable of registering and attending to all the perceptual stimuli that assault our senses; we simply see, hear, smell, and even feel and taste too much for our brains to account for all the information our senses transmit to them. Instead, our brains quickly and efficiently filter through the stimuli, dumping what seems irrelevant or unimportant and focusing on what seems relevant and important. (I say "seems" because, often enough, our brains misjudge the significance of perceptual data, for example when we can't find an item we're actively looking for even when it's right in front of us.) Interpretation, therefore, isn't simply a secondary activity performed on data that we have perceived apart from the prejudices and biases we impose on that data. Our prejudices already form the lenses through which we see the world, and it is a constant risk that we will fail even to see or hear data that our biases are ill-equipped to register.

Jesus's followers, then, didn't observe the events of Jesus's life and later fuse their shared memory of those events with biblical words, images, and precedents. Biblical echoes and allusions provided the lenses through which Jesus and his contemporaries perceived and interpreted the world around them. At the same time, the world around them also affected their understanding of Israel's biblical traditions.[13] The early Christians didn't overlay a secondary interpretive framework onto a series of events (say, Jesus's suffering and death) that they first understood apart from that framework. Instead, that framework enabled them to see Jesus's suffering, to understand it in certain ways, and to infer or attribute appropriate meaning to it. Certainly it would be *possible* to observe and describe Jesus's crucifixion as an event apart from Israel's biblical traditions. The Romans

---

12. Anthony Le Donne ("Theological Memory Distortion," 165) has brought considerable attention to this point: "historical interpretations does not begin with the historian, but within the perceptions, memories and articulations of the first witnesses" (see also idem, *The Historiographical Jesus: Memory, Typology, and the Son of David* [Waco, TX: Baylor University Press, 2009], esp. chapters 2 and 3).

13. The phenomenon of mutual interpretation is ubiquitous, but perhaps one clear example is the interpretation of prophetic scriptures and present circumstances in the so-called *pesharim*, or running commentaries, among the Dead Sea Scrolls. For technical but ground-breaking discussions, see the essays in George J. Brooke, *Reading the Dead Sea Scrolls: Essays in Method*, EJL 39 (Atlanta: Society of Biblical Literature, 2013), esp. chapters 9 and 10.

didn't crucify criminals in order to convey a biblical message.[14] None of our surviving data, however, describe the events of Jesus's life—whether his teachings, his healings and exorcisms, or the events of his Passion and resurrection—apart from the influence of Hebrew scripture, especially its translation in the Greek Septuagint.[15]

We have no evidence for thinking the events of Jesus's life were perceived *first* apart from the interpreting influence of Israel's scriptural traditions and only *later* were made to conform to scriptural patterns. Like the refracting prescription lenses worn every day, the early Christians perceived Jesus's life and teaching through scriptural lenses. There never was a layer of Jesus tradition free of the interpretive influence of Israel's scriptures. Interpretations of the facts, in other words, are always going to be part of the data with which historians must work.[16] We have no other option, therefore, but to participate in the growing resistance to what Anthony Le Donne calls the "false dichotomy between 'veracity' and distortion."[17] Unfortunately, the negative connotations of the word *distortion* are so entrenched that Le Donne employs a euphemism, *memory refraction*, to refer to distortion's positive, enabling effects.[18] We use the phrase "interpretive work" to similar effect.

John's Interpreted Jesus

Jesus as he is portrayed in the Gospel of John is under heavy suspicion from many historians of being a distortion, a misrepresentation, or at least a *biased* representation of Jesus that is inconsistent with the "real Jesus." Historians of Jesus have long dismissed the historical value of the Fourth Gospel. Though there have always been defenders of John or aspects of

---

14. See Joel Marcus's discussion in "Crucifixion as Parodic Exaltation," *JBL* 125 (2006): 73–87.

15. For an introductory discussion of the significance of the Septuagint for the development of Christian theology and Western civilization, see Timothy Michael Law, *When God Spoke Greek: The Septuagint and the Making of Western Civilization* (Oxford: Oxford University Press, 2013).

16. This is similar to James Dunn's emphasis on the irreducible faith-element in the Jesus tradition. For an introductory discussion see his *A New Perspective on Jesus: What the Quest for the Historical Jesus Missed* (Grand Rapids: Baker Academic, 2005), esp. pp. 15–34.

17. Le Donne, "Theological Memory Distortion," 168.

18. See, e.g., Le Donne, *Historiographical Jesus*, 13n50, passim.

John's image of Jesus, in the twenty-first century we've observed a significant uptick of historical interest in Johannine traditions and the value of John's testimony to Jesus as a figure in history.[19]

We're prepared now to recognize that *every* act of remembering and representing the past—literally, *re*-presenting, or making present *again*—involves interpretation of the past. The eyes with which John sees Jesus are not the same eyes with which the Synoptic Gospels see Jesus. The Jesus who comes into view in the Fourth Gospel is manifestly not identical with the portraits of Jesus by Mark, Matthew, and Luke. That is hardly a mark against the Johannine Jesus, because John is an autonomous account of Jesus's life and teachings.[20] Whether or not the Fourth Evangelist was familiar with one or more of the Synoptic Gospels, he didn't feel constrained to repeat or replicate their account of events of Jesus's life.[21]

Pastoral Imagery in the Gospels

The pastoral configuration of Jesus is one of the more flexible and powerful concepts characterizing the Fourth Gospel's portrayal of Jesus. (The word *pastor* comes from Latin, where it means "herdsman" or "shepherd.") The Synoptic Gospels employ pastoral imagery for Jesus, but not to the same extent nor to the same effect as does John. On two occasions Mark mentions sheep and the shepherd (Mark 6:34; 14:27), which refer to the crowds or disciples and to Jesus, respectively. Matthew greatly expands on the Israel-as-sheep imagery; he also includes a third allusion to Jesus-as-shepherd (Matt 25:31-46). Luke also implicitly

---

19. See Paul N. Anderson, Felix Just S.J., and Tom Thatcher, eds., *John, Jesus, and History*, 3 vols. (Atlanta: Society of Biblical Literature, 2007–2016); Paul N. Anderson, *The Fourth Gospel and the Quest for Jesus: Modern Foundations Reconsidered*, T&T Clark Biblical Studies (London: Bloomsbury T&T Clark, 2008).

20. See Rafael Rodríguez, "What Is History? Reading John 1 as Historical Representation," *JSHJ* 16 (2018): 31–51.

21. Richard Bauckham ("John for Readers of Mark," in *The Gospels for All Christians: Rethinking the Gospel Audiences*, ed. Richard Bauckham [Grand Rapids: Eerdmans, 1998], 147–71) has argued the Fourth Gospel appears to assume its readers are familiar with Mark and so should interpret the Fourth Gospel with the First Gospel near to hand; for a critical response, see Wendy Sproston North, "John for Readers of Mark? A Response to Richard Bauckham's Proposal," *JSNT* 25 (2003): 449–68. Whether or not Bauckham is right, the point we're making here is simply that John is not *derivative of* or secondary to the Synoptic Gospels, a point with which, as far as I know, Bauckham would agree.

refers to "tax collectors and sinners" as a sheep that wanders off from the rest of the flock, with the never-endangered ninety-nine sheep standing in for the main part of Israel. He never, however, explicitly calls Jesus "shepherd," and in fact he appears to make an unintentional allusion to Jesus-as-sheep that is unique among the Synoptic Evangelists (Acts 8:32).

John's use of pastoral imagery stands out from the same imagery in the Synoptic Gospels. The Fourth Gospel uses pastoral terms about as much as the other three Gospels combined.[22] The largest cluster of pastoral terms occurs in John 10, Jesus's discourse on the shepherd and the flock.[23] Here John expands on a theme that we see in the other Gospels, namely that the people of God are the flock, and Jesus is the shepherd who cares for the flock. We saw this theme even in Luke, though we noted Luke's reticence to call Jesus a shepherd, good or otherwise. Both Mark and Matthew, however, bear witness to this metaphor within the Jesus tradition, that the people of God are sheep, and Jesus is the shepherd who guides and protects them. John takes this metaphor and distorts it, not like a fun house mirror but like a telescope, bringing new dimensions into view.

Jesus, the Gate and Good Shepherd

John 10 begins with a distinctive metaphor: Jesus is "the gate of the sheep," an image that is too easily eclipsed by the more familiar (and popular) metaphor of Jesus-as-Shepherd.[24] The Jesus-as-gate metaphor

---

22. I searched for the following words in NA28: *amnos, arēn, arnion, poimainō, poimēn, poimnē, poimnion,* and *probaton.* Mark, Matthew, and Luke employ pastoral imagery thirty times in twenty-three verses; if we include Acts, the numbers are thirty-five times in twenty-six verses. The Fourth Gospel, all by itself, uses pastoral terms thirty times in twenty-one verses. The numbers are not greatly affected by text-critical variants. Some manuscripts may interchange synonymous pastoral terms (e.g., *probation* for *probaton*); the original hand of Codex Sinaiticus lacks the phrase *hōs probata* at Mark 6:34 (though the words were added by a later corrector); some manuscripts add *tēs poimnēs* in Mark 14:27; some manuscripts read *hoi anthrōpoi* instead of *hoi poimenes* at Luke 2:15.

23. Pastoral terminology (see the previous footnote) occurs twenty-two times (in fourteen verses) in John 10 alone.

24. See, e.g., George R. Beasley-Murray, *John,* 2nd ed., WBC 36 (Nashville: Nelson, 1999), 169–70, who conflates the two images. For a treatment that respects and explores the two different images, see Christopher W. Skinner, "'The Good Shepherd Lays Down His Life for the Sheep' (John 10:11, 15, 17): Questioning the Limits of a Johannine Metaphor," *CBQ* 80 (2018): 97–113.

appears to have two applications. The primary application, the one that occupies Jesus's attention early in John 10, is that Jesus mediates interaction between the people of God (= the sheep in the pen) and their shepherds. John 10 invites the reader to identify the Pharisees from 9:40-41 with the "thieves and outlaws," setting up a clear if yet implicit contrast with Jesus.[25] "In what is clearly a figure of speech, Jesus describes himself in metaphorical terms that are meant to draw a contrast between himself and the Pharisees."[26] Unlike these Pharisees, who are illicit "shepherds" who inflict harm on the flock, Jesus provides entrance for good shepherds, who are known by guard and flock alike.

> "I assure you that whoever doesn't enter into the sheep pen through the gate but climbs over the wall is a thief and an outlaw. The one who enters through the gate is the shepherd of the sheep. The guard at the gate opens the gate for him, and the sheep listen to his voice. He calls his own sheep by name and leads them out. Whenever he has gathered all of his sheep, he goes before them and they follow him, because they know his voice. They won't follow a stranger but will run away because they don't know the stranger's voice." Those who heard Jesus use this analogy didn't understand what he was saying. So Jesus spoke again, "I assure you that I am the gate of the sheep. All who came before me were thieves and outlaws, but the sheep didn't listen to them." (John 10:1-8)

Jesus's contrast between those who enter through the gate and "all who came before me" throws the Jewish leaders into a bad light. They—the Pharisees, but also presumably the chief priest(s) and "the Jews" when that phrase applies to Jewish leaders[27]—are strangers whose voice is alien to the sheep. Jesus, in contrast, grants access to legitimate leaders, shepherds who have entered through the gate, who know the name of the sheep, and

---

25. Beasley-Murray, *John*, 169, 170.

26. Skinner, "Good Shepherd," 101–2.

27. See Malcolm F. Lowe, "Who Were the IOYΔAIOI?" *NovT* 18 (1976): 101–30, esp. pp. 123–24. This topic is the subject of vigorous debate, and not just for the Fourth Gospel. For an extensive introduction to the discussion, see Steve Mason, "Jews, Judaeans, Judaizing, Judaism: Problems of Categorization in Ancient History," *JSJ* 38 (2007): 457–512; see also the three-part discussion in David M. Miller, "The Meaning of *Ioudaios* and Its Relationship to Other Group Labels in Ancient 'Judaism,'" *CurBR* 9 (2010): 98–126; idem, "Ethnicity Comes of Age: An Overview of Twentieth-Century Terms for *Ioudaios*," *CurBR* 10 (2012): 293–311; idem, "Ethnicity, Religion and the Meaning of *Ioudaios* in Ancient 'Judaism,'" *CurBR* 12 (2014): 216–65.

whose voice is known to the sheep.[28] He mediates interaction between the people of God and their shepherds. He sends his disciples to feed the sheep, and in this way his disciples are unlike other reputed leaders of the Jewish people.[29]

There is a secondary application of the Jesus-as-gate metaphor. In addition to mediating interaction between licit shepherds and the flock and keeping out illicit "shepherds," Jesus grants access for other sheep to enter the pen. Sheep who are outside the flock enter the sheep pen through Jesus-the-gate and join the flock within. This idea follows immediately after John 10:1-8, discussed above: "I am the gate. Whoever enters through me will be saved. They will come in and go out and find pasture. The thief enters only to steal, kill, and destroy. I came so that they could have life—indeed, so that they could live life to the fullest" (vv. 9-10). In these verses, those who enter through Jesus-the-gate are not licit shepherds but rather are other sheep! This idea will find expression later, in the Upper Room Discourse of John's Gospel, when Jesus tells the disciples, "I am the way, the truth, and the life. No one comes to the Father except through me" (John 14:6). In John 10, however, access is granted through Jesus not to "the Father" but rather to the sheep pen, to the flock itself. Jesus, in other words, provides access to the people of God. As the gate, lost sheep are found and restored to their proper place when they enter the sheep pen through Jesus.

The Jesus-as-gate image appears to be a unique configuration of pastoral imagery in the Jesus tradition. Nowhere else in the Jesus tradition is Jesus "a door," whether for the sheep to enter the sheep pen or for shepherds to find access to the sheep.[30] As John 10 continues, however, the

28. J. Ramsey Michaels, *The Gospel of John*, NICNT (Grand Rapids: Eerdmans, 2010), 583.

29. The metaphorical referent(s) in John 10 are notoriously complicated, perhaps even confused. Is Jesus the gate? Or is he the shepherd? The Johannine Jesus claims to be both (John 10:7, 9, 11, 14). But whereas some readers (e.g., Gary T. Manning Jr., *Echoes of a Prophet: The Use of Ezekiel in the Gospel of John and in Literature of the Second Temple Period*, LNTS [London: T&T Clark, 2004], 108–9) mistakenly read 10:1–10 in terms of Jesus-as-shepherd, we must be careful to appreciate that in these verses Jesus is the gate that grants admission to shepherds and sheep alike. In other words, in the parable (*paroimia*) of John 10:1-5, Jesus isn't the shepherd who enters through the gate but rather the gate through which licit shepherds enter.

30. The nearest parallel to John's Jesus-as-gate metaphor is Luke 13:24-25, where Jesus says, "Make every effort to enter through the narrow gate. Many, I tell you, will try to enter and won't be able to. Once

Fourth Gospel reverts to more traditional uses of pastoral imagery. John, like Mark and Matthew especially but also Luke, identifies Jesus as the shepherd over the flock that is Israel:

> I am the good shepherd. The good shepherd lays down his life for the sheep. When the hired hand sees the wolf coming, he leaves the sheep and runs away. That's because he isn't the shepherd; the sheep aren't really his. So the wolf attacks the sheep and scatters them. He's only a hired hand and the sheep don't matter to him. I am the good shepherd. I know my own sheep and they know me, just as the Father knows me and I know the Father. I give up my life for the sheep. (John 10:11-15)

The Fourth Gospel deploys pastoral imagery in this passage in completely traditional ways, likening Jesus to the good or noble (*kalos*) shepherd, in implicit contrast to wicked or ignoble shepherds. We saw in chapter 2 that the Gospel of Mark contrasts Antipas, the wannabe king of Galilee, with Jesus, the rightful king who gathers his flock and feeds them in the wilderness. The Markan narrator gives the reader insight into Jesus's internal emotional response to the crowd: "he had compassion on them because they were like sheep without a shepherd" (Mark 6:34). John's portrayal of Jesus-as-shepherd can be read profitably in light of Mark's. Just as Antipas abandoned John the Baptist when his [step-]daughter, on her mother's instruction, asked for John's head on a platter,[31] so the hired hand abandons the sheep when he sees the wolf approaching. Unlike the hired hand (= Antipas), the good shepherd (= Jesus) has compassion on the sheep

---

the owner of the house gets up and shuts the door, then you will stand outside and knock on the door, saying, 'Lord, open the door for us.' He will reply, 'I don't know you or where you are from.'" Nowhere, however, does Luke equate the "narrow gate" to Jesus.

31. The description of the young dancing girl in Mark 6 is conflicted in the surviving manuscripts. Antipas's wife is named Herodias in Mark 6:17, 19, and the dancing girl is clearly Herodias's daughter in Mark 6:24. But the manuscripts disagree whether the dancing girl who pleased Herod Antipas in Mark 6:22 is "Herod's daughter Herodias" (so some early Greek manuscripts, including Sinaiticus and Vaticanus) or "the daughter of Herodias [herself]," as in other early Greek manuscripts (e.g., Alexandrinus and the miniscule manuscripts in Family 1) and the majority of (later) manuscripts. The NA28 and UBS5 both opt for the former, while the SBLGNT opts for the latter. This verse's difficulties are evident in Bruce Metzger's comments (*A Textual Commentary on the Greek New Testament.*, 2nd ed. [Stuttgart: German Bible Society, 1994], 77): "A majority of the Committee decided, somewhat reluctantly, that the reading with *autou*, despite the historical and contextual difficulties, must be adopted on the strength of its external attestation." The Committee, however, gave this reading only a {C} ranking. See also Adela Yarbro Collins, *Mark: A Commentary*, Hermeneia (Minneapolis: Fortress, 2007), 295, 308–11.

(Mark 6:34) and, rather than sacrificing [one of] the sheep, lays down his own life for the sheep. The image of Jesus-as-good-shepherd in John 10, then, is thoroughly traditional. Sure, John expands on this traditional image, explicitly contrasting the good shepherd with its inverse, the hired hand. Even so, it is thoroughly traditional.

The Johannine innovation comes in John 10:16: "I have other sheep that don't belong to this sheep pen. I must lead them too. They will listen to my voice and there will be one flock, with one shepherd." Jesus doesn't clarify the identity of these "other sheep"; all we learn about them is (i) they don't belong to "this sheep pen"; (ii) Jesus is committed—or obligated—to leading these "other sheep," just as he is to the first set of sheep"; and (iii) like the sheep in verse 14 who "know" Jesus, these "other sheep" "will listen to [his] voice." Some readers understand the "other sheep" as a reference to Christians outside the particular circle of Johannine Christians, whose view of Jesus is more like that in the Synoptic Gospels and the teaching of the Twelve (esp. Peter).[32] Others interpret the "other sheep" as a reference to Jewish Christians who had been excluded from the synagogue.[33] The most popular interpretation, however, is that Jesus refers to the inclusion of gentiles, non-Jews, within the sheep pen that represents the people of God.[34]

This latter interpretation makes the most sense within the broader scope of Christian origins; the inclusion of the gentiles—and especially the *how* of the gentiles' inclusion[35]—was perhaps the most freighted and conten-

---

32. Raymond E. Brown, *An Introduction to the Gospel of John*, ed. Francis J. Moloney (New Haven: Yale University Press, 2003), 67, 178; see also Tom Thatcher, *The Riddles of Jesus in John: A Study in Tradition and Folklore*, SBLMS 53 (Atlanta: Society of Biblical Literature, 2000), 251n39.

33. See Francis Moloney's summary of J. Louis Martyn's position in Brown, *Introduction*, 71. Alan Culpepper (*Anatomy of the Fourth Gospel* [Philadelphia: Fortress, 1983], 65–66) lists five interpretations of the "other sheep" of John 10:16, and he prefers "the gathering of Jewish Christians excluded from the synagogues" because of narrative context (the healing of the blind man in John 9 and the "fear of the Jews" and of being put out of the synagogue in 9:22).

34. Maurice Casey, *Is John's Gospel True?* (London: Routledge, 1996), 112–13; Beasley-Murray, *John*, 171; Thatcher, *The Riddles of Jesus in John*, 251n39; Andreas J. Köstenberger, *John* (Grand Rapids: Baker Academic, 2004), 306–7; Manning, *Echoes of a Prophet*, 110; Craig R. Koester, *The Word of Life: A Theology of John's Gospel* (Grand Rapids: Eerdmans, 2008), 200; Michaels, *John*, 588; Paul N. Anderson, *The Riddles of the Fourth Gospel: An Introduction to John* (Minneapolis: Fortress, 2011), 186.

35. See my discussion in Rafael Rodríguez, "Paul and Social Memory," in *Paul in the Greco-Roman World: A Handbook*, ed. J. Paul Sampley, 2nd ed. (London: T&T Clark, 2016), 346–68, esp. pp. 361–63.

tious issue in first-century Christianity. Unfortunately, nothing in John 10 suggests either Jesus or the Johannine narrator has gentiles in mind. Instead, the context of John 10 as well as the use of pastoral imagery elsewhere in the Jesus tradition leads us to understand the "other sheep" of John 10:16 along similar lines as the "lost sheep" of Matthew 18:10-14 and Luke 15:3-7. That is, they are Israelites whom Jesus and his disciples call to enter the sheep pen through the gate of the sheep. Though they are currently outside "this sheep pen," Jesus calls them in. "They will listen to my voice," Jesus says, "and there will be one flock, with one shepherd" (John 10:16).

"Sheep," however, "are a common biblical metaphor for Israel,"[36] and Jesus's language in John 10 resonates with uses of that metaphor in Israel's sacred traditions and texts. The pastoral metaphor in biblical tradition performed political functions. Biblical authors used pastoral images to express the relationship between the people and their leaders (the sheep and the shepherds, respectively) as well as to critique those leaders when they failed their responsibilities to the people and/or to God. John 10 deploys pastoral imagery precisely for this latter purpose.[37] Gary Manning identifies two biblical traditions as particularly relevant for understanding John 10's pastoral imagery: Moses's request for God to appoint someone to succeed him as leader over the people (Num 27:15-17), and the oracle of judgment against "Israel's shepherds" in Ezekiel 34.[38] The echoes of Ezekiel 34 are especially resonant in John 10. Both Ezekiel and Jesus confront Israel's unfaithful leaders. In the former those leaders are "shepherds who tended themselves" (Ezek 34:2), while in the latter they are "hired hands" who care for themselves rather than for the sheep (John 10:12-13). Both Ezekiel and Jesus note the danger posed by "wild animals" or "wolves" (Ezek 34:5, 8; John 10:12). Both Ezekiel and Jesus seek out lost

36. George W. E. Nickelsburg, *1 Enoch 1: A Commentary on the Book of 1 Enoch, Chapters 1–36; 81–108*, Hermeneia (Minneapolis: Fortress, 2001), 377.

37. Manning, *Echoes of a Prophet*, 102–3.

38. See Manning, *Echoes of a Prophet*, 100–135. Manning goes against the consensus and argues echoes of Numbers 27 dominate in John 10 on the basis of verbal links between two passages. His own analysis, however, supports the exact opposite conclusion: John 10's pastoral imagery levels a critique against the Jewish leadership (see pp. 102–3, 114), which dynamic is at work in Ezekiel 34 but not in Numbers 27. Richard Hays (*Echoes of Scripture in the Gospels* [Waco, TX: Baylor University Press, 2016], 318–20) rightly emphasizes John 10's critique of the Jewish leaders, though he overinterprets certain features of our pericope (esp. Jesus's location in Solomon's Portico).

or scattered sheep (Ezek 34:11, 16; John 10:16). Both Ezekiel and Jesus anticipate the restoration of the sheep into one flock, under the care of one shepherd (Ezek 34:23; John 10:16).

The resonance with Ezekiel, however, is surprising precisely because Ezekiel anticipates YHWH, the God of Israel, taking upon himself the shepherding responsibilities and functions that the leaders of the people had left derelict.[39] Ezekiel 34's grammar features thirty-two first-person singular verbs, in which God repeatedly declares, "I will..."[40] Examples include, "*I* myself *will search* for my flock and *seek* them out" (34:11, emphasis added). "*I will gather* and *lead* them out from the countries and peoples, and *I will bring* them to their own fertile land" (34:13, emphasis added). "*I will rescue* my flock so that they will never again be prey" (34:22, emphasis added). The most striking verse is Ezekiel 34:16, which features six first-person verbs: "I will seek out the lost, bring back the strays, bind up the wounded, and strengthen the weak. But the fat and the strong I will destroy, because I will tend my sheep with justice." In Ezekiel 34, YHWH sends forth his prophet to announce God's judgment against the unjust leaders of the people. The Lord also declares to the people that he himself will care for the people where their leaders had previously failed.

So it would have been unexceptional for the Johannine Jesus to remind those around him of God's pastoral role vis-à-vis the people, in contrast to the Pharisees (who, you'll remember, are "thieves and outlaws"). As the CEB's subheading over Ezekiel 34 explains, *God* is "the good shepherd." God's good-shepherd-ness was available for the Johannine Jesus to hold up in contrast to the Pharisees and chief priests, had he wanted to make that particular contrast.

But he doesn't make that particular contrast.

"*I* am the good shepherd. *I* know my own sheep and they know *me*" (John 10:14). Rather than contrasting the Pharisees with God, Jesus contrasts them with himself. They are "thieves and outlaws" (10:1, 8) or,

---

39. See Skinner, "Good Shepherd," esp. p. 98 and the texts cited in nn. 2, 3.

40. The Greek translation of Ezekiel 34 has thirty-seven first-person singular verbs, thirty-two of which take the future tense. Thirty-one of those first-person singular future Greek verbs correspond to thirty-one of the first-person singular Hebrew verbs mentioned in the main text. One Greek verb, *diakrinō* in verse 17, translates a Hebrew participle (*shopet*), and one finite Hebrew verb (*dibarti* in v. 24) is rendered with a first-person *aorist* verb, *elalēsa*.

perhaps less damningly but no less inadequately, "hired hands" (10:12-13). They are unknown to the sheep and unrecognized by them. In contrast to the thieves, outlaws, and hired hands, Jesus "lays down his life for the sheep" (10:11).

This is the achievement of John's handling of both the Jesus tradition and Hebrew biblical tradition: he brings both together so that the one interprets the other, and vice versa.[41] The Synoptic Jesus tradition used pastoral imagery to express Jesus's relationship, as shepherd, to Israel (the sheep). The Prophets' anticipation of a "good shepherd" who would banish wicked shepherds, restore wandering sheep, and lead the flock is mapped onto Jesus's conflict with Jewish leaders, his compassion for people on the margins, and his royal status in Mark, Matthew, and Luke. John uses pastoral imagery to similar effect, though he uses the pastoral metaphor to reinforce another aspect of the Jesus tradition: Jesus's relationship with God. The Johannine Jesus is conscious of being loved by God (John 15:9), of being in tune with God (5:19-23), of being "in" God even as God is "in" him (17:21). In John 10, Jesus not only fulfills YHWH's pastoral role as good shepherd; he also plainly declares, "I and the Father are one" (10:30). John's use of pastoral imagery, therefore, capitalizes on and extends the Jesus tradition's portrayal of Jesus as shepherd and also advances the Johannine presentation of Jesus as "in" and "one with" the Father.

Feed My Sheep

The Fourth Gospel contains two instances of pastoral imagery besides the Good Shepherd discourse. Jesus appears as a shepherd-figure in Jesus's threefold (re)commissioning of Peter in John 21. After eating a meal of bread and fish with the disciples (John 21:13), the risen Jesus engages Peter and gives him a task:

> Jesus asked Simon Peter, "Simon son of John, do you love me more than these?" Simon replied, "Yes, Lord, you know I love you." Jesus said to him, "Feed my lambs." Jesus asked a second time, "Simon son of John,

---

41. For a similar claim made with respect to the Johannine Prologue (John 1:1-18), see Rafael Rodríguez, *Oral Tradition and the New Testament: A Guide for the Perplexed* (London: T&T Clark, 2014), 94–100.

do you love me?" Simon replied, "Yes, Lord, you know I love you." Jesus said to him, "Take care of my sheep." He asked a third time, "Simon son of John, do you love me?" Peter was sad that Jesus asked him a third time, "Do you love me?" He replied, "Lord, you know everything; you know I love you." Jesus said to him, "Feed my sheep. I assure you that when you were younger you tied your own belt and walked around wherever you wanted. When you grow old, you will stretch out your hands and another will tie your belt and lead you where you don't want to go." He said this to show the kind of death by which Peter would glorify God. After saying this, Jesus said to Peter, "Follow me." (John 21:15-19)

With each affirmation of Peter's love for him, Jesus tells Peter, "Feed my sheep."

What catches our interest here isn't the different Greek words for "sheep" (*ta arnia mou* [21:15] or *ta probata mou* [21:16, 17]) nor even the different words for "love" (*agapaō* in Jesus's first two questions; *phileō* in each of Peter's responses and in Jesus's final question). Jesus's words to Peter remind us of his parable of the sheep pen in John 10:1-8. As Raymond Brown notes, "It is quite understandable that John 21:15-17 has been interpreted as the granting to Peter of some of both the responsibility for the flock and the authority over it that Jesus himself possessed as the model shepherd (ch. 10)."[42] As we noted above, Jesus is the gate that grants access to legitimate shepherds. This idea finds its ultimate expression in John's commissioning scene, where the risen Jesus tells his disciples, "As the Father sent me, so I am sending you" (John 20:21). In John 21, however, Peter is the licit shepherd who enters the sheep pen through the gate, who is sent by Jesus and who comes to feed the sheep. How interesting to note, then, that 1 Peter (a letter we'll discuss in the next chapter) contains the following exhortation from the Petrine author to the older readers among his audience:

Like shepherds, tend the flock of God among you. Watch over it. Don't shepherd because you must, but do it voluntarily for God. Don't shepherd greedily, but do it eagerly. Don't shepherd by ruling over those

42. Raymond E. Brown, *The Gospel According to John XIII–XXI*, AB 29A (New York: Doubleday, 1970), 1114.

entrusted to your care, but become examples to the flock. And when the chief shepherd appears, you will receive an unfading crown of glory. (1 Pet 5:2-4)[43]

Peter, far from *replacing* Jesus as the good shepherd, *fulfills* Jesus's promise to be the gate through whom "the shepherd of the sheep" (John 10:2) enters in order to feed and guide and protect them.

The Lamb of God

In the beginning of the Fourth Gospel, John the Baptist gives his testimony on behalf of "the true light that . . . was coming into the world" (John 1:9). The Baptist begins by testifying about himself: he is neither the Christ nor Elijah nor the prophet (1:19-21). Instead, he is the voice from Isaiah 40:3, crying out in the wilderness and calling the people to prepare the way of the Lord (John 1:23), and he comes in advance of someone greater, someone who comes after him, someone none of them (including John himself!) recognizes.

The Fourth Gospel then explains how John came to recognize Jesus. Having recognized him, John offers his testimony:

> The next day John saw Jesus coming toward him and said, "Look! The Lamb of God who takes away the sin of the world! This is the one about whom I said, 'He who comes after me is really greater than me because he existed before me.' Even I didn't recognize him, but I came baptizing with water so that he might be made known to Israel." John testified, "I saw the Spirit coming down from heaven like a dove, and it rested on him. Even I didn't recognize him, but the one who sent me to baptize with water said to me, 'The one on whom you see the Spirit coming down and resting is the one who baptizes with the Holy Spirit.' I have seen and testified that this one is God's Son." (John 1:29-34)

When John says, "Look! The Lamb of God" (John 1:29), he isn't addressing the Jewish leaders from Jerusalem who were questioning him in 1:19-28; neither is he addressing his own disciples (see 1:35-37). Instead, he

---

43. Raymond Brown (*John XIII–XXI*, 1111) notes, "The association of shepherd imagery with Peter is found independently in I Pet v 1–4."

seems to be addressing the audience of the Fourth Gospel, letting *us* know who Jesus is and what he does, and so inviting us to avoid the path taken by "the world" and by "his own people" (see 1:10-11). John, however, is also presenting Jesus *to Israel* and testifying that "[t]he 'hidden Messiah' is no longer hidden."[44] John's baptismal ministry results in a twofold revelation: first, that Jesus is the messiah/christ, and second, that as messiah/ christ Jesus removes the world's sin. To this we should probably add a third revelatory dimension: Jesus is the Son of God, "the one who baptizes with the Holy Spirit" (John 1:33-34).

The Fourth Evangelist *intentionally* applies pastoral imagery to Jesus, identifying Jesus as "the Lamb of God" (*ho amnos tou theou*; John 1:29, 36) and drawing a vital inference from that metaphor ("who takes away the sin of the world!"; 1:29). Recall that the author of Luke-Acts *accidentally* innovated within the Jesus tradition, applying pastoral imagery to Jesus but doing so with Jesus as sheep/lamb (Acts 8:32, citing Isa 53:7) rather than as shepherd. Luke doesn't expand on or make use of this innovation; instead, his interest is in aligning Jesus with the Isaianic tradition as a whole rather than with its pastoral metaphor in particular.[45] The Gospel of John takes full advantage of this innovation, even to the point of aligning the death of Jesus with the slaughter of the Passover lamb, as Jesus will be handed over for crucifixion at "about noon on the Preparation Day for the Passover" (19:14). John, then, takes full advantage of the pastoral association of Jesus not just with the good shepherd (John 10) but also with the lamb (John 1).

The Apocalyptic Lamb, Slaughtered and Conquering

The Gospel of John and the Revelation of John belong together, so we will consider them together here. The identification of both Gospel and Apocalypse as "Johannine" is fairly secure, even if the precise details remain unclear. The Fourth Gospel never claims that the author was named John;

---

44. Michaels, *John*, 108.

45. See also Luke 4:16-21; 24:25-27, 44-48.

it only claims a connection with the testimony of the so-called beloved disciple (John 21:24), whom Christian tradition has identified as John, the son of Zebedee.[46] Only later, perhaps early in the second century, were the Gospels attributed to specific authors (Matthew, Mark, Luke, and John).[47] Unlike the Gospel, the Apocalypse identifies the author at the very beginning: "Christ made it known by sending it through his angel to his servant John, who bore witness to the word of God and to the witness of Jesus Christ, including all that John saw" (Rev 1:1-2; see also 1:4, 9; 22:8).[48] The links between the Gospel and the Apocalypse extend beyond the former's title and the latter's protagonist. Despite differences in genre and vocabulary, the Gospel and the Apocalypse exhibit a "deep harmony in outlook and symbolization."[49]

Pastoral imagery, which is prominent in the Fourth Gospel, is emphasized to an extreme in the book of Revelation. The only reference to "sheep" (*probata*) occurs in Revelation 18:13 in a list of commercial items that will no longer find eager buyers when God judges Rome—John refers to the city using the code name "Babylon"—for its "loose and extravagant ways" (18:3, 7, 9). Unlike the Gospels (including the Fourth Gospel), nowhere does Revelation refer to the people of God as "sheep." It does, however, use shepherding imagery on multiple occasions. Three times Revelation says that Jesus "will shepherd" (*poimanei*) the persecuted faithful (7:13) as well as all the nations (12:5; 19:15),[50] which implicitly portrays those who fall under Jesus's authority as sheep. Similarly, in the letter to the church in Thyatira (2:18-29), the exalted Jesus promises, "To

---

46. Irenaeus, *Haer.* 3.1.1; see also John Painter, "Beloved Disciple," *DJG*2, 69–72, esp. §6 (p. 71).

47. Harry Y. Gamble, *Books and Readers in the Early Church: A History of Early Christian Texts* (New Haven: Yale University Press, 1997), 153–54.

48. According to the church historian Eusebius, the second-century bishop Papias identifies *two* men named John: the son of Zebedee who was also a disciple of Jesus, and another John, whom Papias calls "the elder" (see Eusebius, *Hist. eccl.* 3.39.4). Ascribing any or all of the Johannine books (the Fourth Gospel, the three Johannine letters, and the Apocalypse) to one or the other of these Johns has been the subject of much scholarly discussion.

49. Luke Timothy Johnson, *The Writings of the New Testament: An Interpretation*, 3rd ed. (Minneapolis: Fortress, 2010), 513–15 (p. 513 quoted).

50. The CEB translates *poimanei* in Revelation 12:5 and 19:15 with "he will rule" (see also 2:27, discussed immediately below). This is a legitimate translation (see L&N §37.57), followed by the other English versions, though it obscures the shepherding imagery from the English reader.

those who emerge victorious, keeping my practices until the end, I will give authority over the nations—to rule [or shepherd, *poimanei*] the nations with an iron rod and smash them like pottery—just as I received authority from my Father" (2:26-28). These latter three uses of pastoral terms (Rev 2:27; 12:5; 19:15) don't convey pastoral overtones as much as they promise the exercise of wrath against injustice and the restoration of justice over wayward "sheep."[51] We have not heard this resonance in Johannine pastoral imagery up to this point. Shepherding "with an iron rod," and the related actions of "smashing like pottery" (2:27) and "trampling the winepress of the Almighty God's passionate anger" (19:15), are utterly foreign to the Fourth Gospel's pastoral imagery.

We do, however, see another idea that is quite at home with the use of pastoral imagery in the Fourth Gospel. You'll recall that, in addition to being the "good shepherd" himself, the Johannine Jesus sends good shepherds to pasture his sheep. We saw this in two places: first, in Jesus's self-depiction as the gate through which licit shepherds enter (John 10:7-8) and, second, in the thrice-repeated call for Peter to "feed my sheep" (21:15-19). In his promise to the church in Thyatira, Jesus similarly delegates pastoral authority to his followers. Not Jesus himself but rather "those who emerge victorious, keeping my practices until the end" will shepherd and rule the nations. In Revelation as also in John, both Jesus and his followers fulfill shepherding roles. In Revelation as also in John, both Jesus and his followers work for and bring about justice (both the consolation of the oppressed and the correction or condemnation of the oppressors). In this way, Jesus and his followers are one, just as Jesus and the Father are one (John 17:20-23).

Besides the one reference to "sheep" in Revelation 18:13 and the four references to "shepherding" (or "ruling") in 2:27; 7:17; 12:5; and 19:15, the apocalypse of John portrays Jesus as a lamb (or Lamb) twenty-eight times, on average a little more than once per chapter. We've already seen Jesus likened to a lamb in two other texts. Luke unintentionally portrays

---

51. Perhaps in Rev 12:5 and certainly in Rev 2:27 and 19:15, those whom Jesus "will shepherd" are not the faithful people of God but rather the nations who suffer God's wrath. See Gregory K. Beale, *The Book of Revelation*, NIGTC (Grand Rapids: Eerdmans, 1999), 267–68, 962–63, for comments on 2:27; 19:15 and the allusion to Ps 2:9.

Jesus as a lamb in a quotation from Isaiah 53:7, and John the Baptist, in the Fourth Gospel, intentionally portrays Jesus as a paschal lamb who takes away the world's sin. Both Luke and John use the word *amnos*, "lamb." Revelation never uses *amnos*; its word for "lamb" is *arnion*, which by the time of the NT can refer to "a sheep of any age."[52] There isn't any apparent difference between *amnos* and *arnion*; both terms refer or can refer to lambs.[53] Revelation, a text filled with and driven by the most exalted NT imagery for Jesus, utilizes the image of a lamb for its primary representation of Jesus.

This is a striking observation. At the beginning of Revelation, Jesus speaks with "a loud voice," one that sounds "like a trumpet" (1:10), and John's description of Jesus is jaw-dropping:

> I turned to see who was speaking to me, and when I turned, I saw seven oil lamps burning on top of seven gold stands. In the middle of the lampstands I saw someone who looked like the Human One. He wore a robe that stretched down to his feet, and he had a gold sash around his chest. His head and hair were white as white wool—like snow—and his eyes were like a fiery flame. His feet were like fine brass that has been purified in a furnace, and his voice sounded like rushing water. He held seven stars in his right hand, and from his mouth came a sharp, two-edged sword. His appearance was like the sun shining with all its power. (Rev 1:12-16)

Even with this cosmic, exalted language in hand, the Johannine apocalypse prefers to portray Jesus as a lamb.

The first appearance of the lamb occurs in John's vision of the throne-room of God in Revelation 4–5. After transcribing Jesus's letters to the seven Asian churches in Revelation 2–3, John sees an open door granting access from earth to heaven. He hears Jesus's voice, "which sounded like a trumpet" (4:1), summoning him in through the door, and John finds himself in the throne room of God. The unnamed monarch "seated on the

---

52. BDAG, s.v. Outside Acts 8:32 and John 1:29, 36, the only other use of *amnos* in the NT is found in 1 Peter 1:19 ("you were liberated by the precious blood of Christ, like that of a flawless, spotless lamb"), which aligns well with the Johannine use of *amnos*. Outside Revelation, the only use of *arnion* in the NT comes in Jesus's first command for Peter to "feed my lambs" (John 21:15).

53. Moisés Silva, "ἀμνός; ἀρήν; ἀρνίον," *NIDNTTE* 1:267–68.

throne" (4:2) is surrounded by twenty-four elders who also sit on thrones. In the midst of the elders were four living creatures, which resembled a lion, an ox, a human being, and an eagle, though each creature has six wings and is covered with eyes (4:6-8). These creatures, whose striking descriptions understandably threaten to draw our eye toward themselves, direct our attention throne-ward. They sing out, "Holy, holy, holy is the Lord God Almighty, who was and is and is coming," and the twenty-four elders fall prostrate before the throne, casting their crowns and singing God's worth (4:8-11).

It can be difficult for us to appreciate the awe and wonder and splendor John conveys in his vision of the heavenly throne room. We simply don't have spaces of power or awe or dread in our own cultural spheres to provide helpful analogs to what John sees or how he reacts to it. Our centers of political or economic power or of historical significance are available to visitors, offering public tours and viewing galleries so that the average person can see what goes on inside. The effect is to demystify such spaces, to make them accessible to the populace. We may continue to experience a sense of awe or wonder standing in the residence of an executive of state or touring the remains of a significant site of battle, but few of us will feel out of place, as though we don't belong here.

John doesn't react to the vision of the heavenly throne room like a visitor to the Houses of Parliament or a tourist at the Gettysburg Battlefield. As his vision begins to focus and his head clears in the face of what he's seeing, John sees "a scroll in the right hand of the one seated on the throne. It had writing on the front and the back, and it was sealed with seven seals" (Rev 5:1). An angelic herald cries out, asking who, if anyone, could take the scroll, break its seals, and read its contents, and after a search no one was found, not in heaven or on earth or under the earth. The seven-sealed scroll was filled completely with some revelation from God—"it had writing on the front and the back"—but it looks like that revelation will not be made known and the word from God will remain sealed and under wraps. God wants to disclose some decree to creation; after all, he has written or dictated the contents of the scroll and prepared it for sending. But now that act of communication seems impossible, since no messenger or courier can be found to take the scroll from God and disclose its contents to creation. Shall the will of God remain undisclosed, even unaccomplished?[54]

The scene conveys a remarkable, nearly palpable tension. On one hand, all of creation is deemed unworthy of the word of God, as no one can even take the scroll, let alone open it and read it. The unsuccessful search for someone, *anyone*, worthy to open the scroll "underscores the differences between creatures and their Creator. All creatures prove to be inadequate for the carrying out of God's purposes."[55] The gap between God and creation appears unbridgeable. On the other hand, John himself has been permitted to bridge that gap, being invited through the door into heaven and permitted to see and describe for others the hidden realities of the throne room of God. John succumbs to the tension and sobs uncontrollably: "I began to weep and weep, because no one was found worthy to open the scroll or to look inside it" (Rev 5:4).

As John weeps, one of the elders who had been seated on the thrones surrounding the throne of God—who had gotten off their thrones, thrown down their crowns, and fallen prostrate before the one who sits on the center throne (Rev 4:4, 9-11)—notices him and consoles him in his despair. He tells John: "Don't weep. Look! The Lion of the tribe of Judah, the Root of David, has emerged victorious so that he can open the scroll and its seven seals" (5:5). At this point it might be useful to remind ourselves that we're talking about *pastoral* imagery in Revelation, that is, imagery relating to sheep and shepherding. We already noted that Revelation's dominant portrayal of Jesus is as a lamb (or perhaps, Lamb; *arnion*). Here in verse 5, we have a different image of Jesus: he is a *lion* (or perhaps, *Lion*); he is also a "root" that continues to live in the safety of the soil even after the rest of the plant has been destroyed by wind or fire or axe.

As a metaphor for Jesus, "the Lion of the tribe of Judah" seems more appropriate than a lamb. It *feels* right that Jesus, "the King of Beasts,"

---

54. Beale (*Revelation*, 338–48) rightly argues that the plot of Revelation concerns not just the *disclosure* but also the *accomplishment* of the contents of the book/scroll in chapter 5.

55. Craig R. Koester, *Revelation and the End of All Things* (Grand Rapids: Eerdmans, 2001), 77. I would add that all creatures prove to be inadequate for the *disclosure* of God's purposes, in addition to *carrying out* his purposes."

should be "a lion—*the* Lion, the great Lion."[56] How surprising, then, that Revelation 5:5 is *the only time in the NT* that Jesus is likened to a lion,[57] that the NT authors didn't, apparently, feel the regal "king of beasts" was a useful representation for portraying the King of kings. The imagery of "the Lion of the tribe of Judah" comes from the patriarchal narratives in Genesis. Abraham's grandson Jacob (= Israel), as he was nearing death, summoned his sons and, according to the LXX, prophesied over them "what will happen to you in the last days" (Gen 49:1 LXX).[58] After addressing Reuben and Simeon and Levi, Jacob turns to Judah:

> Judah, my son, a lion's cub. You sprang up from a shoot; when you laid down, you slept as a lion, even as a lion's cub. Who will disturb him? A ruler will not fail [to arise] from Judah, nor one who governs [to issue forth] from his loins, until what is his shall come, and he shall be the expectation of nations. (Gen 49:9-10 LXX)

We can see the same mixed metaphors in Genesis 49 as in Revelation 5: both Judah and Jesus are lions, like shoots rising from roots.[59] The one who steps forth "in the last days" (remember Gen 49:1 LXX) to take hold of the scroll in God's right hand (remember Rev 5:1) is the promised lion (or Lion) of Judah, the hope of nations (see Gen 49:10; Isa 11:10).

So after the elder eases John's grief by pointing out the presence of the Lion of Judah, John turns to see this Lion. What he sees surprises him. Rather than an Aslan-type figure[60] who approaches the throne with a quiet and fearful dignity, John sees a lamb (or Lamb), whose features distinguish him from any other lamb that might come to mind: "I saw a Lamb, standing as if it had been slain. It had seven horns and seven eyes, which

---

56. C. S. Lewis, *The Chronicles of Narnia* (New York: HarperCollins, 2004), 146. Upon learning that Aslan isn't a man but a lion, Susan and Lucy ask if he's safe. Mister Beaver responds incredulously: " 'Safe?' said Mr Beaver; 'don't you hear what Mrs Beaver tells you? Who said anything about safe? 'Course he isn't safe. But he's good. He's the King, I tell you.' "

57. The other references to a *leōn* in the NT refer either to an opponent—or the Opponent—of the people of God (see 2 Tim 4:17; Heb 11:33; 1 Pet 5:8; Rev 13:2) or the agent of God's wrath (Rev 9:8, 17; 10:3) or one of the divine creatures attending God's royal court (Rev 4:7).

58. The translation of the LXX in this section is my own, rendered from the Rahlfs edition of the Greek text.

59. This mixing of metaphors in Genesis 49:9 LXX helps explain the echo of Isa 11:1, 10 in Rev 5:5.

60. Cf. C. S. Lewis, *The Chronicles of Narnia*.

are God's seven spirits, sent out into the whole earth" (Rev 5:6). There is much to say about the Lamb John sees standing near the throne.

First, and most conspicuously, the Lamb is "standing as if it had been slain." The image is fundamentally contradictory: standing livestock hasn't been slaughtered, and slaughtered livestock doesn't stand. The Lamb John sees, however, simultaneously lives and has been slaughtered. The slaughtered-but-still-standing Lamb readily calls to mind John the Baptist's description of Jesus as "the Lamb of God" (John 1:29, 35), as well as the Fourth Gospel's synchronization of Jesus's execution with the slaughter of the Passover lambs in John 19:14.[61] This slaughtered Lamb clearly has atoning significance: in Revelation as in the Fourth Gospel, the Lamb "takes away the sin of the world." But the obsolete sense of *atonement*— that is, "harmony, reconciliation, or being 'at one'"—is also at work here, as the slaughtered Lamb traverses and closes the gap that separates the one who holds the scroll and those for whom the scroll is intended.

Second, the Lamb has two distinct and distinctive groups of seven: its seven horns and its seven eyes. The description of the Lamb's horns and eyes is suggestive rather than representational. Rather than trying to *see* in our minds what a ram with seven horns and seven eyes would look like, we ought to grasp the significance of horns and eyes, on the one hand, and of the number seven on the other. The horn (*ceras*) was a symbol of strength and power, whether of an animal or of a human being. For example, when Hannah leaves her firstborn son, Samuel, in service at the Lord's tent, she sings, "My heart is strengthened in the Lord; my horn is uplifted in my God. My mouth is opened wide upon my enemies, and I am made glad in your salvation" (1 Sam 2:1 LXX).[62] Especially in the Prophets, horns are a symbol of strength, as in this oracle from the prophet Micah to Zion: "Get up and thresh them, daughter of Zion, for I will make your horns as iron, and I will make your hooves as copper. You will thrash nations with them and crush many peoples. Then you will dedicate their wealth to the Lord, and their strength to the Lord of all the earth" (Mic 4:13 LXX). The horn

---

61. Koester, *Revelation and the End of All Things*, 78–79.

62. See also 1 Samuel 2:10 LXX, where Hannah declares that the Lord "will exalt the horn of his anointed one" (*hypsōsei keras christou autou*), which is a literal translation of the Hebrew *veyarem qeren meshikho*.

is a symbol of strength, whether of the people of Israel and/or Judah or of their enemies.[63] That the Lamb has seven horns is a symbol of the Lamb's incomparable, perfect strength.

In addition to seven horns, the Lamb has seven eyes, which John explains as "God's seven spirits, sent out into the whole earth" (Rev 5:6). That the Lamb's eyes/spirits encompass "the whole earth" suggests either that God sees and watches over his people no matter where they are or that he is with them no matter where they are. Perhaps both of these are intended. John's vision of the Lamb echoes with the vision of the prophet Zechariah, who saw a golden lampstand with seven lamps (Zech 4). The seven lamps "are the seven eyes of the LORD, surveying the entire earth" (4:10). The seven-eyed Lamb resonates with Zechariah's vision of Israel's restoration, which God will accomplish "neither by power, nor by strength, but by my spirit" (4:6). The Lamb also serves as the point of connection between the heavenly throne room and "the whole earth." That is, the Lamb stands in the center of heaven, in the midst of the four creatures and the twenty-four elders. But the presence and awareness of God isn't restricted to this most holy place; in the eyes of the Lamb the presence of God issues forth throughout all of creation. The LORD's seven eyes survey the entire earth and encourage a people returning from exile, ensuring them that they have not been exiled so far from home that they are beyond God's attention or awareness. The Johannine echo of Zechariah's vision extends God's attention and awareness even further, so that "every creature in heaven and on earth and under the earth and in the sea" comes under God's purview and, in response, sings praises "to the one seated on the throne and to the Lamb" (Rev 5:13).

This Lamb—with seven eyes, seven horns, standing as if it had been slain—is John's dominant image for Jesus through the rest of the book of Revelation. I can't help thinking that Judah's Lion rather than John's Lamb would have been a more appropriate image, especially as the Lamb wages war, wins victory, and has his power and worth acknowledged by friend and foe alike.[64] None of these things sounds pastoral to me; they sound

---

63. See also Jer 31:12, 25; Lam 2:3, 17; Ezek 29:21; Dan 7:7-27; 8:3-26.

64. The references in Revelation to the Lamb and his power and/or victory and/or authority are nearly universal. Of Revelation's twenty-eight references to Jesus as *to arnion*, at least twenty-three of them portray him as powerful, victorious, and/or worthy of the worship that the creatures in heaven, on earth,

more lion-like and less lamb-ish. John, however, clearly preferred the image of a slaughtered Lamb to a stately Lion, and our job as readers must be both to notice and to understand this preference.

Through the rest of Revelation we see the Lamb in proximity to the throne. The Lamb stands "in the midst of the throne and the four living creatures and among the elders" (Rev 5:6, CEB modified). The innumerable crowd "from every nation, tribe, people, and language" stands before both the throne and the Lamb (7:9), and the Lamb is identified by his position near the throne (7:17). The "river of life-giving water" in the New Jerusalem flows "from the throne of God and the Lamb" (22:1). The Lamb and the throne are two images that appear together throughout Revelation.

We could emphasize the distinction between the Lamb *next to* the throne and the one sitting *on* the throne. Such a distinction, however, would be overdrawn and unhelpful. Instead, we ought to understand the Lamb as the symbol through which the presence of God is made available to creation. As such, the Lamb has one characteristic that no other entity in Revelation has. John's slaughtered Lamb is *worshipped*. No one else in Revelation receives worship. Even the revelatory angel rebukes John for bowing before him: "Then I fell at his feet to worship him. But he said, 'Don't do that! I'm a servant just like you and your brothers and sisters who hold firmly to the witness of Jesus. Worship God!'" (Rev 19:10). Even so, the Lamb regularly receives the same deference and worship offered to God, from humans, from angels, and from the creatures who attend God's throne. In Revelation, the one who sits on the throne both is distinct from and yet shades into the Lamb, and vice versa. As the Lamb shepherds his people and metes justice upon his enemies (Rev 7:17), we find the fulfillment of the prophetic promise that God himself would shepherd his people.[65]

The presence of the Lamb becomes identical with the presence of God. Where the Lamb is, there too is God. In Revelation 7, for example, John sees "a great crowd that no one could number . . . from every nation,

---

and beneath the earth offer to God (see Rev 5:6, 8, 12, 13; 6:16; 7:9, 10, 17; 12:11; 13:8; 14:1, 4 [2x], 10; 15:3; 17:14 [2x]; 19:7, 9; 21:14, 27; 22:1, 3).

65. Ezek 34; see also Jer 23:3.

tribe, people, and language" (7:9). This multitude stands before the throne *and before the Lamb*, and they give worship "to our God who sits on the throne, and to the Lamb" (7:9-10). Later, in Revelation 14, John sees the Lamb "standing on Mount Zion" (14:1), surrounded by 144,000 who have been separated ("purchased") from the rest of humanity as firstfruits for both God and the Lamb (14:4). The 144,000 who stand with the Lamb have God's name inscribed on their foreheads (14:1); their facial tattoos marking them as belonging to God and to the Lamb as well as distinguishing them from those who "worship the beast and its image, and receive a mark on their foreheads or their hands" (14:9).

John's vision of the Lamb evokes themes and images from the vision of four beasts and the one like a son of man in Daniel 7. This evocation is perhaps nowhere more prevalent than in Revelation 14. The Danielic vision is difficult in its own right; both the referent and the intentions of its unrelenting imagery spark considerable discussion and debate among readers. (The same is true, of course, of Revelation.) Daniel sees a dream-vision in which "the four winds of heaven" stir up chaos in "the great sea" (Dan 7:2). He then sees "four giant beasts emerg[ing] from the sea, each different from the others" (7:3). The description of each is both other-worldly and terrifying. Daniel's description of the beasts "paints a picture of these kingdoms *as monstrous eruptions of chaos*, in order to convey a sense of terror far beyond anything suggested by the flat statement of the interpretation."[66] In other words, the point of the description of Daniel's vision isn't simply to convey information (four kingdoms are coming; they're not the nicest). His description elicits an emotional response among his readers; it terrifies them before it introduces the resolution to their terror. That terror describes the present as much as it describes the future.[67] As a result, whenever readers have found Daniel's terror relevant

---

66. John J. Collins, *The Apocalyptic Imagination: An Introduction to the Jewish Matrix of Christianity* (New York: Crossroad, 1987), 80; my emphasis.

67. It is commonly noted that Daniel's vision describes—and dates from—the Jews' experience of persecution under Antiochus IV in the second century BCE (see Collins, *Apocalyptic Imagination*, 68–92). In other words, Daniel 7 steps backward into the past to describe the present terror of the "Hellenistic Reforms" rather than predicts those terrors from within the relative tranquility of the Babylonian exile. If this note is wrong and Daniel does in fact date from the Babylonian period, then at least we can say that Daniel's prediction of terror found meaningful reception in the second-century BCE.

for their own situations, Daniel 7's beastly vision has provided a frame enabling readers to understand their present and to express their expectations and hopes for the future. Daniel's vision is, then, a vehicle of hope for the hopeless. Its terror provides the language and conceptual categories for people who find themselves in turmoil and chaos and, after explaining that turmoil, offers a path toward resolution and hope.

The resolution to the beastly terror comes in the form of "one like a human being coming with the heavenly clouds," who approaches "the ancient one" who sits on his throne and receives "rule, glory, and kingship," an eternal, indestructible kingdom (Dan 7:13-14). Daniel is playing with images from the creation account in Genesis 1. When creation was still "good," God created the beasts and animals and then appointed the human being to rule over them. In Daniel's vision, the order of creation is inverted, to disastrous effect. During the exile, beasts rise up from out of the sea to rule, and their reign is terrible. But it isn't permanent. Daniel's "one like a human being" resumes his rightful place; he rules over the beasts and brings their beastly rule to an end. And creation will once again be good, as it was in the beginning.

Revelation picks up Daniel's terrifying-and-consoling dream-vision and enacts it anew. Revelation 13 describes the advent—if that is the right word—of two beasts; Daniel, of course, saw four. But the difference hardly matters, any more than do the differences in Daniel's and Revelation's descriptions of the beasts. Both achieve the same emotional effect: terror. More importantly, both resolve that effect in the same way: by replacing the beasts with one like a human being. Revelation first opposes the two beasts from chapter 13 with the Lamb standing on Mount Zion in the beginning of chapter 14. As we already noted, the Lamb is accompanied by a retinue of 144,000. He is also attended by three angels (Rev 14:6-11) who summon creation to worship the creator God. They also announce the judgment of God upon the beast and those who worship it. Revelation ultimately drops the image, for the time being, of Jesus-as-Lamb in order to bring its presentation of Jesus more fully in line with Daniel's vision of one like a human being: "Then I looked, and there was a white cloud. On the cloud was seated someone who looked like the Human One" (14:14).

For our purposes, the CEB's translation is a bit unfortunate. Both Daniel and Revelation refer to "one like a son of a human," so that Revelation's "Human One" refers to the same individual as Daniel's "human being."[68] Daniel's "Human One," now a figure in John's Revelation, sends out an angel to gather the faithful to God's presence (14:15-16), and he sends a second angel to bring his wrath on the unfaithful (14:17-20).[69] For our purposes, however, we note that Revelation has set aside its portrayal of Jesus as an animal (here, the Lamb) in order to echo Daniel's vision of a human being, an image-of-God-bearing ruler whose rule contrasts with the terrifying, beastly power of those who oppose Israel's God. The switch in figurative representation, from Lamb to human being, was dictated by the dynamics of Daniel's vision. The whole point of Daniel's vision is that the animalistic kingdoms of the gentiles are supplanted and replaced by the human (and humane) reign of the one who bears God's image. Revelation respects that point by laying aside, temporarily, the animalistic representation of Jesus-as-Lamb.

Even so, Revelation returns to its favorite image of Jesus in the very next scene. John sees "another great and awe-inspiring sign in heaven," which includes the crowd of "those who gained victory over the beast, its image, and the number of its name" (Rev 15:1-2). This crowd sings "the song of Moses, God's servant, and the song of the Lamb" (15:3). John envisions the climactic manifestations of God's wrath against the whole earth (Rev 16) and against the "great prostitute" and the "scarlet beast...covered with blasphemous names" (Rev 17). The beast, with its seven heads and ten horns, represents kings arrayed against the rule of God and his people (17:9, 12), and the prostitute is "the great city that

---

68. The standard phrase, in Greek, for "the Son of Man" (CEB = "the Human One") is *ho huios tou anthrōpou* (seventy-eight times in the NT). Only four times in the NT do we find the phrase *huios anthrōpou* (see John 5:27; Heb 2:6; Rev 1:13; 14:14), which matches the LXX of Daniel 7:13 (cp. the Hebrew *bar 'enash*). For discussions of "the Son of Man problem," see the essays gathered in Benjamin E. Reynolds, ed., *The Son of Man Problem: Critical Readings*, T&T Clark Critical Readings in Biblical Studies (London: T&T Clark, 2018).

69. See Beale, *Revelation*, 773–80. Beale interprets both angels' harvest as a singular scene of judgment, which is possible. I read the angelic harvests in Revelation 14 as parallels to the parable of the weeds (Matt 13:24-30), though in Matthew the order of the harvests is reversed. For discussion, see Richard Bauckham, *The Theology of the Book of Revelation*, New Testament Theology (Cambridge: Cambridge University Press, 1993), 94–98.

rules over the kings of the earth" (17:18). In a strange twist of imagery, the prostitute and her beast "will make war on the Lamb, but the Lamb will emerge victorious" (17:14). Lambs are not normally portrayed as adept or fearsome animals of war. This Lamb, however, "is Lord of lords and King of kings" (17:14), and his victory over the kings reminds us of another twist of imagery from earlier in Revelation: "the kings of the earth, the officials and the generals, the rich and the powerful, and everyone, slave and free...called to the mountains and the rocks, 'Fall on us and hide us from the face of the one seated on the throne and from the Lamb's wrath! The great day of their wrath has come, and who is able to stand?'" (6:15-17).

Who's afraid of the big, bad Lamb? Apparently, everybody.

In Revelation 18, the final judgment against Babylon echoes across creation, and a voice from heaven calls the people of God away from the godless city. Heaven rejoices at her condemnation and the vindication of the faithful who suffered under her influence (19:1-5). Suddenly, as John is listening to the heavenly chorus, he hears a "huge crowd, like rushing water and powerful thunder," singing praise to God and declaring a celebratory event: "Hallelujah! The Lord our God, the Almighty, exercised his royal power! Let us rejoice and celebrate, and give him the glory, for the wedding day of the Lamb has come, and his bride has made herself ready. She was given fine, pure white linen to wear, for the fine linen is the saints' acts of justice" (19:6-8). The Lamb gets married; having defeated his enemies in war, he is united with his bride. With the old celestial and terrestrial orders condemned, a new heaven and a new earth, with a new Jerusalem, unfolds before John. Thirst and hunger and death and sorrow disappear, and a new order appears, in which God and humanity dwell together again as they did in Eden. Everywhere this new order bears the marks of the Lamb. The twelve foundations of the city wall are inscribed with "the twelve names of the Lamb's twelve apostles" (21:14). Even more striking is John's description of the city as lacking a temple:

> I didn't see a temple in the city, because its temple is the Lord God Almighty and the Lamb. The city doesn't need the sun or the moon to shine on it, because God's glory is its light, and its lamp is the Lamb. The nations will walk by its light, and the kings of the earth will bring

their glory into it. Its gates will never be shut by day, and there will be no night there. They will bring the glory and honor of the nations into it. Nothing unclean will ever enter it, nor anyone who does what is vile and deceitful, but only those who are registered in the Lamb's scroll of life. (Rev 21:22-27)

The final chapter, Revelation 22, unveils a "river of life-giving water, shining like crystal, flowing from the throne of God and the Lamb" (22:1). He sees "the tree of life, which produces twelve crops of fruit, bearing its fruit each month. The tree's leaves are for the healing of the nations" (22:2). With this the curse of sin is completely unraveled. (The tree of life became especially dangerous after the original curse of sin in Genesis 3. In order to prevent humans from eating the fruit of the tree of life, the LORD God "stationed winged creatures wielding flaming swords to guard the way to the tree of life" [see Gen 3:20-24]. In Revelation, the curse of Genesis comes to an end.)

Revelation ends with John realizing (or being reminded) that all of this is a vision, that it is not yet reality, that it is yet to come. As he begins to awaken, he hears the voice of Jesus encouraging him: "Look! I'm coming soon. Favored is the one who keeps the words of the prophecy contained in this scroll" (Rev 22:7). God's Spirit, Christ's bride, and John's readers all bid Christ, saying, "Come," and they hear in response the invitation: "let the one who is thirsty come" (22:17). The last thing John hears is Jesus, saying, "Yes, I'm coming soon," to which John says, "Amen. Come, Lord Jesus" (22:20). He closes the book by asking the grace of the Lord Jesus for all his readers (22:21).

This brings the NT to an end, with a slaughtered-yet-victorious Lamb united with his bride and their enemies brought under control. It's a strange image, really. Lambs don't get married. Lambs don't wage war. Lambs don't inspire terror and fear in their enemies. For that matter, lambs don't typically have enemies. For all these things (well, for most of them), the image of Judah's Lion would seem more appropriate.

Surely it tells us something, though, that John's preferred representative symbol for Jesus is a lamb, an animal fit for sacrifice but not much else. Perhaps this explains the rest of the NT's reluctance to liken Jesus to a lamb; "fit for sacrifice but not much else" is hardly how the early Christians perceived Jesus. We saw that Luke could accidentally stumble into portraying Jesus as a lamb, but Luke seems not to have found that portrayal theologically suggestive for his account of Jesus's life or the advance of the gospel on Rome. The Fourth Gospel embraced the image of Jesus-as-Lamb more fully than did Luke, both in the twice-repeated exclamation, "Look! The Lamb of God!" (John 1:29, 35) and in the realignment of Jesus's death with the slaughter of the Passover lambs. But none of these texts pushed against connotative load of their imagery. For the Third and Fourth Gospels, lambs were fit for sacrifice but not much else. When the Gospels wanted to do something else with pastoral imagery—especially to portray Jesus as the one who guides, protects, and provides for the people of God—they switched from Jesus-as-Lamb to Jesus-as-Shepherd.

But Revelation isn't like the Gospels. Not even the Fourth Gospel. Revelation runs roughshod all over the connotative load of its pastoral imagery. On a few occasions Jesus (or those he sends) shepherded the sheep, and of course the slain Lamb has clear sacrificial, atoning resonance. But otherwise and for the most part, John allows his view of Jesus—his Christology—to drive his use of Lamb imagery rather than the other way around. In other words, Revelation's pastoral imagery expresses his Christology but doesn't generate or create it. Revelation's Lamb does what sheep don't do because Jesus does what sheep don't do, and Revelation doesn't respect the limits of its imagery. Instead, Revelation explodes those limits.

Pastoral imagery in the Fourth Gospel and especially in Revelation justifies this chapter's subtitle: "Johannine Innovations as Memory." The NT's Johannine literature remembers Jesus in innovative, sometimes surprising ways. The early church responded to the surprise by allegorizing the Gospels. Irenaeus, who died around 202 CE, associated each of the four evangelists with the four creatures described in Revelation 4:6-7.[70] At about the same time, Clement of Alexandria compared John with the

---

70. Irenaeus (*Haer.* 3.11.8) likens Matthew to a human being, Luke to an ox, Mark to an eagle, and John to a lion. The Latin scholar Jerome, in his revision of Victorinus's *Commentary on Revelation*, reassigns the Markan and Johannine symbol, so that now Mark is the lion and John is the eagle. See Francis Watson, *The Fourfold Gospel: A Theological Reading of the New Testament Portraits of Jesus* (Grand Rapids: Baker Academic, 2016), 90–95.

Synoptic Gospels, describing the first three Gospels as accounts of the "bodily facts" of Jesus's life and Fourth Gospel as a "spiritual Gospel."[71] In the wake of the Enlightenment, NT scholars have responded to the surprise by ignoring (or at least displacing) the Fourth Gospel in favor of the Synoptic Gospels.

We may understand and respond to the similarities and differences between our four Gospels in any number of ways. When we reduce the Gospels' plurality to an imagined singularity of "what really happened," we literally set aside the word of God in favor of human tradition (Mark 6:6-13). The gospel can't be reduced to singularity; it is always plural, always multiform. Sometimes the differences between them provoke little more than a raised eyebrow or a yawn, as in the different ways that the Synoptic Gospels and the Fourth Gospel connect John the Baptist to Isaiah's voice crying in the wilderness (Isa 40:3).[72] At other times that plurality levels questions against the veracity of major parts of the entire Jesus tradition, as in the various accounts of Jesus's birth and genealogy.[73] But in both moments and in every moment between them, the Gospel is plural.[74]

The differences between them are not distortions in the sense of Señora Giménez's "repair" of García Martínez's *Ecce Homo*. The differences are distortions in the sense of a refracting lens that enables us to see what had been invisible, or to see in a new light what had been obscured. The fourfold Gospel canon sets, in some sense, limits on what the church can remember about Jesus; it would be difficult, for example, to find in the Gospels a Jesus who is the friend of religious hypocrites and an oppressor of the poor. But the fourfold Gospel canon also authorizes a multiform memory of Jesus, a Jesus who speaks to evangelical American Christians as well as liberationist Latino/a Christians, and others besides. We may not

---

71. Clement of Alexandria, cited by Eusebius, *Hist. eccl.* 6.14.7; see Judith Lieu, "How John Writes," in *The Written Gospel*, ed. Markus Bockmuehl and Donald A. Hagner (Cambridge: Cambridge University Press, 2005), 171–83 (171–73).

72. Compare Mark 1:3//Matt 3:3//Luke 3:4-6 with John 1:23.

73. Compare Matthew 1–2 and Luke 1–2, including the two genealogies of Jesus in Matthew 1:2-17 and Luke 3:23-38.

74. See Francis Watson, *Gospel Writing: A Canonical Perspective* (Grand Rapids: Eerdmans, 2013), esp. the chapters in Part One ("The Eclipse of the Fourfold Gospel," pp. 13–113).

be free to remember Jesus in any way we might like, but neither are we constrained to remember Jesus in just one particular way.

The Johannine Jesus opens up the possibility that memory of Jesus can be authentic even as it is also innovative. The hairy and sometimes unpleasant task of discerning when and how and why certain memories of Jesus exceed the bounds of authentic representations of Jesus still remains. But perhaps that hairy and sometimes unpleasant task is an important part of remembering Jesus faithfully.

Chapter 4
Reimagining Jesus: The General Epistles and Hebrews

Men make their own history, but they do not make it just as they please; they do not make it under circumstances chosen by themselves, but under circumstances directly encountered, given and transmitted from the past. The tradition of all the dead generations weighs like a nightmare on the brain of the living.[1]

Breaking the Rules

It's one of my favorite memes. On the left, Alexander Gardner's photograph of Abraham Lincoln, the sixteenth president of the United States, taken on 8 November 1863, less than two weeks before he would deliver the Gettysburg Address. On the right, the following quote, attributed to Lincoln: "Don't believe everything you read on the internet just because there's a picture with a quote next to it."[2]

---

1. Karl Marx, cited in Clifton Crais, *History Lessons: A Memoir of Madness, Memory, and the Brain* (New York: Overlook, 2014), 243–44.

2. A poster can be purchased from Amazon: https://www.amazon.com/Believe-Internet-Lincoln -Humor-Poster/dp/B00EAYHCW6.

Indeed.

As a commemorative activity, the meme provides an interesting example of both the constraints and the malleability of the past and the present. We should acknowledge, first, that Abraham Lincoln never said anything like "Don't believe everything you read on the internet." The meme only "works" for readers who get this point and who also appreciate its absurdity.

But it also raises a number of questions. What is gained by invoking Abraham Lincoln when urging wisdom and discernment while online? What is the link between critical skepticism and the sixteenth president of the United States? And why are "readers" of this meme able to get the point and, in the end, appreciate it as an authentic—if still deliberately ironic—act of communication?

Abraham Lincoln "makes sense" as an advocate for wisdom and a healthy dose of skepticism online because he is the paradigmatic representation of American wisdom, integrity, and discernment. Lincoln may never have urged incredulity when consuming online information, but neither did any of his mid-nineteenth-century contemporaries, including his most famous rhetorical adversary: Stephen A. Douglas. But the creators of our meme invoked Lincoln rather than Douglas because Douglas lacks any symbolic value for Americans on the internet. Lincoln, on the other hand, exudes symbolic value. As a result, Lincoln's image adds value to the words of the meme; it invokes Lincoln's persona even as it knowingly winks at the reader. After all, both author and audience know Lincoln never said these words.

Still. Be like Lincoln. I mean...c'mon.

In this final chapter, we will look at representations of Jesus in texts from the remaining section of the NT canon: the General Epistles. In previous chapters we looked at texts that had some unifying element, whether of authorship (the Pauline letters; see chapter 1), literary influence (the Synoptic Gospels and Acts; see chapter 2), and/or worldview (the Johannine literature; see chapter 3). The material covered in this chapter, however, lacks any unifying element other than none of it is a Gospel, and none of it claims to have been written by Paul (not even

Hebrews[3]). As Luke Timothy Johnson explains, "Th ˙ writings all present themselves…as letters," though not all of them   through on this presentation consistently.[4] Unlike Paul's letters (bu┌──────────ospels), these texts are not addressed to specific audiences, and ˙   ˙ ˙n grouped together as "General" or "Catholic Epistles." (Th *katholikē*, from which we get "catholic," means "general, ur─── Catholic Letters include Hebrews, James, 1 and 2 Peter, an. Johannine Epistles (1–3 John) are also grouped with the Cathc and sometimes Revelation is included as well, though these la─── also have theological and stylistic similarities to the Fourth Gospe are grouped with the "Johannine literature." Paul's letters are identified by their intended recipients (e.g., the letter to the Romans is called Romans, that to the Philippians is called Philippians); none of them are named after their author. The Catholic Epistles are reversed. The General Epistles are known by the name of their textually encoded author (e.g., the letter that James wrote is called James), in part because they don't name their intended audience.[5]

As with previous chapters, we don't have the time or space to consider each of the Catholic Epistles. In chapter 2, we considered the Synoptic Gospels in the order in which they were written (first Mark, then Matthew, then Luke-Acts), rather than in canonical order. We will follow the same procedure here. Unfortunately, assigning a date to the Catholic Epistles is particularly difficult, and scholars are not agreed on when or in what

---

3. Some within the early church attributed Hebrews to Paul. For example, the papyrus manuscript 𝔓46 (late-second/early-third century CE) arranges Paul's letters from longest to shortest and includes Hebrews between Romans and 1 Corinthians. Today, Pauline authorship of Hebrews is universally (or nearly universally) rejected among credible scholars.

4. Johnson, *Writings of the New Testament*, 403–4.

5. Hebrews and the Johannine Epistles are exceptions. The ascription that is printed at the head of Hebrews, *pros Hebraios* ("To the Hebrews") was likely attached to the text secondarily and was not part of the original text. Nowhere in the body of the text does the author address his readers as *hoi Hebraioi* (or even as *hoi Ioudaioi* or *hoi Israēlitai*). The shorter Johannine Epistles identify their intended reader, first vaguely ("To the chosen gentlewoman and her children"; 2 John 1) and then by name ("To my dear friend Gaius"; 3 John 1). The longest Johannine Epistle regularly addresses its readers directly, for example through seven second-person plural imperative verbs (1 John 2:15, 28; 3:1, 13; 4:1 [2x]; 5:21), but it never explicitly identifies them, either by name or by locale.

115

order these letters were written.[6] In this chapter, we will discuss the letter of James, then the book of Hebrews, and finally the First Epistle of Peter.

Each of these three texts has something in common with the Abraham Lincoln meme we discussed at the start of the chapter. They "break the rules," in a way. And yet, despite breaking the rules, they each—in their own ways—commemorate Jesus in ways that take advantage of the symbolic value and potential afforded by the Jesus tradition and bring the *memory* of Jesus forward into new contexts.

James, Jesus, and Faith[fulness]

James is an interesting little letter. Like many of the Catholic Epistles, James is sometimes subject to benign neglect in favor of its weightier Pauline cousins. It doesn't help that Martin Luther referred to James as "a right strawy epistle," a letter more concerned with works than faith (and especially justification by faith) and so comparatively unconcerned with the good news that Luther found in Paul's letters and the Gospels.[7] Though not many today would join in Luther's overt marginalization of James, few of us have given to James anything like the attention we give to Romans or Matthew or John.

Perhaps a few words about the author would help orient us toward this letter. Christian tradition identified the author as James, the brother

---

6. In addition to *when* the Catholic Epistles were written, scholarship has raised serious questions about *who* wrote them. Hebrews is an anonymous text whose author never identifies himself (or herself, if Priscilla is the author). The author of James identifies himself as "James, a slave of God and of the Lord Jesus Christ" (Jas 1:1), and the author of Jude identifies himself as "Jude, a slave of Jesus Christ and brother of James." Though James never makes this claim, most scholars identify the intended author as James the Just, the brother of Jesus who was an important leader in the church in Jerusalem (see Gal 2; Acts 15, 21), which would imply Jude, also, was a brother of Jesus. The author(s) of 1–2 Peter identifies himself as "Peter, an apostle of Jesus Christ" (1 Pet 1:1) and "Simon Peter, a slave and apostle of Jesus Christ" (2 Pet 1:1). The author of 1 John never identifies himself, while the author(s) of 2–3 John refers to himself simply as "the elder." There are questions about the identity of some of these figures (e.g., does Jas 1:1 refer to James the brother of Jesus or a different James?). Even when the identity is pretty clear (e.g., in the cases of 1–2 Pet), scholars doubt whether any of these texts were written by the person to whom they are ascribed. These doubts, as in the cases of the disputed Pauline Epistles, are never conclusive, though in some, even many, cases they are quite serious.

7. Dan Otto Via, "The Right Strawy Epistle Reconsidered: A Study in Biblical Ethics and Hermeneutic," *JR* 49 (1969): 253–67. Luther's epithet for James is found in the preface to his German New Testament, though it was apparently removed in later editions.

of Jesus, whom the early Christians called "James the Just." Since the Reformation and the rise of critical biblical scholarship, however, students of the Bible have raised questions about whether this James could possibly have written our letter. As it happens, the Jewish historian Josephus, who had been a general in the Jews' war against the Romans in 66–70 CE, reports that a Jewish high priest named Ananus the Younger had "James, the brother of Jesus who was called the Christ," stoned along with certain other men.[8] This Ananus served as high priest for only three months in 62 CE, so we can probably date the death of James the brother of Jesus to that year CE.[9] Moreover, Josephus adds that Ananus's murder of James was not popular with pious Jews in Jerusalem: "Those of the inhabitants of the city who were considered the most fair-minded and who were strict in observance of the law were offended at this."[10] We can infer, then, that James was also considered "fair-minded and strict in observance of the law." This is an important inference given James's prominence in the leadership of the earliest Christian movement: James, the brother of Jesus, was both a prominent first-generation Christian and a pious Jew on the eve of the war between the Jews and the Romans.

The letter of James fits this scenario fairly well. In previous generations, when it was fashionable to make stark and clear distinctions between early Christianity and first-century Judaism (with Paul and Pauline ideas providing the quintessential expression of the former), scholars frequently noted that James is a thoroughly Jewish text.[11] (Usually, they were referring to the fact that James doesn't make much of Jesus, his death, or his resurrection. In fact, the text only mentions Jesus twice, a point to which we will return shortly.) In the last two decades of the twentieth century and the first two of the twenty-first, the boundaries between ancient

---

8. See Josephus, *Ant.* 20.200–201 (LCL).

9. Steve Mason, *Josephus and the New Testament*, 2nd ed. (Peabody, MA: Hendrickson, 2003), 240.

10. Josephus, *Ant.* 20.201 (LCL).

11. James has even been accused of exhibiting a theology of "non-Christian character" (see Martin Dibelius, *James*, trans. Michael A. Williams, Hermeneia [Philadelphia: Fortress, 1976], 22, as well as Dibelius's rebuttal on pp. 23–26).

Judaism and early Christianity have become blurred.[12] Scholars have been rediscovering the "thoroughly Jewish" nature of all the NT texts, including the Gospels and, perhaps surprisingly, even Paul's letters.[13] In an interpretive environment where scholars are reading Paul's letter to the Romans as a Jewish text, James's Jewish tenor is especially easy to appreciate.

We should, then, take note of the fact that James only mentions Jesus twice. First, in the letter's opening, the author identifies himself as "a slave of God and of the Lord Jesus Christ" (Jas 1:1). Second, at the beginning of the second chapter, the author warns his readers not to allow favoritism to affect how they express or live out their faith. The verse itself is awkward, though at least we can say that it links "faith" with "our glorious Lord Jesus Christ" (2:1).[14] This may seem an obvious point. After all, who would be surprised to learn that a letter in the NT draws strong connections between "faith" and "our Lord Jesus Christ"?!

But that connection isn't at all obvious in James, who only mentions Jesus in James 1:1 and 2:1. Contrast this with Paul's letter to the Philippians, which is just a bit shorter than James. Paul mentions Jesus twice *in the very first verse* of Philippians: "From Paul and Timothy, slaves of Christ Jesus. To all those in Philippi who are God's people in Christ Jesus, along with your supervisors and servants" (Phil 1:1). Paul mentions Jesus's name twenty more times in the rest of the letter, sometimes alone (2:10, 19) but usually either as "Jesus Christ" or "Christ Jesus."[15] Philippians refers to

---

12. See, for example, Daniel Boyarin, *Dying for God: Martyrdom and the Making of Christianity and Judaism*, Figurae: Reading Medieval Culture (Stanford, CA: Stanford University Press, 1999); idem, *Border Lines: The Partition of Judaeo-Christianity*, Divinations: Rereading Late Ancient Religion (Philadelphia: University of Pennsylvania Press, 2004). See also the essays in Adam H. Becker and Annette Yoshiko Reed, eds., *The Ways That Never Parted: Jews and Christians in Late Antiquity and the Early Middle Ages* (Minneapolis: Fortress, 2007).

13. The literature is vast; for a helpful, multi-voiced discussion of Paul as a Jew, see Mark D. Nanos and Magnus Zetterholm, eds., *Paul within Judaism: Restoring the First-Century Context to the Apostle* (Minneapolis: Fortress, 2015).

14. The Greek text, despite its awkwardness, is largely free of significant textual questions. The ESV translates James 2:1, "My brothers, show no partiality as you hold the faith in our Lord Jesus Christ, the Lord of glory." Most English translations resemble the ESV and render the phrase *tou kyriou hēmōn Iēsou Christou* as the *object* of *tēn pistin*, so that "the faith" of which James speaks is "*in* our Lord Jesus Christ." The CEB, however, renders the same phrase as the *subject* of *tēn pistin*, so that James is speaking not of *our* faith but of *Jesus's* faith (or faithfulness): "My brothers and sisters, when you show favoritism you deny the faithfulness of our Lord Jesus Christ, who has been resurrected in glory."

15. See Phil 1:2, 6, 8, 11, 19, 26; 2:5, 11, 21; 3:3, 8, 12, 14, 20; 4:7, 19, 21, 23.

"Christ" (without the name Jesus) an additional seventeen times,[16] which means Paul refers to Jesus thirty-nine times in a letter seventeen hundred words long. James refers to Jesus only twice, in a letter of about eighteen hundred words.

If James is sparing in his explicit references to Jesus, he is voluminous in his references to "faith" (*pistis*). He uses the word *pistis* sixteen times, more than nearly any other significant word.[17] James opens with an encouragement to consider various trials as joy, because "the testing of your faith [*pistis*] produces endurance" (1:3). To the one who may lack wisdom, James urges them to ask God: "They should ask in faith [*pistis*], without doubting" (1:6). The one who approaches God "in faith" can be confident to receive what has been requested; the one who doubts God's goodness should not expect to receive anything (1:5-7). At the end of the letter, James recommends to his readers "the prayer of faith" (*pistis*; CEB = "prayer that comes from faith"), which "will heal the sick" (5:15). Faith opens and closes James's letter. Faith is woven into the fabric of James.

So what can we say about faith—*pistis*—in James? We've already said it: James ties "faith" in with "our glorious Lord Jesus Christ" (2:1). The faith that confidently approaches God, that asks for wisdom, and that heals the sick is faith defined by, rooted in, and modeled after the Lord Jesus Christ. The Christ-centered, Christ-shaped character of faith in James finds its fullest discussion in James 2: of James's sixteen uses of the word *pistis*, thirteen of them occur in James 2! As a result, we will focus most of our attention on the second chapter of James.

Protestant and Evangelical Christians who affirm the doctrine of "justification by faith alone" may find James 2 a surprising chapter. James speaks plainly and without qualification: "a person is justified by works and not by faith alone" (Jas 2:24 NRSV).[18] The alleged conflict between James and Paul has attracted significant attention. But we will misunderstand

---

16. See Phil 1:10, 13, 15, 17, 18, 20, 21, 23, 27, 29; 2:1, 16, 30; 3:7, 8, 9, 18.

17. James uses the word "God" (*theos*) sixteen times and "brother [and sister]" (*adelphos*) nineteen times. Otherwise, the only words he uses more than *pistis* are words like "I," "you," "and," and "I am."

18. The CEB renders the same passage: "a person is shown to be righteous through faithful actions and not through faith alone" (Jas 2:24). We will have to spend some time addressing what James—and Paul!—means when they refer to a person "being justified/shown to be righteous" (*dikaioutai anthōpos*).

James's portrayal of a Christ-shaped faith if we jump straight to the second half of James 2 and his discussion of faith and works. The first half of the chapter sets the scene and provides some crucially important context. Moreover, we've already noted that the opening of James 2 closely links his readers' experience and practice of faith with "our glorious Lord Jesus Christ." This might be important.

The first half of James 2 focuses on favoritism or partiality and, as we've seen, urges readers to live out their faith in or imitate the faithfulness of Jesus by refusing to show favoritism. James then illustrates the problem of partiality in 2:2-7. First, he portrays a scenario in which two very different people join the gathering of James's readers:[19]

> Imagine two people coming into your meeting. One has a gold ring and fine clothes, while the other is poor, dressed in filthy rags. Then suppose that you were to take special notice of the one wearing fine clothes, saying, "Here's an excellent place. Sit here." But to the poor person you say, "Stand over there"; or, "Here, sit at my feet." Wouldn't you have shown favoritism among yourselves and become evil-minded judges? (Jas 2:2-4)

This scenario is unacceptable to James. The problem isn't simply the preferential treatment of the rich over the poor (though that is certainly problematic). The problem is that the people of God show themselves to be at cross-purposes to God; they *betray* rather than *reflect* the judgment of God.

Readers with ears to hear may pick up resonances of Samuel's enthusiasm for Saul, the first king of Israel, and his hesitation to anoint David, the second king of Israel. Saul was tall, handsome, and rich (1 Sam 9:1-2), standing head and shoulders above his peers, and although he was from "the littlest of the families" of "the smallest Israelite tribe" (9:21) he was without equal among the people (10:24). Samuel may not have been happy about the people's demand for a king, but he had no trouble understanding why God should choose this Benjamite for the job.

---

19. We should probably note that James refers to *synagōgēn hymōn*, literally "your synagogue" or "your gathering together." The English word *synagogue* refers almost exclusively to a Jewish place of worship or worship gathering. The Greek word *synagōgē* didn't refer narrowly to Jewish meetings; both pagan and Christian assemblies could be referred to as "synagogues" (see BDAG s.v.).

Contrast that to Samuel's response to David, the son of Jesse. First Samuel 16 lacks any description of Jesse's family that compares with the description of Saul's in 9:1-2. Moreover, Samuel objects to anointing a second king of Israel, saying, "How can I do that? When Saul hears of it he'll kill me!" (1 Sam 16:2). When he does finally go to Bethlehem and meets Jesse and his sons, immediately he's impressed with Jesse's oldest son, Eliab, and he thinks to himself, "That must be the Lord's anointed right in front" (16:6). This brings us to one of the few—perhaps the only!—rebukes of Samuel the prophet in the Hebrew Bible. When Samuel finds himself impressed by the eldest son of Jesse, God says to him, "Have no regard for his appearance or stature, because I haven't selected him. God doesn't look at things like humans do. Humans see only what is visible to the eyes, but the Lord sees into the heart" (16:7). So Samuel examines each of Jesse's sons in turn and, after some delay, discovers that God has chosen the youngest, an easily overlooked shepherd-boy with a dark complexion and beautiful eyes (16:12-13).

Humans see what is visible to the eyes, but the Lord sees into the heart.

This is the problem James sets before his readers. Not just that they give in to a preference for the wealthy over the poor, but that they see what is visible to the eyes and fail to see into the heart. James explains the problem of being at cross-purposes with God in the very next paragraph:

> My dear brothers and sisters, listen! Hasn't God chosen those who are poor by worldly standards to be rich in terms of faith? Hasn't God chosen the poor as heirs of the kingdom he has promised to those who love him? But you have dishonored the poor. Don't the wealthy make life difficult for you? Aren't they the ones who drag you into court? Aren't they the ones who insult the good name spoken over you at your baptism? (Jas 2:5-7)

"Hasn't God chosen the poor?" James asks; his question expects an affirmative answer: Yes, God has indeed chosen the poor. But God's people—"the twelve tribes who are scattered outside the land of Israel" (Jas 1:1)—dishonor the poor. They dishonor those whom God has chosen.

Did you notice how James reintroduces the concept of faith into the discussion? You'll recall that he is illustrating the problem of his readers having faith with "favoritism" (Jas 2:1), whether that faith is their own belief in and allegiance to Jesus or Jesus's faithfulness to YHWH's covenant with Israel. What the world counts as poverty—whether that be material, social, or political poverty—God considers bountiful as faith. James isn't celebrating poverty *as* poverty, for its own sake. James is warning his readers that their preference for wealth (again, material, social, or political wealth) and those who wield it renders them at odds with what God is doing in the world and puts them at risk of missing the blessing of God in their own lives.[20] Indeed, preferential treatment toward the rich privileges "the ones who drag you into court... [and] who insult the good name spoken over you at your baptism" (2:6-7). Favoritism, in James's view, marginalizes those who may turn out to be faithful even as it privileges those who oppress the people of God. The practice of partiality aligns the readers, the supposed people of God, with the enemies of the people of God and puts them at odds with YHWH.

In the next six verses, James anchors his moral exhortation regarding favoritism in Israel's Torah:

> You do well when you really fulfill the royal law found in scripture, *Love your neighbor as yourself.* But when you show favoritism, you are committing a sin, and by that same law you are exposed as a lawbreaker. Anyone who tries to keep all of the Law but fails at one point is guilty of failing to keep all of it. The one who said, *Don't commit adultery,* also said, *Don't commit murder.* So if you don't commit adultery but do commit murder, you are a lawbreaker. In every way, then, speak and act as people who will be judged by the law of freedom. There will be no mercy in judgment for anyone who hasn't shown mercy. Mercy overrules judgment. (Jas 2:8-13)

---

20. This last point deserves some repetition. The point in James 2 is not that poverty = faith*ful*ness and wealth = faith*less*ness; this is as empirically false as its converse assumption (viz., that wealth = faith*ful*ness and poverty = faith*less*ness). The point in James 2 is that faithfulness and wealth are two different and distinct variables. Judging others on the basis of wealth, therefore, is *mis*judging them because it evaluates them on the wrong variable, on "what is visible to the eyes" rather than "see[ing] into the heart" (1 Sam 16:7).

We might reasonably read this section of James as being very concerned with legal questions and how (or even whether) we are law-abiding people. After all, those three letters, L-A-W, occur six times in these six verses. Five of those occurrences translate the Greek word *nomos*.

We discussed the word *nomos* in chapter 1. The people who translated the Hebrew Bible into Greek rendered the Hebrew word *torah* (which is rendered "Instruction" throughout the CEB Old Testament) using the Greek word *nomos*. And most people who translate Greek into English render the word *nomos* using the English word *law*. But in chapter 1, I opted to translate *nomos* with its Hebrew equivalent, "Torah." Torah, after all, includes laws (e.g., "Do not steal"; Exod 20:15), but it includes much else in addition to laws. For example, the Ten Commandments don't begin with a Thou-shalt or Thou-shalt-not; the Ten Commandments actually begin with the recollection of God's redemptive intervention on behalf of his people, an act of mercy that *preceded* his people's obedience or disobedience: "Then God spoke all these words: 'I am the LORD your God who brought you out of Egypt, out of the house of slavery. You must have no other gods before me'" (Exod 20:1-3). In addition to laws, then, Torah includes promises and covenants, narratives, teachings and instructions, and much else besides.[21] In order to appreciate the subconscious effect of interpreting *nomos* as "law," let's replace "law" in James 2:8-13 with "Instruction":

> You do well when you really fulfill the royal Instruction found in scripture, *Love your neighbor as yourself.* But when you show favoritism, you are committing a sin, and by that same Instruction you are exposed as a transgressor of the Instruction.[22] Anyone who tries to keep all of the Instruction but fails at one point is guilty of failing to keep all of it. The one who said, *Don't commit adultery*, also said, *Don't commit murder.* So if you don't commit adultery but do commit murder, you are a transgressor of the Instruction. In every way, then, speak and act

---

21. See Rafael Rodríguez, *If You Call Yourself a Jew: Reappraising Paul's Letter to the Romans* (Eugene, OR: Cascade, 2014), 4n8.

22. The CEB renders *parabatai* in James 2:9 as "lawbreaker." Since we're obscuring the notion of "law" in this passage, I've chosen to modify the translation of *parabatai* ("violator, transgressor"; BDAG s.v.) to bring out its covenantal (rather than legal) significance. The point in James 2:9 is not that the person who shows favoritism is a *criminal*; the point is that they are *unfaithful*.

as people who will be judged by the Instruction of freedom. There will be no mercy in judgment for anyone who hasn't shown mercy. Mercy overrules judgment. (Jas 2:8-13)

James's exhortation to his readers not to show favoritism is rooted in his *covenantal relationship* with God and the Instruction (= *torah*) that formalizes that relationship. God has chosen the poor to be rich in faith (Jas 2:5). If the people of God imitate God's behavior, they are faithful to that Instruction. If they behave at cross-purposes to God's behavior, they are unfaithful to that Instruction.

In the traditional reading of James 2:10-11, the "Law of Moses" is a unified whole that requires perfect obedience. The slightest misstep in even the slightest matter renders someone a lawbreaker. For example, the parents who circumcise their son on the ninth day (instead of the eighth; see Gen 17:12) are as guilty as the person who kills his neighbor. Therefore, no one is capable of keeping the Law; in fact, God didn't really intend anyone to keep the Law, since he already knew no one would be able to do so. In this reading, God gave the Law not so that people would obey it but so that they would recognize how incapable of obedience they really are. Thus, the Law drives us toward the gospel of Jesus Christ. This is a fairly traditional Christian line of interpretation.

But there are real problems with this way of thinking about Judaism and reading NT texts. For one thing, the Torah makes numerous and conspicuous provisions for reconciling imperfect Israelites with a perfect, holy God. In fact, the whole of Torah presupposes that the people will run afoul not just of its ceremonial requirements but also of its moral requirements. In the Jewish texts written between 70 and 200 CE,[23] disobedience to this or that commandment didn't cut a person off from the covenant; the covenant itself provided mechanisms for renewing one's standing within the covenant. Occasional, even regular disobedience didn't terminate a

---

23. These texts are known as "Tannaitic literature," named after the so-called tannaim ("repeaters"), Jewish teachers who "repeated" their teachings and those of their rabbis orally rather than writing them down; see Brad H. Young, *Meet the Rabbis: Rabbinic Thought and the Teachings of Jesus* (Grand Rapids: Baker Academic, 2007), 180–94; 232–33.

person's place among the people of God; "the cure for non-obedience is repentance."²⁴

Was James 2 *really* saying that violation of one part of Torah was the same as violating the whole of Torah? I don't think so. Instead, as we have already seen, James is addressing his readers' penchant for showing favoritism, a practice that puts them at cross-purposes with God. Let's imagine that these same readers highly valued their pious observance of Torah. They worshipped YHWH. Their sons were circumcised at the right time. They observed the Sabbath. They understood themselves to be observant of and obedient to Torah. James tells these readers that their Torah-observance is inadequate, because while keeping parts of Torah (e.g., worship YHWH alone, circumcise their sons, keep the Sabbath holy) they violate Torah in their partiality. Because of their favoritism they are at cross-purposes with God, and their other acts of Torah-piety don't negate that fact.

This explains verses 12-13, where James urges his readers to "speak and act as people who will be judged by the Instruction [*nomos*] of freedom." We might be surprised that James would identify the *nomos* as being "of freedom," especially since Christians have developed a robust tradition of associating the law (or Law) with slavery, condemnation, and death. We saw in chapter 1, however, that Paul says Torah was "intended to give life" (Rom 7:10). Here James does something similar, associating Torah not with slavery but with freedom. James's readers will be judged by Torah, but that judgment isn't necessarily condemnation. If they behave mercifully, they will receive mercy, *even as they are judged by Torah*!

In all of this, then, James urges his readers to give their faith concrete expression by avoiding favoritism, by receiving the poor, whom God has chosen to be rich in faith. If they don't forsake favoritism, they will be judged as those who deny the covenant as surely as will adulterers and murders. But if they do put aside partiality, they will find mercy. And, as we have seen, James has already associated this kind of faith with "our glorious Lord Jesus Christ" (Jas 2:1, NRSV).

24. E. P. Sanders, *Paul and Palestinian Judaism: A Comparison of Patterns of Religion* (Philadelphia: Fortress, 1977), 112; see also p. 147.

This brings us to the famous discussion of faith and works in the second half of James 2. On the face of it, James seems to be diametrically opposed to Paul and/or the Pauline tradition. Compare the following:[25]

James 2:24	Ephesians 2:8-9
You see that a person is made righteous by works [*ex ergōn*] and not by faith [*ouk ek pisteōs*] alone.	For you have been saved by grace, through faith [*dia pisteōs*]—and this not of your own; it is a gift from God—not by works [*ouk ex ergōn*], lest anyone should boast.

One says "by works, not by faith alone"; and the other says "through faith, not by works." We can appreciate why readers have read James and Paul against each other.

We should not, however, forget James 2:1-13 when we read 2:14-26. James has just urged his readers to avoid partiality, to make judgments on the basis of people's heart rather than their appearance, and to keep the "Instruction of freedom" by aligning themselves with God's acts of mercy rather than putting themselves at cross-purposes with God. The second half of James 2 drives home the point that a person's acts of piety don't count as Torah obedience if one's actions are misaligned with the Instruction of freedom and mercy. James introduced the example of a poor person in 2:2-6, and he reintroduces the poor person again in 2:15-16. In the second half of James 2, that person isn't dressed dirtily, "in filthy rags" (2:2). Now that person is "naked and never has enough food to eat" (2:15). James doesn't imagine a situation where his readers would curse or abuse such a person. As James portrays it, "one of you" blesses the poor person, saying, "Go in peace! Stay warm! Have a nice meal!" (2:16). That blessing would be nice as far as it goes, if only it went somewhere.

James is nearly incredulous at the hypocrisy of such a faith expressed with partiality: "What good is it if you don't actually give them what their body needs?" (Jas 2:16). A faith that is unwilling to act is an invisible faith,

---

25. The following translations of Ephesians and James are my own. The CEB, unfortunately, translates the word *erga* in both passages in a highly interpretive, nonliteral fashion.

and an invisible faith is no faith at all. "How can I see your faith apart from your works? Instead, I'll show you my faith by my works" (2:18, CEB modified). James returns to Torah to illustrate his point. Both Abraham the patriarch and Rahab the prostitute believed God and brought that belief into expression through their actions. In the same way, James's readers should avoid denying their faith by showing partiality, by speaking empty blessings while refusing to work out or produce those blessings in their actual deeds and conduct (*erga*). Such behavior is akin to favoritism, and "when you show favoritism you deny the faithfulness of our Lord Jesus Christ" (2:1).

Recall that James refers to Jesus Christ quite infrequently, in fact only twice. But James has thicker, more resonant echoes of Jesus's teaching, especially from the Sermon on the Mount, than nearly any other letter in the NT.[26] James never cites Jesus's teaching with a source, such as, "As Jesus taught," or "As the Lord says." Neither does he refer to any written Gospels by name or quote from any known written Gospel. James echoes teachings of Jesus that we find in Matthew and Luke but not in Mark, which might indicate that James was familiar with a written account of Jesus's teaching that Matthew and Luke used as a literary source.[27] What matters, however, is that this letter, despite rarely referring explicitly to Jesus, extends and/or applies Jesus's teachings throughout each of its five chapters.[28]

In his discussion of faith, James echoes Jesus's blessing on the poor as he cautions his readers not to show partiality.

---

26. Peter H. Davids, *The Epistle of James*, NIGTC (Grand Rapids: Eerdmans, 1982), 16.

27. See Alicia J. Batten, "The Jesus Tradition and the Letter of James," *RevExp* 108 (2011): 381–90, who argues that James "had access to a form of the Jesus tradition prior to its incorporation into the gospel narratives, perhaps some manifestation of the source Q" (382).

28. For a chart that identifies parallels between James and the Synoptic tradition (and the prevalence of so-called Q-material), see Davids, *James*, 47–48. The parallels between James and the Synoptic tradition occur in each of James's five chapters.

Matthew 5:3, 5 (CEB modified)	James 2:5	Luke 6:20
Happy are people who are poor in spirit, because the kingdom of heaven is theirs....Happy are people who are humble, because they will inherit the earth.	My dear brothers and sisters, listen! Hasn't God chosen those who are poor by worldly standards to be rich in terms of faith? Hasn't God chosen the poor as heirs of the kingdom he has promised to those who love him?	Happy are you who are poor, because God's kingdom is yours.

According to both Matthew and Luke, Jesus blessed the poor, declaring that God's kingdom belonged to them. James, in chastising his readers, reminds them that God has named the poor as "heirs of the kingdom."

Instead of showing partiality, James urges his readers to fulfill "the royal *nomos*" (Torah, Instruction) and then cites Leviticus 19:18, which Jesus identifies as among the greatest commandments.[29]

Mark 10:31	James 2:8	Matthew 22:39-40
The second is this, "You will love your neighbor as yourself." No other commandment is greater than these.	You do well when you really fulfill the royal law found in scripture, "Love your neighbor as yourself."	And the second is like it: "You must love your neighbor as you love yourself." All the Law and the Prophets depend on these two commands.

It isn't clear what James means when he refers to Leviticus 19:18 (or to Jesus's teaching on the greatest commandment) as "the royal *nomos*." While he might be referring to Jesus's authoritative interpretation of the whole Torah,[30] it is more likely that James is elevating the command to love one's neighbor above other commandments, so that failure to love one's neighbor (= showing partiality) outweighs other acts of covenantal piety. In

---

29.   Luke also has a version of this tradition, but in Luke it isn't Jesus who identifies the two greatest commandments but rather a "legal expert" (see Luke 10:25-28).

30.   Davids, *James*, 114.

other words, the commandment to love in Leviticus 19:18 "reigns over" the rest of Torah's statutes.

Finally, James warns his readers they will receive the same standard of judgment they apply to others, which again echoes Jesus's teaching:

James 2:13	Matthew 5:7; 6:14-15
There will be no mercy in judgment for anyone who hasn't shown mercy. Mercy overrules judgment.	Happy are people who show mercy, because they will receive mercy....If you forgive others their sins, your heavenly Father will also forgive you. But if you don't forgive others, neither will your Father forgive your sins.

There are other instances where Jesus teaches a similar principle (e.g., "Go and learn what this means: *I want mercy and not sacrifice.* I didn't come to call righteous people, but sinners"; Matt 9:13). See how closely James links faith that doesn't show favoritism with Jesus Christ, not just in James 2:1 but throughout the entire chapter.

How does this "break the rules"? Well...perhaps it doesn't. After all, James exhibits a similar approach to the teachings of Jesus that we see in the roughly contemporaneous letters of Paul (e.g., Rom 12:9-21), which echo Jesus's teaching but don't usually identify Jesus as the source being echoed. At the same time, however, Paul is much more explicit about the central role Jesus plays in his understanding of Torah and the history of God's interaction with Abraham and his descendants. James mentions Jesus twice, but otherwise it takes those "with ears to hear" to pick up James's indebtedness to the teachings of Jesus.

This is nothing compared to the rule-breaking we will see when we turn to the book of Hebrews.

Jesus, the Judean High Priest?

When studying Christian origins and ancient Judaism, we are puzzled by the Greek word *Ioudaios*.[31] The word may have an ethnic, political, or geographical connotation, in which case it refers to people, things, or

---

31. See chapter 3, note 28, above.

ideas from or associated with the region of Judea, and we should translate it "Judean." In this sense, "Judean" is analogous to the modern term *Israeli*, which denotes a person, thing, or idea associated with the modern state of Israel. *Ioudaios*, however, may also have a religious or cultural connotation. In such instances, we quite understandably translate *Ioudaios* as "Jew" or "Jewish." In contemporary English we can easily appreciate that not all Israelis are Jewish and not all Jews are Israelis. In Koinē Greek, the word *Ioudaios* can convey either the ethnic or the religious connotation, or both. It's even possible that the distinction between the two, which is appropriate in contemporary English, is *in*appropriate for the ancients,[32] because there was something fundamentally ethnic about being (or even becoming!) a religious Jew, and there was something fundamentally religious about being (or becoming) an ethnic Judean.

Whether we call them Jews or Judeans, one of their most distinctive traits (when compared to other peoples in the ancient Mediterranean world) was their devotion to one god (monotheism), with only one temple and one altar (in Jerusalem),[33] whose priesthood was restricted on genealogical grounds to descendants of Moses's brother, Aaron. Jewish/Judean priests came from the tribe of Levi. Actually, Jewish/Judean priests came from a particular line *within* the tribe of Levi. All priests might be Levites, but not all Levites could be priests.

Jesus, however, was widely identified as a member of the tribe of Judah and not of the tribe of Levi. Despite their significant differences, the genealogies of both Matthew and Luke have Jesus coming from the line of Judah (Matt 1:2-3; Luke 3:33), and as we saw in chapter 3, Revelation 5:5 identifies the exalted Jesus in the throne room of God as "the Lion of the tribe of Judah." The illustrious king of Israel, David, was also a Judahite, so the broad and popular acclamation of Jesus as "the son of David" (Rom

---

32. See, for example, Paula Fredriksen, *Paul: The Pagans' Apostle* (New Haven: Yale University Press, 2017). I am very sympathetic to Fredriksen on this point.

33. Despite the ideology of a single Judaic temple (on the Temple Mount in Jerusalem), there were, in fact, other temples of YHWH in antiquity, including the Samaritan temple on Mount Gerizim in Samaria (which was in competition with the Jerusalem temple) and two temples in Egypt (Elephantine and Leontopolis; neither seems to have been in competition with Jerusalem). Even so, the fact of the annual half-shekel temple tax sent to Jerusalem from around the Jewish Diaspora attests that, even in antiquity, Jews around the known world avoided erecting local altars to offer sacrifices and thought of the Jerusalem temple as the one temple of YHWH.

1:3; Mark 10:47-48; Matt 1:1; and throughout the NT) further reinforces the identity of Jesus as a Jew from the tribe of Judah.

Hebrews both knows of and accepts the identification of Jesus as belonging to the tribe of Judah. Moreover, Hebrews acknowledges head-on that Jewish/Judean priests don't come from the tribe of Judah. "The person we are talking about belongs to another tribe, and no one ever served at the altar from that tribe. It's clear that our Lord came from the tribe of Judah, but Moses never said anything about priests from that tribe" (Heb 7:13-14). The genealogical identity of Jewish priests (descendants of Aaron the Levite) as well as their geographical location (serving at the altar in Jerusalem) made Jewish priesthood an exclusive club.

Even so, Hebrews devotes significant space to portray Jesus in priestly hues. Jesus isn't just *a* Jewish/Judean priest. He is *the* priest, the "great high priest" (Heb 4:14) who serves at the really-real altar in heaven (i.e., not at the seemingly real altar on earth/in Jerusalem; 8:1-6). We would be surprised had Hebrews simply cast Jesus in the role of any old priest, just as we are surprised when Paul—a Jew from the tribe of Benjamin (Rom 11:1; Phil 3:5)—casts himself in priestly terms.[34] But the author of Hebrews goes even further and positions Jesus at the very top of the priestly order; he's the *high* priest (*archiereus*; the "arch-priest") who surpasses and even replaces all other priests and priesthoods.

As a result, readers of Hebrews have often interpreted this anonymous and undated text as a polemic or attack against the priestly system in Jerusalem.[35] This reading depends on a number of assumptions, but it also makes powerful sense of the text. For example, traditional Christian readings of Hebrews often assume or infer that the text is addressing Jewish Christians (Jews who have professed faith in Jesus as Israel's messiah). These Jewish Christians are inferred to be wavering in their Christian faith

34. This is a fairly significant aspect of Paul's self-presentation in Romans (e.g., Rom 1:1-7; 12:1-2; 15:15-16); see my discussion of these passages in Rodríguez, *If You Call Yourself a Jew*.

35. Hebrews used to be attributed to Paul, though the text itself never claims to be Pauline. No credible student today holds to Pauline authorship (for discussion, see Paul Ellingworth, *The Epistle to the Hebrews*, NIGTC [Grand Rapids: Eerdmans, 1993], 3–12). We will return to the question of dating Hebrews.

and attracted back to a non-Christian form of Judaism.[36] These Jewish Christians have found their Christian faith difficult, apparently, whether because it brings with it opposition from others (non-Christian Jews? non-Christian gentiles? [see Heb 10:32]) or because it takes from them the things they found attractive about their previous Jewish lifestyles.

Although this sermon to the Hebrews never explicitly affirms these assumptions, they have provided a powerful context for understanding the text. For example, the author makes a rather openly negative claim about the Torah of Moses and its mechanisms for approaching God: "On the one hand, an earlier command is set aside because it was weak and useless (because the Law made nothing perfect). On the other hand, a better hope is introduced, through which we draw near to God" (Heb 7:18-19). The CEB translation accurately represents the strong language of the Greek text; the phrase "set aside" translates the word *athetēsis*, which denotes "the refusal to recognize the validity of something."[37] Similarly, the phrases "weak," "useless," and "made nothing perfect" are all responsible interpretations of the Greek. These verses, then, provide a fairly striking attack against the *nomos*, the covenant of Moses, whose efficacy pales in comparison to the "better hope" offered by the gospel.[38]

However, Hebrews's picture of Jesus as high priest "is a *metaphor which grew out of a re-presentation of the traditional Christian 'story' in cultic terms because of a perceived need*."[39] This claim, though dense, provides a helpful perspective from which to reevaluate our reading of Hebrews.

First, for some people the word *metaphor* implies "unreal" or "false." Metaphors, however, are not untrue things; they are nonliteral things. If

---

36. Respected twentieth-century NT scholar F. F. Bruce (*The Epistle to the Hebrews*, rev. ed., NICNT [Grand Rapids: Eerdmans, 1990], 6) described Hebrews's intended audience as "still trying to live under [the old covenant], or imagin[ing] that, having passed beyond it, they could revert to it."

37. BDAG s.v.

38. So, again, F. F. Bruce: "It was inevitable that the earlier law should be abrogated sooner or later; for all the impressive solemnity of the sacrificial ritual and the sacerdotal ministry, *no real peace of conscience was procured thereby, no immediate access to God*" (Bruce, *Hebrews*, 169; my emphasis). He immediately walks back from this surprising statement, but he does not shy away from the idea that the God-given mechanisms for approaching God laid out in Torah were always and intrinsically ineffective.

39. Kenneth L. Schenck, *Cosmology and Eschatology in Hebrews: The Settings of the Sacrifice*, SNTSMS 143 (Cambridge: Cambridge University Press, 2007), 183. In addition to his previously published work, Professor Schenck has shared with me some of his current work in pre-publication form. I would like to thank him for his generosity.

my daughter says one of her teachers "bled all over her homework," I don't worry about her teacher's well-being; neither do I accuse my daughter of saying something untrue. Instead, I recognize that she's saying something nonliteral and yet still true. Despite the fact (hopefully!) that no blood was shed in the grading of my daughter's homework, her choice of metaphor says something real, something true.

So also in the case of Hebrews. Jesus, of course, was never a Jewish high priest, whether as a successor of a previous high priest or as a rival of an illegitimate high priest. There is no sense in which Jesus of Nazareth literally was appointed to the office of a Jewish priest, let alone a Jewish high priest. Jesus's high-priesthood is a metaphor that conveys the moral and/or spiritual truth of Jesus's function vis-à-vis both God and humans. The high priest in Jerusalem stands between the Israelites who bring their sacrifices and gifts and offerings to the temple, on one hand, and God, on the other. Hebrews' metaphor of Jesus-as-high-priest puts Jesus in the same position, standing between humanity and God, and offering the sacrifice that reconciles the two to each other.

Second, the metaphor of Jesus-as-high-priest "grew out of a re-presentation of the traditional Christian 'story.'" The story Hebrews is telling isn't new or innovative. As early as Paul we find evidence that the Christian story already began to assume a clearly identifiable narrative shape (1 Cor 11:23-26; 15:3-8). The details of that story could and did vary between different performances (compare the accounts of the Last Supper and of appearances of the risen Jesus in the Gospels), but the story's shape is recognizable even in these diverse texts. On the other hand, Hebrews offers a *re*-presentation of that story, an innovative interpretation of the gospel that responds to a new situation. Since Hebrews spends the better part of six chapters discussing Jesus's high-priesthood (Heb 4:14–10:18), we can safely say that the Jesus-as-high-priest metaphor is a central aspect of the author's "re-presentation of the traditional Christian 'story.'"

Third, Hebrews offers a retelling of the Christian story in "cultic terms." In popular usage, the word *cult* refers to a false or even dangerous religious sect. In the study of religion and history, however, *cult* refers to any religious system, especially its liturgical rituals. The book of Hebrews puts Jesus squarely at the center of Israel's cult: he is the law-giver who mediates a better covenantal system (Heb 7:22; 8:6-13; 9:15), he is the better priest who ministers faithfully and gently but without the guilt of sin (2:17; 5:1-10; 7:4-16), and he is the better sacrifice that is actually effective for purifying a holy people and removing their sin (9:23-28; 10:12).

It would be easy for us to read the word *better* in the previous paragraph as suggesting that Jesus competes with or replaces the earlier law-giver (Moses), the earlier priests (the sons of Aaron), and the earlier sacrifices (the Levitical sacrificial system). In other words, it would be possible for us to read the argument in Hebrews as an anti-Jewish polemic (or attack) arguing that Judaism is weak and ineffectual.[40] Hebrews, however, is a thoroughly Jewish text that makes its christological claims on the basis of careful and thorough interpretation of Israel's biblical traditions even as it relentlessly critiques aspects and institutions of Judaic religion and culture. In this respect, "Hebrews is no more supersessionist than Jeremiah"[41] or the Jewish community at Qumran, who leveled blunt critiques against the Jews they considered unfaithful to Torah.[42]

Fourth, the author of Hebrews responds to a perceived need by developing an innovative image of Jesus as high priest. Unfortunately, Hebrews doesn't give any explanation of the perceived need to which the author responded by writing the text we have in our Bibles today. All we can do is read the text itself and infer what problem(s) our author thought he (or she) was addressing through this sermon. As we have already seen, some readers interpret Hebrews as a warning to Jewish Christians against abandoning their faith in Jesus and returning to a non-messianic or non-Christian form of Judaism. In this case, the perceived need motivating

---

40. Richard Hays (*Echoes of Scripture in the Letters of Paul* [New Haven: Yale University Press, 1989], 98–99) describes Hebrews as "relentlessly supersessionist," meaning that Hebrews thoroughly replaces the Judaic religious system with its Christian counterpart. Twenty years later, Hays repented of this reading of Hebrews (see idem, "'Here We Have No Lasting City': New Covenantalism in Hebrews," in *The Epistle to the Hebrews and Christian Theology*, ed. Richard Bauckham et al. [Grand Rapids: Eerdmans, 2009], 151–73).

41. Hays, "New Covenantalism," 165.

42. For a helpful introduction to the Jews at Qumran and their opposition to the Jewish leadership in Jerusalem, see C. D. Elledge, *The Bible and the Dead Sea Scrolls*, ABS 14 (Atlanta: Society of Biblical Literature, 2005), esp. pp. 33–54, 97–114.

our author is the need to persuade Jewish Christians not to abandon their Christian faith and revert to their Jewish past. This reading of Hebrews is inherently supersessionist, meaning it explicitly construes Hebrews as an argument against returning to Judaism. The argument, in this case, has to be that Christianity is better than Judaism, that Christianity *replaces* Judaism.

But what if another "perceived need" was the prompt for this sermon? What if we could read Hebrews not as an attempt to persuade Jewish Christians from abandoning Christianity in favor of Judaism but rather as a "message of encouragement" (Heb 13:22) to remain faithful to a God who is faithful even when he appears distant? Was there a time or an event in the first century CE where we might expect Jews (whether or not they professed faith in Christ) to wonder if they had been abandoned by God, or if the promises and covenants in Torah had come to naught?

In fact there is. In 66 CE the Jews revolted against the Roman Empire and attempted to drive the Romans out of Judea. For two years the war looked hopeful as the Jews early on were able to defeat the Romans, first the forces garrisoned in Judea and then the legions that came south from Syria. In 67 CE, however, the Roman general Vespasian invaded Galilee. In the wake of the political turmoil that followed the Roman emperor Nero's suicide in June 68 CE (68–69 CE is known among Roman historians as the "Year of the Four Emperors"), Vespasian would leave Judea to become emperor in 69 CE. His son, Titus, would continue the offensive against the Jews, laying siege to Jerusalem and, in 70 CE, destroying the city and the temple.[43]

The significance and importance of the temple's destruction is difficult to overestimate. This was not the first such catastrophe, of course. The first temple, built by David's son Solomon was destroyed six and a half centuries earlier by the Babylonians in 586 BCE. The second temple was built seventy years later (in 515 BCE). This second temple was defiled in the 160s BCE by the Hellenistic king Antiochus IV and again in 63 BCE by the Roman general Pompey. (The purification and rededication

---

43. The Jewish general-turned-historian Josephus recounts the destruction of the temple in *War* 6.220–315.

of the temple after the defilement by Antiochus is still celebrated today in the Jewish holiday of Hanukkah.) Herod the Great, in 20 BCE, began an extensive renovation and expansion of the temple complex that made the Jerusalem temple a significant site in the Roman Empire. Jonathan Klawans has helpfully described the Jerusalem temple as "the fulcrum of ancient Jewish religion," and so he attempts to recover the sanctity and prominence of the temple not just for those Jews who worshipped in the temple but also for Jews (e.g., at Qumran, or also the early Christians) who levelled serious charges against the Jerusalem temple and its leadership.[44] The temple was the beating heart of Jewish religion, culture, politics, and economics, and problems with or threats against that heart were as serious as (pardon the pun) a heart attack.[45]

The first generation of Christians—those who lived and worshipped between Jesus's death and resurrection in 30 CE and the destruction of the temple in 70 CE—shared in the broader Jewish commitment to the temple and offering worship there. Most of the evidence is indirect or dates to after 70 CE, but not all of it. Paul, for example, who was martyred in Rome while the temple still stood in Jerusalem, wrote to gentile Christians in Rome in the spring of 57. When he wrote Romans, he was in Corinth, Greece, on his way to Jerusalem "to serve God's people" and to deliver "a contribution for the poor among God's people in Jerusalem" (Rom 15:25, 26). The book of Acts, which was written after the destruction of Jerusalem and the temple (perhaps in the 80s or early 90s CE), offers an account of Paul's trip to Jerusalem (Acts 19:21–21:17). Importantly, Paul's decision to go to Jerusalem was "guided by the Spirit" (19:21) and was motivated especially by his desire to get to Jerusalem, "if possible, by Pentecost Day" (20:16). Pentecost, of course, was a major Jewish holiday, and readers of Acts 2 will remember that the temple was a prominent place for celebrating Pentecost. Luke never says whether Paul arrived in time for Pentecost, but he does portray Paul as going quickly to the temple (on the second day

44. Jonathan Klawans, *Purity, Sacrifice, and the Temple: Symbolism and Supersessionism in the Study of Ancient Judaism* (Oxford: Oxford University Press, 2005); p. 104 quoted.

45. In addition to Klawans (cited in the previous note), see Wright, *New Testament*, 224–26 (Wright also employs the heart metaphor for the temple on p. 226).

after his arrival; see 21:18-26).[46] According to Luke, then, Paul continued to value the Jerusalem temple and worshipped Israel's God there even after his encounter with the risen Jesus on the road to Damascus.

Moreover, Paul isn't unusual for continuing to worship in the temple even after Jesus's death and resurrection. First, of course, we should note that Paul doesn't go to the temple in Acts 21 by himself. He is accompanied at least by four Jewish men who had made a solemn promise (Acts 21:23-24), and perhaps also by his gentile companions (though these latter, if they had come into the temple complex, would not have proceeded past the Court of the Gentiles; see 21:27-29). Earlier in Acts, Luke represented the followers of Jesus as worshipping in the temple, whether on the feast-day of Pentecost[47] or on an average day (3:1). Finally, we've already seen that Josephus preserves evidence that Jesus's brother, James, whom Paul calls a "key leader" (or "acknowledged pillar"; *hoi dokountes styloi*) of the church in Jerusalem (Gal 2:9), was popular among "the most fair-minded and who were strict in observance of the law."[48] For James to have been reckoned among the pious and strictly law-observant Jews in Jerusalem, I find it likely that he also participated regularly in worship in the temple.[49]

---

46. Scholars have rightly pointed out that Luke has his own literary and theological perspective, so his portrayal of Paul's activities doesn't necessarily align with Paul's. In other words, Luke may portray Paul's temple piety in terms or to a degree to which Paul himself would object. For a classic expression of this perspective, see Philipp Vielhauer, "On the 'Paulinism' of Acts," trans. William C. Robinson Jr. and Victor P. Furnish, *PSTJ* 17 (1963): 5–18. Our point here, however, is not that Luke is portraying Paul rightly but rather that Luke, writing approximately two decades after the temple's destruction, valued the temple to such a degree that he portrayed Paul as worshipping in the temple. This point becomes all the more significant if Luke is distorting Paul's actual practice or beliefs!

47. Luke is ambiguous regarding where the disciples were gathered at the beginning of Acts 2. He says the disciples "were all together in one place" (2:1) and then mentions the sound of a violent wind filling "the entire house where they were sitting" (2:2). Verse 5 gives no indication of a shift in location (i.e., Luke never says anything like, "Filled with the Holy Spirit, the believers went up to the temple courts..."), but by verse 6 a crowd gathers and debates what they're hearing and seeing, and in verse 14 Peter and the other apostles address the crowds. Were the apostles originally gathered in a private residence in verses 1-2? Or do the "one place" in verse 1 and the "house" in verse 2 refer to (some part of) the temple complex?

48. Josephus, *Ant.* 20.201 (LCL).

49. Hegesippus, a second-century Christian chronicler, preserved an account of the death of James in which James is thrown down from "the battlement of the temple" (*to pterygion tou naou*). James survives the fall, so the Jewish leadership begin stoning him. Ultimately, James dies when he's struck in the head by a club (see Eusebius, *Hist. eccl.* 2.23.1–19 [LCL quoted]). This version of James's martyrdom is considerably embellished and dramatized vis-à-vis the account we read in Josephus, *Antiquities* 20.

It appears that the earliest Christians shared in the broader Jewish commitment to the temple and offering worship there. As a result, the destruction of the temple in 70 CE was as catastrophic for the earliest Christians as it was for their non-Christian Jewish neighbors. When Roman soldiers set the temple on fire, the flames threatened more than wood and plaster and stone. The very possibility of worshipping YHWH, the God of Israel, was threatened.

This threat seems small in retrospect, not least because rabbinic Jews were able to reconstitute Judaic worship in terms of the study and practice of Torah and Christians were able to reconstitute worship in terms of following Jesus. This is not to say that Jews didn't study Torah and Christians didn't follow Jesus before 70 CE. Rather, Torah-study and discipleship took on added significance in the wake of the loss of the temple.

In the aftermath of the temple's destruction, Jews—Christian and otherwise—faced the uncertainty of a world without a holy site for coming into the presence of God, without an altar for presenting one's offering to God, without a priest to mediate between oneself and God, and without a sacrifice for reconciling one to God. This was certainly an uncertain world for God's people.

Given the uncertainty of the loss of the temple and the question of whether or not the connection between earth and heaven, between humanity and God, had been severed—we return to Hebrews 7. The chapter begins with praise for the greatness of Melchizedek, the king of righteousness and of peace, and the greatness of his priesthood (Heb 7:1-10). In fact, the author takes special note that the Levitical priests die, in contrast to the Melchizedekian priest who never dies: "in one case a tenth is received by people who die, and in the other case, the tenth is received by someone who continues to live, according to the record" (7:8). The author may be referring to nothing more spectacular than that Levitical priests all experience death. But if we are right to date Hebrews to the aftermath of the temple's destruction, the author may be alluding to the death not of Levitical *priests* but of the Levitical *priesthood*.

Our author goes on to ask a key question: "So if perfection came through the levitical office of priest (for the people received the Law under

138

the priests), why was there still a need to speak about raising up another priest according to the order of Melchizedek rather than one according to the order of Aaron?" (Heb 7:11). If the question was asked before Rome conquered Jerusalem, it sounds polemical and aggressive. But if the question is asked after 70 CE, it takes on a different connotation. In the wake of the end of the Levitical liturgy and the daily sacrifices, our author asks if that liturgy and those sacrifices really were the linchpin securing the connection between God and God's people. The scriptures themselves attest to a greater priesthood, first in the narrative of Abraham's encounter with Melchizedek in Genesis 14 and then again, long after the revelation of Torah at Sinai, in the oath sworn to the king of Israel: "You are a priest forever in line with Melchizedek" (Ps 110:4). The king of Israel, of course, comes from the tribe of Judah. So when the writer of Hebrews slots Jesus, a Judahite Jew, into the Melchizedekian priesthood, he isn't acting arbitrarily or without precedent. The scriptures themselves (so our author argues) anticipate an eternal priesthood, sustained "by the power of a life that can't be destroyed" (Heb 7:16), which provides a measure of comfort and reassurance to anyone who despairs over the loss of the Jerusalem temple and the Levitical priesthood.

God through Jesus has introduced "a better hope...through which we draw near to God." In this encouraging sermon, Jesus-the-high-priest isn't a metaphor that Hebrews uses to win a battle against the God-given priesthood operating in Jerusalem. Instead, Jesus-the-high-priest is a metaphor that Hebrews uses to console a people mourning the loss of the focal point of their religious, cultural, economic, and political world. To these people, Hebrews says, "Jesus has become the guarantee of a better covenant....He holds the office of priest permanently because he continues to serve forever....The solemn pledge, which came after the Law, appointed a Son who has been made perfect forever" (Heb 7:22, 24, 28). And they can be confident of this priest's service on their behalf: "he can completely save those who are approaching God through him, because he always lives to speak with God for them" (7:25).

In all of this, Hebrews's presentation of Jesus the high priest reminds me of Lincoln's admonition for a healthy skepticism toward online information. Hebrews "breaks the rules," because no Jew from the tribe of Judah can serve in the priesthood that comes from Levi. Jesus was not and could not have been Israel's high priest any more than the sixteenth president of the United States could urge kids to be smart about what they read on the internet.

And yet, by the time of the temple's destruction, Jesus already served as the connection between his followers and God. Paul, who wrote all of his letters while the temple still stood, already argued that "it is Christ Jesus who also pleads our case [to God] for us" (Rom 8:34). In the wake of the temple's destruction, our author takes the same idea—"he always lives to speak with God for them" (Heb 7:25)—and expresses it in liturgical terms: Jesus's intercession is a specifically priestly service. Thus, while Hebrews's Jesus-as-high-priest metaphor is, perhaps, the most conspicuously innovative aspect of his "re-presentation of the traditional Christian 'story'" (Schenck), it nevertheless remains thoroughly traditional, part of and at home in both the established patterns of speaking about and portraying Jesus Christ and also part of and at home in established patterns of interpreting Israel's biblical traditions.

Gentiles, God's Chosen Strangers in the Diaspora?

The last of the Catholic Epistles we will consider is 1 Peter. The apostle Peter, like Paul, was said to have been martyred in Rome during the reign of Emperor Nero, probably in the early 60s CE. For obvious reasons, then, Peter was not likely to have written many letters after the destruction of the temple in 70 CE. Even so, NT scholars largely conclude that 1 Peter was written near the end of the first century CE, which means it was written well after Peter was executed.[50] First Peter is literarily and rhetori-

---

50. Eugene Boring ("First Peter in Recent Study," *WW* 24 [2004]: 358–67) notes that evangelical scholars increasingly accept that certain NT texts are pseudonymous and, in this context, writes: "First Peter is now generally accepted as pseudonymous" (360). Earlier on the same page Boring summarizes the view of ten 1 Peter commentaries: "The prevailing view is either that Simon Peter wrote it himself or that it was written in his name by a teacher in the Roman church some years after Peter's death, *with most critical scholars clearly opting for pseudonymity*" (emphasis added). Of the ten commentaries Boring considers, only two advocate for Petrine authorship. Earl Richard ("Honorable Conduct among the Gentiles: A Study of the Social Thought of 1 Peter," *WW* 24 [2004]: 412–20) is even more emphatic: "modern scholarship, employing linguistic, social, and theological factors, is virtually unanimous in arguing for pseudonymity" (413). My thanks to Travis Williams for these references.

cally elegant when compared with other NT texts, and for this reason NT scholars largely question whether Peter, a fisherman from Galilee whom Acts describes as "uneducated and inexperienced" (Acts 4:13), could actually have written this letter.[51] However, the text itself identifies a possible amanuensis, a scribe or secretary who physically wrote the letter while Peter dictated its contents: "I have written and sent these few lines to you by Silvanus. I consider him to be a faithful brother" (1 Pet 5:12).[52] Still, it seems likely 1 Peter was written in the late first century, and the text makes good sense in that context.

The more interesting question, however, focuses on 1 Peter's intended *audience*, which is where the author "breaks the rules."[53]

The opening verse of 1 Peter identifies its intended readers using overtly Jewish descriptors: "To God's chosen strangers in the world of the diaspora, who live in Pontus, Galatia, Cappadocia, Asia, and Bithynia" (1 Pet 1:1). The geographical places may not be immediately familiar; they describe a roughly clockwise circuit beginning in northern Asia Minor (modern-day Turkey) and ending in northwest Asia Minor near the border of Asia and Europe. First Peter presents itself, then, as a circulating letter intended for communities of Jesus's followers in the northern and western regions of Asia Minor, sent from an (even *the*) apostolic figure, Peter, in the capital city, Rome.[54]

More interesting than his readers' location, however, is Peter's description of his readers as "God's chosen strangers in the world of the diaspora." On the one hand, we shouldn't be surprised to find that 1 Peter is a "diaspora letter." The Greek word *diaspora* ("scattering, dispersion") refers to

---

51. See, e.g., Bart D. Ehrman, *The New Testament: A Historical Introduction to the Early Christian Writings* (Oxford: Oxford University Press, 1997), 373–74.

52. The use of an amanuensis to write a dictated letter is not uncommon; see Paul's letter to the Romans, where Paul's amanuensis breaks into the text to send his own greetings to the readers: "I'm Tertius, and I'm writing this letter to you in the Lord—hello!" (Rom 16:22). Even so, "[t]he reference to Silvanus in [1 Peter] 5:12…is now almost universally taken as referring to the one responsible for delivering the letter, not to the secretary who assisted in its composition" (Boring, "First Peter," 359).

53. For the sake of simplicity, the rest of our discussion will refer to the author of 1 Peter as "Peter," without accepting or denying that Simon bar Jonah (see Matt 16:17), also called Peter, was the letter's actual author.

54. First Peter's Roman provenance is widely accepted and is indicated in 1 Peter 5:13: "The fellow-elect church in Babylon [= Rome] greets you, and so does my son Mark."

aspects of Jewish existence outside the land of Israel, and 1 Peter appears as a letter from a Jew in Rome to readers in Asia Minor. What makes 1 Peter unusual, however, is that he isn't actually writing to *Jews* in the diaspora. In fact, there's reason to think his readers are natives in the regions to which he is writing; they are local Pontics, Galatians, Cappadocians, and so on. Peter tells his readers, "Don't be conformed to your former desires, those that shaped you when you were ignorant" (1 Pet 1:14). Peter's readers' "former desires" and their earlier period of "ignorance" begins to suggest they weren't raised in local synagogues, hearing the Torah from Moses and living godly lives.

A few verses later, these suggestions are confirmed: "Live in this way, knowing that you were not liberated by perishable things like silver or gold from *the empty lifestyle you inherited from your ancestors*" (1 Pet 1:18, emphasis added). Peter writes to men and women whose ancestors worshipped idols as representations of their gods but which Peter dismisses as "perishable things like silver and gold" that result in an "empty lifestyle." Toward the end of his letter, Peter admonishes his readers: "You have wasted enough time doing what unbelievers [or gentiles] desire—living in their unrestrained immorality and lust, their drunkenness and excessive feasting and wild parties, and their forbidden worship of idols" (4:3). They used to live among and as the (other) gentiles in northern and western Asia Minor, but the time for that way of living has passed. "Now," Peter tells them, "none of you should suffer as a murderer or thief or evildoer or rebel" (1 Pet 4:15). Instead, should they suffer, they should suffer as "Christians" (*Christianoi*).[55]

But what does it mean for Peter's readers to be "Christians" and, if necessary, for them to suffer as Christians? The word *Christianos* means "one who is associated with Christ" and can be translated "Christ-follower, Christ-partisan" or simply transliterated into English as "Christian."[56] The

---

55. If Simon Peter wrote 1 Peter, this is the first extant use of the word *Christianos* in history. If our letter was written nearer the end of the first century, it is roughly contemporaneous with the two uses of *Christianos* in Acts 11:26; 26:28. These are the only three times this word is used in the NT (perhaps obviously, it never occurs in the Hebrew Bible/Old Testament); it will appear again in the texts of Apostolic Fathers (Ignatius, *Magn.* 4.1; Mart. Pol. 12.1; Diogn. 2.6, 10; 6.5) along with the related word *Christianismos* (Ignatius, *Magn.* 10.1, 3; *Rom.* 3.3; *Phld.* 6.1; Mart. Pol. 10.1).

56. BDAG s.v.

evidence suggests that the label *Christianos* was originally used as a scorn or even a criminal accusation. In the early second century CE (and so just a couple decades after 1 Peter was written), the Roman-appointed governor of Bithynia and Pontus (part of the ambit Peter addresses in 1 Pet 1:1) was a man we call Pliny the Younger. Pliny governed Bithynia and Pontus on behalf of the Roman emperor Trajan (98–117 CE) around the year 110 CE. During his time in office, Pliny wrote numerous letters to the emperor. Trajan wrote letters back to Pliny, and Pliny saved the emperor's replies. Famously, one of Pliny's letters asks for advice about how to deal with anyone accused of being a Christian (Lat.: *Christianus*). Pliny clearly thinks anyone who persists in their allegiance to Christ deserves punishments, but he's not sure how vigorously he should seek out or punish suspected Christians.[57] The point here is that the charge of being a *Christianus* could result in someone being brought before the local governor and questioned under torture.

The gentile Pontics, Bithynians, Asians, and others to whom Peter is writing have left behind the practices that identified them as local gentiles, including worship at pagan temples and participation in pagan festivals. In place of these practices, these gentiles have adopted practices that align themselves much more visibly with a *Jewish* identity. When they call upon a deity as "Father," they are calling upon YHWH, Israel's covenant God, who raised Jesus Christ from the dead (1 Pet 1:17-21). From a modern perspective, these former gentiles are clearly Christians. But from the perspective of their local families and friends, they would appear to have "Judaized," to have adopted Jewish practices and beliefs, including their new and strange refusal to worship the traditional gods and their devotion to a once-executed Jew named Jesus. (Refusal to worship the local gods, rather than to acknowledge them even if one were devoted to a god or gods from another locale, was a peculiarly Jewish practice that sometimes led to the accusation that Jews were atheists!) Now, Peter's readers receive instruction from the Jewish Torah (including, "You will be holy, because I am holy"; Lev 19:2, cited in 1 Pet 1:16). To us they appear to be Christians, but to

---

57. See Pliny, *Ep. Tra.* 10.96 (Trajan's response appears in 10.97).

their neighbors they seem to have adopted the practices and customs of the Jews.

Strange as it may seem to us today—after all, the labels "Jew" and "Christian" identify two different kinds of people; Jews are not Christians and Christians are not Jews—Peter leans into this counterintuitive characterization of his (remember: *gentile!*) readers. That is, *Peter portrays his readers as Jews*, as descendants of Abraham and members of the covenant people of God. This portrayal is every bit as much "breaking the rules" as was Hebrews' portrayal of Jesus as high priest. In antiquity, some Jews rejected the idea that non-Jews (= non-descendants-of-Abraham) could become Jews (= descendants of Abraham).[58] In fact, not even all the descendants of Abraham qualified as "descendants of Abraham." From a covenantal perspective, neither the children of Ishmael nor of Esau (a son and grandson of Abraham, respectively) were counted as children of Abraham. Even so, here's Peter, portraying his *gentile* readers in western Asia Minor as full-fledged Jews, Israelites, members of the covenant people of God.

Peter's re-ethnicization (if I may use such an ungainly word) of his readers begins in the very first verse: "To God's chosen strangers in the world" (1 Pet 1:1). The word *chosen* (*eklektos*) reverberates with notions of Israel's election, her status as *the* people of God, in distinction from all other peoples. The theme of Israel's election runs right through the narratives, poetry, and prophecies of Israel's Torah, but we see it clearly expressed on the eve of the giving of the Ten Commandments, those twin stone tablets inscribed by the finger of God (Exod 31:18; see also Deut 9:10). As the descendants of Abraham's grandson, Israel, camp at the base of Mount Sinai, God summons Moses to join him on the summit. In preparation for the coming covenant, YHWH gives Moses a message to pass on to the people: "You saw what I did to the Egyptians, and how I lifted you up on eagles' wings and brought you to me. So now, if you faithfully obey me and stay true to my covenant, *you will be my most precious possession out of all the peoples*, since the whole earth belongs to me. You will be a kingdom of priests for me and a holy nation" (Exod 19:4-6, emphasis added). We will have more to say about this passage shortly. For now, we

---

58. See the excellent discussion of this question in Thiessen, *Contesting Conversion*.

note God's promise that, though all the nations of the earth belong to God, the assembled tribes of slaves in the desert are God's special people, his "most precious possession." Like Israel in the wilderness, Peter addresses his gentiles in Asia Minor as God's "chosen." Thus begins, in this short letter, the blurring of the boundary between Israel in her covenant and gentiles "in Christ" (see 1 Pet 3:16; 5:10, 14).

The blurring continues in the very next word: "To God's chosen *strangers*" (1 Pet 1:1). The Greek word behind the CEB's "strangers" is *parepidēmos*, which describes a person who is "staying for a while in a strange or foreign place."[59] A *parepidēmos* is a vulnerable person, a visitor or sojourner who depends on the hospitality of natives for their well-being. A foreign exchange student, a migrant worker, or even a more permanent immigrant are all good, modern examples of contemporary *parepidēmoi* (the plural of *parepidēmos*). Also refugees and asylum seekers.

The word isn't common in the NT. Outside of 1 Peter, it only occurs once, in the famous list of scriptural examples of faith in Hebrews 11. "All of these people died in faith without receiving the promises, but they saw the promises from a distance and welcomed them. They confessed that they were strangers and immigrants [*parepidēmoi*] on earth" (Heb 11:13). In fact, Hebrews itself taps into the covenantal connotations of the word *parepidēmos*. Abraham had been called to leave home and live as a migrant visitor in a strange land. "By faith Abraham obeyed when he was called to go out to a place that he was going to receive as an inheritance. He went out without knowing where he was going. By faith he lived in the land he had been promised as a stranger.[60] He lived in tents along with Isaac and Jacob, who were coheirs of the same promise. He was looking forward to a city that has foundations, whose architect and builder is God" (11:8-10). The status of being a *parepidēmos* was a sign of being in covenant with YHWH, and more importantly of being faithful (remember Hebrews' repeated "by faith...") to that covenant despite the apparent absence of what God has promised. Being a stranger or immigrant is a sign that one

---

59. BDAG s.v.

60. The CEB's "stranger" does not appear in the Greek text. Instead, the Greek text describes the land Abraham inhabited as "a strange" or "foreign land" (*gēn...allotrian*), in which Abraham "sojourned" (*parōkēsen*) and lived "in tents" (*en skēnais*).

trusts YHWH to be faithful to his word even when the fruits of that faith are still in the future.

Peter applies this status to his (remember: *gentile!*) readers. When Sarah died in their land of sojourn, Abraham appealed to his Hittite natives: "I am an immigrant and a temporary resident [LXX: *parepidēmos*] with you. Give me some property for a burial plot among you so that I can bury my deceased wife near me" (Gen 23:4). A widower begging for land to bury his dead wife . . . this is the vulnerability of the *parepidēmos*, of the one who trusts God to be *eventually* (rather than *immediately*) faithful. This, also, is the analog to Peter's readers' surprising condition in late-first-century CE Asia Minor: though they used to be natives among the gentiles living in these regions, now they are not. More than immigrants or strangers or temporary residents, they have left their fathers' land in response to the covenant of YHWH, the God of Israel. They have left their fathers' houses and, as such, are imitating Abraham. They therefore show that they are, in fact, children of Abraham.[61]

We should look again at Abraham's self-designation in Genesis 23:4. In his appeal to the local natives for a place to bury his wife, Abraham calls himself "an immigrant and a temporary resident." The Hebrew word for "temporary resident" is *toshav*, which the Greek translators of the Septuagint rendered *parepidēmos*. The Hebrew word for "immigrant" is the common Hebrew word *ger*, *paroikos* in the Septuagint, which "pertains to being a resident foreigner."[62] Abraham calls himself a *ger* and a *toshav*, or in Greek a *paroikos* and a *parepidēmos*. The illustrious King David would use the same two words to describe himself when he appealed to God in a time of distress: "Hear my prayer, LORD! Listen closely to my cry for help! Please don't ignore my tears! I'm just a foreigner [Heb.: *ger*; Grk.: *paroikos*]—an immigrant [Heb.: *toshav*; Grk.: *parepidēmos*] staying with you, just like all my ancestors were" (Ps 39:12). Like Abraham, even like "all my ancestors," David is a foreigner and an immigrant, a *paroikos* and a *parepidēmos*. These two words align David with Abraham and locate him within the circle of God's covenant promise. In fact, these two words

---

61. See the very similar argument Paul makes in Romans 4, which I discuss in my essay, "Paul and Social Memory."

62. BDAG s.v.

nearly hum with covenantal resonance, giving meaning to a difficult present and hope for a promised future.

Our ears, then, should hear this resonance when Peter turns to urge his readers to continue to live in the covenantal space of trust in God's *eventual* if not *immediate* faithfulness. "Dear friends, since you are immigrants [*paroikos*] and strangers [*parepidēmos*] in the world, I urge that you avoid worldly desires that wage war against your lives" (1 Pet 2:11). These "worldly desires" (or "fleshly desires") characterize the former lives of Peter's readers, who used to live as gentiles in the land. The connection between worldly desires and gentiles is made explicit in the very next verse, where Peter instructs his readers to "live honorably among the unbelievers" (lit. "gentiles"; 2:12). The contrast should be clear to everyone: on one hand we have Peter's readers' former way of life, which continues on in the lives of their gentile neighbors, and on the other their current way of life, which is modeled on the example of Israel's covenant relationship with YHWH. The re-ethnicization (there's that word again) of Peter's readers is more than a narrative fiction, more than overlaying the story of Israel in Canaan onto the biographies of gentiles in Asia. Peter is describing the transformation brought about by the sanctifying (or "making holy") work of the Spirit (see 1:2; 4:14). The Spirit of God transforms Peter's gentile readers, unmaking them as gentiles and remaking them into a covenantal people, a people like Israel (perhaps even as Israel itself).[63]

The re-ethnicization and (to use an even more ungainly term) Israelization of Peter's gentile readers is clearly displayed in 1 Peter 2:4-10. Peter

---

63. I am hesitating to identify Peter's gentile readers, who are urged to be faithful as "Christians" (1 Pet 4:16), as the "new Israel" because I want to avoid any implication that Christianity replaces Judaism as the people of God or supersedes any putative "old Israel." These ideas—known as "replacement theology" and/or as "supersessionism"—have done much harm in the history of the church and of Jewish-Christian relations. But more than that, they are unbiblical. In Paul's famous olive tree metaphor (Rom 11:16-32), Paul does not portray God as "chopping down" or otherwise abandoning his olive tree in favor of a new tree that replaces the old. Instead, the point is that branches that don't belong to the covenantal tree are grafted onto and become part of that original tree. To say that gentiles are "grafted onto" the family of Abraham and/or that they become part of Israel is not to say that gentiles/the church *replace* Jews as God's covenantal people; it is, rather, to say that they *join* them. Paul, after all, is explicitly concerned with the depths of "God's riches, wisdom, and knowledge" (11:33), as well as his mercy, which has accomplished the salvation of all Israel (11:26), not its replacement or supersession. So also here in 1 Peter, the transformation of the gentiles into Israel does not suggest they *replace* Israel; instead, they *join* Israel, participating in the same covenantal mercy that God first showed his people in the wilderness to the east of Egypt and which is now (in the first century CE) advancing throughout the world in the form of the gospel.

forges an explicit link between his readers, on one hand, and Christ. They are "living stones" that are "being built...into a spiritual temple" (2:5), and they come before Christ who is himself "a living stone" (2:4). The Christ-stone was "rejected by humans" but declared "chosen, valuable" by God (2:4), a description of Jesus that takes its cue from the scriptures (Isa 28:16; see also Ps 118:22) but that also resonates with the experiences of 1 Peter's readers (see 1 Pet 2:12, 21-25, and throughout). They, like Christ, were rejected by humans but declared chosen and valuable by God. They, like Christ, are living stones making up the temple in which God dwells. They, like Christ, ought to remain faithful precisely when remaining faithful is most difficult.

The surprising thing is that Peter applies the memory of Israel's election to his gentile (= non-Israelite) readers. We've already discussed Exodus 19:4-6, in which God declares to the gathered tribes encamped at the base of Mount Sinai that they will be "my most precious possession out of all the peoples" (19:5). You will recall that God declares to them, "You will be a kingdom of priests for me and a holy nation" (19:6). Peter takes this decisive moment of election and overlays it onto his non-Israelite (= non-chosen-people-of-God) readers! "But you are a chosen race, a royal priesthood, a holy nation, a people who are God's own possession" (1 Pet 2:9).

If we ask how Peter can think he can use such quintessentially Israelite language to describe his non-Israelite readers, we are brought back to the second verse of the entire letter: they were chosen "because of what [God the Father] knew beforehand. He chose you through the Holy Spirit's work of making you holy and because of the faithful obedience and sacrifice of Jesus Christ" (1 Pet 1:2). The obedience and death of Jesus are given sacrificial significance; that is, Jesus's obedience and death bridge the divide between God and Peter's gentile readers and reconciles them. In the aftermath of this reconciliation, the Spirit of God works to take these pagan gentiles and transform them into the covenant people of God. When our Petrine author thinks of or describes the covenant people of God, he thinks of and describes the people of Israel.

Peter marvels at the work of God among these gentiles of Asia Minor, and he expects that his readers, too, will find God's works both marvelous and noteworthy. "You have become this people so that you may speak of the wonderful acts of the one who called you out of darkness into his amazing light" (1 Pet 2:9). In Christ, God has expanded his work of election to include non-covenantal people within the scope of his covenant.

This surprising paragraph comes to a close with one more unexpected move, though (perhaps paradoxically) this latest move restores a sense of consistency to Peter's reading of Torah and his understanding of God. Israelite covenantal theology included a robust understanding of God's mercy for his imperfect people. (The Christian idea that "obedience to the law" had to be *perfect* obedience or it was only *dis*obedience, which is often buttressed with references to James 2:10-11, is foreign to Jewish texts.) In his final charge to the people of Israel, on the eve of their crossing over the River Jordan into the land of Canaan, Moses sets before the people a lengthy list of covenantal curses that God will visit upon the people if or when they disregard his instruction and commandments (his *Torah*) and worship foreign gods (Deut 28:15-68). Moreover, Moses even anticipates that the people will experience both the blessings and the curses of the covenant. Moses promises the people that God will hear their repentance whenever they cry out to him. God punishes a wayward people, but he doesn't reject a penitent people (30:1-10).

Both the wrath and the mercy of God are repeatedly on display in Israel's story, but perhaps nowhere so poignantly as in the story of the prophet Hosea. In the book that bears his name, Hosea is instructed to "marry a prostitute and have children of prostitution" (Hos 1:2). Hosea's unfaithful wife is a symbol of YHWH's unfaithful people, and the children of their union are given wretched names: a son named Jezreel ("for in a little while I will punish the house of Jehu for the blood of Jezreel, and I will destroy the kingdom of the house of Israel. On that day I will break the bow of Israel in the Jezreel Valley"; Hos 1:4-5), a daughter named No-Compassion, and a son named Not-My-People. The two younger children, like their older brother, were named according to God's judgment against the northern kingdom of Israel for their abandonment of the covenant. Israel had gone off to worship other gods, and God was none too pleased. But then God remembers his promise to Abraham ("Yet the number of the people of Israel will be like the sand of the sea, which can be neither measured nor numbered"; 1:10; see Gen 22:17; 15:5), and he reverses the names of Hosea's children:

> In the place where it was said to them, "You are not my people," it will be said to them, "Children of the living God." The people of Judah and the people of Israel will be gathered together, and they will choose one head. They will become fruitful in the land. The day will be a wonderful one for Jezreel. Say to your brother, My People, and to your sister, Compassion. (Hos 1:10–2:1)

In his wrath, God punishes a wayward people. But then he remembers his promise to Abraham, and he has mercy on a penitent people.

Hosea's marriage and children provide an explanation for how God deals with his people Israel, with the descendants of Abraham. Peter, however, explains that God deals the same way with other peoples, with those who are not, genealogically speaking, descendants of Abraham. If God can remake a rejected people ("Not-My-People") into a chosen people ("My People"), a people who have been shown no mercy ("No-Compassion") into a people of mercy ("Compassion"), then he can do the same for the gentiles. And so Peter inserts his gentile readers into the story of Hosea's children. "Once you weren't a people, but now you are God's people. Once you hadn't received compassion, but now you have received mercy [or compassion]" (1 Pet 2:10). Paul, who cites the same story from Hosea (Rom 9:25-26), reads it as a story of God's compassion and mercy *for Israel*.[64] Our Petrine author, however, goes even further. He has been overlaying Israel's story onto his gentile readers, and as a result he has found license for reading the gentiles into Israel's story of election, covenant, rebellion, punishment, and restoration.

This is Peter "breaking the rules," which invokes our memory of Peter's controversial vision about eating forbidden foods that almost led to the first church schism in Acts 10–15. Only rather than distorting (in a non-pejorative sense) Jesus into something new, as the author of Hebrews had done, Peter distorts his readers into something new. They are now

---

64. Despite claims that Paul reads Hosea's children onto his gentile readers, see my explanation of the passage in Rodríguez, *If You Call Yourself a Jew*, 187–88.

Israel. Not a "new Israel," but part of the *re*newed Israel. And this, at the end of the day, is how we see Jesus in 1 Peter. That is, if one were to ask where Jesus is, 1 Peter suggests the answer: Jesus is the one who transforms gentiles, folding them into Abraham's and Israel's story. The renewal of the covenant between God and the wayward people of Israel was always going to reach out to fold in non-Israel. After all, hadn't YHWH declared through the prophet Isaiah: "It is not enough, since you are my servant, to raise up the tribes of Jacob and to bring back the survivors of Israel. Hence, I will also appoint you as light to the nations so that my salvation may reach to the end of the earth" (Isa 49:6)? Hadn't God always intended Abraham to be the father not just of a (singular) great nation but even of many nations (Gen 17:5)? Peter begins with the notion that Jesus has brought these scriptures to fulfillment, and the result is nothing less than the remaking of the nations who were once not a people into the chosen people of God.

Thank God for distortion.

Chapter 5
Jesus, Darkly: What We See in the New Testament

Philosophers and psychologists may argue over what's real and what isn't, but most of us living ordinary lives know and accept the texture of the world around us.[1]

Remembering Jesus in an Ordinary Life

You might recall the scene in Charles Dickens's *A Christmas Carol*, where Ebenezer Scrooge is first confronted with the ghost of his now-dead business partner, Jacob Marley. Scrooge sees and hears Marley's ghost, but he's not quite ready to believe his eyes and ears. "Why do you doubt your senses?" asks Marley, to which Scrooge famously (and not inaccurately) replies, "Because a little thing affects them. A slight disorder of the stomach makes them cheats. You may be an undigested bit of beef, a blot of mustard, a crumb of cheese, a fragment of an underdone potato. There's more of gravy than of grave about you, whatever you are!" Our senses are our most immediate avenues to knowledge about the world around us, and yet those senses are so easily misled.

You say, "Seeing is believing"? I say, "Bah! Humbug!"

One needn't know very much about Western philosophy to have heard about René Descartes and his proposition, "I think, therefore I am" (Lat.: *Cogito, ergo sum*). Descartes was in search of an undeniable claim,

---

1. Stephen King, *11/22/63: A Novel* (New York: Scribner, 2011), 32.

something that had to be true and could not be doubted. In Descartes's hands, doubt became an acid test in which every claim of knowledge deduced logically or experienced by our senses was put under suspicion of being fraudulent. Descartes went so far as to pretend that everything he thought he remembered or perceived was false, perhaps an illusion created in his mind by a deceitful deity who wanted him to think he had a body and lived in a physical world perceived by his senses. With such a malevolent demon at large, how could anyone trust anything they thought they knew?

Ultimately, Descartes came to the conclusion that, if nothing else, he must exist. Even if some dastardly deity had nothing else to do but to trick him into thinking the world was real, then it must be true that he existed and was available to be tricked. "If I convinced myself of something (or thought anything at all)," Descartes reasoned, "then I certainly existed.... So, after considering everything very thoroughly, I must finally conclude that the proposition, *I am, I exist*, is necessarily true whenever it is put forward by me or conceived in my mind."[2] Even if everything else is just undigested beef or underdone potato, the reality of Descartes as a reasoning—even if deceived—consciousness was beyond doubt. "I think," Descartes observed, and from that observation he drew the conclusion, "I am."[3] The conclusion is true even if every other thing Descartes thinks is false.

Descartes's proposition and his method of doubt as the acid test of truth is the very bedrock of Western philosophy and epistemology. The scientific revolution and the Enlightenment adopt a fundamentally skeptical stance toward reality. Things are assumed to be not-true until proven otherwise. In order to really know a thing as true, we must first prove that it's not not-true. This thorough-going skepticism has been incorporated into every field of knowledge, including knowledge about Jesus.[4] In the

---

2. Descartes, *Meditations on First Philosophy*, quoted from Lincoln Taiz and Lee Taiz, *Flora Unveiled: The Discovery and Denial of Sex in Plants* (Oxford: Oxford University Press, 2016), 380–81.

3. Perhaps we should not be surprised to learn that philosophers since Descartes have found ways to question even this foundational philosophical proposition.

4. See Gerd Theissen, "Historical Skepticism and the Criteria of Jesus Research: My Attempt to Leap over Lessing's Ugly Wide Ditch," in *Handbook for the Study of the Historical Jesus*, ed. Tom Holmén and Stanley E. Porter, 4 vols. (Leiden: Brill, 2011), 1:549–87.

late twentieth century, historians of Jesus argued about the "burden of proof" in historical Jesus scholarship.[5] Did a historian need to prove a saying or deed of Jesus was authentic in order to continue attributing it to Jesus? Or was that same historian obliged to prove a saying or deed was *in*authentic before she could dismiss it from her portrait of Jesus?[6] These are very different standards of judgment, and the debate has mostly been settled by agreeing that every argument—whether for or against authenticity—bears the burden of proof.[7] We begin with the presumption that any argument is false or wrong or inadequate, and we continue with that presumption until we have no other option but to accept that an argument has been proven true or right or adequate. Descartes doubted even his own existence, until he lit upon an argument that proved it.

I think, therefore I am.

No one lives their life with this level or weight of doubt toward the reality of the information presented to them by their senses. Even Descartes's thought experiment about "a deceiver of supreme power and cunning who deliberately and constantly deceives me" was just that: a thought experiment. In reality, Descartes certainly believed in the existence of the paper on which he wrote his *Meditations* and the ink he used to do so. Just as certainly, Descartes believed in the existence of other actually-thinking, actually-existing human beings who inhabited the world alongside him, who could and would appreciate the irreducible truth of *cogito, ergo sum*. Descartes didn't believe, in other words, that he was an isolated consciousness being deceived at every turn but who had stumbled upon the one undeniable truth of his existence. In actual fact—I can't prove this, but I am certain of it—Descartes accepted the reality and truth of many, probably even most of his sensory perceptions. And so do the rest of us.

Consider Jake Epping, the protagonist in Stephen King's novel *11/22/63*. Epping, a high school English teacher in 2011, is shown a

5. Dagmar Winter, "The Burden of Proof in Jesus Research," in Holmén and Porter, 1:843–51.

6. See the essays in Chris Keith and Anthony Le Donne, eds., *Jesus, Criteria, and the Demise of Authenticity* (London: T&T Clark, 2012). Anthony Le Donne mentions the question of "burden of proof" in the introduction (see pp. 13–14).

7. Dagmar Winter, "Saving the Quest for Authenticity from the Criterion of Dissimilarity: History and Plausibility," in *Jesus, Criteria, and the Demise of Authenticity*, ed. Chris Keith and Anthony Le Donne (London: T&T Clark, 2012), 115–31 (129–30).

portal that takes him back to 11:58 a.m., September 9, 1958. The first
time Epping goes through the portal, of course, he has a difficult time
reconciling what his brain said *could be* true and what his senses told him
was in fact true. His brain told him he was in the pantry of a local diner
in the early twenty-first century, but his senses very clearly reported back
to him that he was outside, that he was in a foreign time, and that the
world was, apparently, quite other than he thought he knew it. "I tried to
tell myself this wasn't happening, *couldn't* be happening, but it wouldn't
wash," Epping says, and then the epigram to this chapter: "Philosophers
and psychologists may argue over what's real and what isn't, but most of
us living ordinary lives know and accept the texture of the world around
us."[8] Perhaps unlike philosophers and psychologists, most of us living ordinary lives have too many other things to do to question the onslaught
of information we receive through our senses from the world around us.
This, though, is probably too self-congratulatory of ordinary people and
too cynical of philosophers and psychologists.[9]

What does a Stephen King character have to do with remembering
Jesus in the NT? The study of memory is, perhaps by definition, geared
toward identifying the failures and flaws of the human ability to recall
the past accurately. For example, Daniel Schacter, a leading memory
researcher, gave his book the title *The Seven Sins of Memory*.[10] Schacter
isn't unusual. He has inherited a century-long scholarly tradition that has
devised ingenious methods for implanting and uncovering false or distorted memories in research subjects; he *reflects* rather than *directs* the bias
among memory studies toward memory's sins.[11] Little wonder, then, that
a magisterial book on Jesus begins with the sobering claim, "The frailty of

8. King, *11/22/63*, 32; italics in the original.

9. The massive popularity of The Wachowski Brothers' *The Matrix* suggests that people "living ordinary lives" are more than happy to engage in Descartes's thought experiment: that the world around us
doesn't exist, that our senses are being actively deceived by a malevolent being (or technology), and that of
all the things we think we know only the fact that we exist is true.

10. Daniel L. Schacter, *The Seven Sins of Memory: How the Mind Forgets and Remembers* (Boston:
Mariner Books, 2002).

11. For a particularly compelling example, see Elizabeth Loftus and Katherine Ketcham, *Witness for
the Defense: The Accused, the Eyewitness, and the Expert Who Puts Memory on Trial* (New York: St. Martin's
Press, 2015).

human memory should distress all who quest for the so-called historical Jesus."[12] Others are even less optimistic about memory.[13] Academics—"philosophers and psychologists"—have demonstrated beyond a shadow of a doubt that human beings *mis*remember the past, and we do it all the time. Experiments conducted in laboratories, in simulations of real life, and in actual real-life situations, *prove* that human memory of events in the past isn't perfect, infallible, or impervious to degradation.

And yet the fictional Jake Epping puts his finger on something fundamentally true. Most of us live our lives in the ordinary, and we don't have any significant trouble navigating the world of our senses or recalling the authentic past. Sure, I misplace my keys or my cell phone almost daily, and the number of sermons I remember is minuscule compared to the number of sermons I've heard. The problem isn't even just that I forget things. The problem is also that I misremember things. My wife and children will be happy to bear witness.[14] But even so—and this is the point—*my senses and my memories are good enough that I'm able to live my life reasonably successfully.* The list of things I remember accurately every single day would be staggering if it weren't so banal. I remember which toothbrush is mine, which drawer my socks are in, where we keep the milk (and even that I prefer the 2% milk to my wife's almond milk), who the three children in my house are, which office is mine, the password to access my computer, and literally dozens or even hundreds of other things. I may be well aware that my memory is imperfect. In fact, my memory may be even more imperfect than I realize. Nevertheless, my memories are good enough for me to get by without using the wrong toothbrush, trying to gain entry into the wrong office, or otherwise misremembering the details of my life. And I suspect yours are too. Even the philosophers and

---

12. Dale C. Allison Jr., *Constructing Jesus: Memory, Imagination, and History* (Grand Rapids: Baker Academic, 2010), 1. Allison chronicles nine of memory's sins (pp. 1–10), with copious footnotes.

13. Zeba Crook ("Memory and the Historical Jesus," *BTB* 42 [2012]: 196–203; see also idem, "Collective Memory Distortion and the Quest for the Historical Jesus," *JSHJ* 11 [2013]: 53–76) is very worried about the prevalence of "invented memory" and the impossibility of separating out invention from authentic memory. Anthony Le Donne offers a brief rejoinder in "The Problem of Selectivity in Memory Research: A Response to Zeba Crook," *JSHJ* 11 (2013): 77–97; see also Zeba A. Crook, "Gratitude and Comments to Le Donne," *JSHJ* 11 (2013): 98–105.

14. For a charming and very interesting example of memory distortion, see Ira Glass's conversation with Robert and Tamar Krulwich, which is available online at https://youtu.be/PxQ9Gx2-ceM.

psychologists among us know and accept the texture of the world around us and the past behind us.

We should be able to acknowledge both of these things at the same time. Yes, we misperceive, misremember, forget, and fabricate details about the world around us and the past behind us. This happens all the time; the imperfection of memory is, to use a Latin word, *quotidian*. But there are limits to our misperceptions and misrememberings. Our memories also work, and they work quite well. Any research program that misses one of these dynamics and overemphasizes the other skews our understanding of memory. It would be foolish to claim that human memory perfectly preserves and recalls events from the past. It would be just as foolish to suppose that memory perfectly corrupts and falsifies events from the past.

The most important thing we might say about memory, then, is that we need to get away from an either/or approach to memory and authenticity: *either* an event happened *or* it didn't. There are multiple ways to recount the past; in fact, there are multiple ways to recount the past authentically. My wife and I tell the story of how we started dating very differently. The differences aren't just a result of our different experiences or perspectives during our early days as a couple; we also have different points to make in how we recount those days. And while we playfully argue in front of our friends over whose version is more accurate, the truth is that "authentic" or "inauthentic" are irrelevant categories for judging the differences between our stories. They are simply different. Either one of us (or both of us) could certainly tell inauthentic versions of our story. For example, sometimes I'll claim she stalked me and manipulated me into marrying her. This is flatly wrong, and we both know it. But there are multiple ways to tell our story truthfully, and forcing our multiform memory into a single narrative disfigures our history together and silences our different perspectives on some of the most important and formative moments in our lives.

Jesus, Darkly: A Retrospect

The previous four chapters have tried to hear the different voices of the various NT authors as they remember Jesus. The differences in their presentations, portrayals, and perspectives of Jesus don't merely stem from their different views of the events of Jesus's life and/or his teachings. They also have different reasons for recalling Jesus and different goals in their presentations. Remembering Jesus involves more than simply recalling facts about the past; remembering Jesus also involves one's perspective on the present and hopes for the future. From Paul and his letters, which provide our earliest extant evidence for Jesus and his influence in the early Roman Empire, to the first three commemorative texts narrating the events of Jesus's life and their aftermath (Mark, Matthew, and Luke-Acts), to the Johannine literature's familiar-but-distinctive presentation of Jesus, to the various and variously rule-breaking authors of the Catholic Epistles, the authors of our NT texts are all engaged in the fundamentally familiar project of standing squarely in the present, marshaling the resources of a common past in order to make sense of and act in the present and move toward a desirable future.

We took the time in the introduction to reorient ourselves to the drama of scripture. Many of us have been raised to read the Bible's story as the redemption of lost souls. But scripture tells a much grander story, the story of creation and the goodness of God and the lengths to which God goes to undo creation's brokenness. In this story, humans aren't a problem to be solved; they are an image to be restored. The goal of this story is nothing less than the freedom of the whole of creation from the bondage to which it has been subjected (Rom 8:19-23). That story runs right through, from creation to rebellion to the promise of restoration beginning with Abraham and his descendants. When we understand this story rightly, the covenants of God—including the Mosaic covenant, the Torah—are not minor plots or obsolete scenes. They move the action along, preparing us, the audience, to follow the plot as the hero brings the story's conflict to resolution and ushers in the celebration of a new heaven and a new earth. Here, at the story's end, just as at its beginning, God dwells among humanity; he will be our God, and we will be his people.

We started with Paul. The most conspicuous fact of Paul's memory of Jesus is that he doesn't actually recall Jesus very much. We get some isolated facts about Jesus, as we saw, and on one or two occasions Paul explicitly recalls some teaching from Jesus. We would, however, be woefully ignorant of the narrative of Jesus's life if the earliest Christians stopped producing written texts after Paul's letters. These are facts, and they can't be disputed.

We can, however, argue about whether Paul had any substantial knowledge about Jesus's life and teaching. So, on the one hand, some scholars infer from Paul's silence that he didn't know much, nor was he very interested to know very much, about the details of Jesus's life. Others, however, make the diametrically opposite inference, that Paul knew the facts about Jesus but simply didn't have need or occasion to narrate those facts in his letters. We may find either one of these options more compelling than the other (personally, I prefer the latter). But when we approach Paul from the perspective of memory studies, we see how thoroughly and completely Paul "thinks with" Jesus, perceiving everything from theology and ethics to identity and hermeneutics through the lens of Jesus Christ.

Perhaps the most conspicuous aspect of Paul's "thinking with" Jesus concerns his own identity and vocation. In one of his earliest letters, Paul describes his vocation as a calling to or toward the gentiles (*ta ethnē*; or "the nations"): "But God had set me apart from birth and called me through his grace. He was pleased to reveal his Son to me, so that I might preach about him to the Gentiles" (Gal 1:15-16). When he went up to Jerusalem he reported the gospel he proclaimed to gentiles (2:2), and an agreement was reached that he, Paul of Tarsus, was called to and responsible for preaching to gentiles just as Peter was called to preach to Jews (2:7-9). In Romans he explicitly calls himself the apostle to the gentiles (*ethnōn apostolos*; Rom 11:13), just as he had also described his apostolic appointment in terms of bringing gentiles to "faithful obedience" and his "responsibility" to different kinds of gentiles (1:5, 13-15). This calling to the gentiles is rooted in Paul's vision of the risen Jesus (Gal 1:16) and in response to Jesus's call to the gentiles (Rom 1:6).

None of this is surprising; the "mission to the gentiles" is one of the most famous aspects of the apostle's legacy. Paul's turn to the gentiles has even led some to argue that Paul is the true founder of Christianity! They argue that Jesus was a Jew who remained a Jew and who pitched his teaching to Jewish audiences, and that it was Paul who took the Jewish teachings of Jesus and fundamentally transformed them into a new religious system, one that left behind its Jewish roots to become something altogether new.[15]

Our own discussion, however, has found that Paul isn't nearly as un- or post-Jewish as this idea would suggest. Yes, Paul is the "apostle to the gentiles" who is engaged in a "mission to the gentiles." But Paul understands that identity and mission in thoroughly Jewish terms. The gospel he proclaims is a fulfillment of Torah (Rom 10:4), and the gentiles who accept that gospel and, as a result, love their neighbors as themselves fulfill Torah (Gal 5:14; 6:2; Rom 13:8-10). Israel's scriptures are about God's Son (Rom 1:2-3), and they bear witness to the revelation of God's righteousness in his raising Jesus from the dead (3:21-22). In the gospel, God has brought to fulfillment his promises to Abraham. He has made Abraham a great nation. He has blessed all the families of the earth through Christ, Abraham's seed. And he has made Abraham the father of many nations.

In none of this is Paul simply concerned to preach a message of "free admission to heaven" to non-Jews. Christians have too often portrayed the apostle's message as a narrative of God rescuing and/or releasing sinners from hell and allowing them into heaven. This portrayal often understands Paul in contrast to his Jewish heritage, as if Judaism and Christianity were two different and distinct ways to pursue the same goal: getting into heaven. In this light, Judaism is portrayed as a deficient and ineffectual avenue, a dead-end that stops short of the Pearly Gates. Christianity, of course, succeeds where Judaism failed. Christianity is the thoroughfare that delivers its travelers to the kingdom of God, the otherworldly place of God's presence.

This isn't the Paul of the letters, neither of the seven undisputed letters nor of the six disputed letters, nor even of Luke's Acts of the Apostles. Instead, we see in Paul a Jewish figure who lived in a world created by the God of Israel. That creator God had called Israel to be his chosen people in

---

15. See Patrick Gray, *Paul as a Problem in History and Culture: The Apostle and His Critics through the Centuries* (Grand Rapids: Baker Academic, 2016), 2–5.

order to reconcile all the families of the earth to himself, and he was faithful to his promises and covenants even when his chosen people had shown themselves unfaithful. Those promises and covenants were narrated in Israel's biblical traditions, and they provided the framework within which Paul understood Jesus's significance, first for the Jew and also for the gentile. And just as Paul understood Jesus from a thoroughly biblical, scriptural perspective,[16] so also Paul understood Israel's biblical traditions from the perspective of Jesus. Paul could not envision Jesus apart from the story of Israel; neither could he envision Israel apart from the story of Jesus.

When we turned to the earliest narratives about Jesus's life and teachings, we made the transition from "thinking with" Jesus to "thinking about" Jesus. Both the Synoptic Gospels and the Johannine texts we discussed in chapters 3 and 4 offer commemorative portraits of Jesus, whether in the guise of biographical narratives (Mark, Matthew, Luke, and John, but also the Acts of the Apostles) or through a highly symbolic, visionary apocalypse (Revelation). For the Synoptic and Johannine texts, we traced the various ways our authors portrayed Jesus as king and/or shepherd over the people of God. Whereas Rome mocked pretenders to royal sovereignty by "lifting up" would-be kings and fixing them to crosses, Mark embraced the parodic sarcasm of crucifixion. Little did Pontius Pilate know that the one he lifted up as "king of the Jews" was indeed the King, the Son of God.

But what does it mean that Jesus is king? One of Mark's most underappreciated ways of showing the character of Jesus's reign is to contrast it with another would-be king, Herod Antipas. "King" Antipas throws a banquet to celebrate his birthday, where the rich and powerful eat and drink their fill and have their senses titillated by a young dancing girl (Mark 6:21-22). And John the Baptist loses his head. Meanwhile, in a very different scene, Jesus has compassion on crowds out in the wilderness, "because they were like sheep without a shepherd" (6:34), and the masses eat bread from heaven, all they can eat. No lusty aristocracy. No vindictive wife. And definitely no dead prophet.

---

16. Remember, the terms "biblical" and "scriptural" here refer to the Hebrew Bible, Israel's scriptures, not to the two-testament Christian canon of texts we refer to as "the Bible."

Death, you'll remember, was the penalty for rebellion. In Antipas's story, of course, the "king" is the one who rebels, but he isn't the one who dies. This is the depth of the tragedy of scripture's drama. God told Adam, "Don't eat from the tree of the knowledge of good and evil, because on the day you eat from it, you will die!" (Gen 2:17). We thought the point was that rebels would be punished with their own death. But we were wrong. The point was that rebellion would introduce death into God's good creation. Rebellion, brokenness, *sin*...these words don't just refer to the evil we *do*; they also refer to the evil we *experience*. In one sense, John was the victim of injustice perpetrated by Antipas and, behind him, his wife Herodias. But in a broader, more fundamental sense, John was simply one more character in scripture's wider drama, where everyone is subject to suffering and death.

This is the real miracle of Jesus's banquet in the wilderness. Unfortunately, we are often distracted by the incredible claim that five thousand people ate and were filled by one small lunch. But don't miss the more significant point: Jesus and his disciples go out to a deserted, secluded place. A crowd follows them, perhaps foolishly, without adequate provisions to sustain life. In the book of Numbers an entire generation died in the wilderness when they failed to believe God and take hold of what he had promised to give them. Here in Mark, death once again lurks just offstage.

But Jesus's banquet isn't like Antipas's banquet. When they come to Jesus, the crowds find life even in a barren wasteland. Like the generation of the exodus, they come out into the wilderness and find that God is able to sustain them and to feed them and, unlike Antipas, to preserve their life. The crowd came out into the wilderness like sheep without a shepherd. They left having been filled by the Good Shepherd.

Israel's scriptural traditions had always anticipated such events, and others besides. The Matthean evangelist is without question the most self-conscious and intentional about the fulfillment of Israel's covenants in Jesus's proclamation of the kingdom of God. From the events of Jesus's birth, his flight to Egypt, and his return to Galilee, to his healing the sick and casting out demons, his teaching in parables, and his betrayal, arrest, and suffering in Jerusalem, Matthew emphasizes the correspondence between the life of Jesus the messiah and the word of God given through its prophets. This is a thoroughly Matthean argument. That is, the author of Matthew is the one performing the interpretive work on the Jesus tradition and focusing our gaze on the links between Jesus and scripture.[17] In one of Matthew's major sources (viz., the Gospel of Mark), Matthew found Jesus himself affirming his fulfillment of the scriptures (Mark 14:49; see also 1:15). In Matthew's Gospel we see one additional instance of Jesus noting the fulfillment of scripture (Matt 8:14); otherwise, the fulfillment formulas are all interpretations of Jesus's life inserted into the narrative by the narrator. In other words, Matthew isn't passively recording "what actually happened"; he's actively interpreting the past for his readers, positioning them to see "what actually happened" from the proper perspective. And that perspective, for Matthew, is thoroughly scriptural.

If Matthew expands an idea he found in Mark, the author of Luke-Acts goes even further. We need to acknowledge, however, that Luke doesn't share Matthew's fulfillment formulas even though he does have a robust theology of fulfillment (see Luke 4:21; 24:44; see also 9:31, 51; 21:24; 22:16). We might suppose, therefore, that Luke's Gospel *de*emphasizes the relationship between Jesus and the scriptures. But we would be wrong. Despite Matthew's focus on Jesus's death as the fruition of scriptural prophecies, he doesn't draw explicit links between Jesus's resurrection and scripture. Perhaps this makes sense; the Hebrew Bible nowhere anticipates a resurrected messiah. But Luke stretches the scriptural blanket taut, like a drumhead, over the whole gospel narrative so that it covers the resurrection. From Abraham's answer in the parable of Lazarus and the rich man and the third of Jesus's predictions of his passion and resurrection to his response to the Sadducees and the post-resurrection announcements by the angel and the risen Jesus that the messiah *must* rise again and the scriptures *must* be fulfilled, Luke's Gospel goes to considerable pains to anchor Jesus's resurrection in Israel's scriptures.

---

17. Scholars differentiate *Jesus's* use of scripture from that of his followers (e.g., see Steve Moyise, *Jesus and Scripture: Studying the New Testament Use of the Old Testament* [Grand Rapids: Baker Academic, 2011]). The distinction is appropriate but difficult to make in practice, in part because Jesus influenced his followers' use of scripture and in part because the evidence doesn't respect this distinction. Our present point is that Matthew's "fulfillment formula" is a feature of *Matthew's* use of scripture.

As the narrative continues into the Acts of the Apostles (i.e., the account of all that Jesus *continued* to do and to teach), the risen Jesus continues his active role in the Bible's drama (which, in Acts, is focused especially on Scene 5 ["Spreading the News of the King: The Mission of the Church"], though the other scenes are also important in Acts, including Scenes 4 and 6). It is true, of course, that Jesus exits the stage early in the first chapter. Even so, he continues to move the plot forward, both directly (via his appearances to Paul) and indirectly (through the agency of the Holy Spirit and of his people). Given the Bible's central problem—the distance set between God and his creation because of human rebellion—the ongoing active presence and working of Jesus becomes especially significant as the resolution of that problem. In Jesus, the God of Israel is present and working to advance his kingdom. As the missiologists like to say: it's not the church of God that has a mission; it's the God of mission who has a church.

We then moved from the Synoptic Gospels and Acts to the comparatively distinctive Gospel of John. We focused our attention on the Fourth Gospel's presentation of Jesus as the Good Shepherd who gives his life that others may have life more abundantly (John 10:10-11). He isn't like the Jewish leaders, hired hands who abandon the sheep in the face of danger. John's use of pastoral imagery goes further than the use of pastoral imagery in the Synoptic Gospels in at least three ways.

First, Jesus is the gate through which other sheep—the lost sheep of Israel—are restored to their Shepherd. A Christian emphasis on faith in Jesus and salvation by that faith may lead us to assume these lost sheep of Israel are Jews who didn't or don't yet believe Jesus is the messiah. And this is certainly part of the picture. Jesus "came to his own people, and his own people didn't welcome him" (John 1:11). For the Johannine narrator, this is a tragedy. But don't forget that the people of Israel had been divided since just after the reign of Solomon, the son of David, and that seven and a half centuries before Jesus the northern kingdom of Israel simply vanished from the land at the hands of the Assyrian Empire. When Jesus says, "I have other sheep that don't belong to this sheep pen. I must lead them too. They will listen to my voice and there will be one flock, with one shepherd," we should hear the promise that God's people, Israel, will be reunited and restored.[18] The people who were divided after Solomon, the son of David, will be united under Jesus, the Son of David.

Second, Jesus is the gate through which faithful shepherds come to the sheep. Immediately before Jesus's Good Shepherd speech in John 10, Jesus heals a man who had been blind from birth. Surprisingly, some of the Jewish leaders and the Pharisees seem perturbed, and they launch an investigation into the man and the events of his healing. As the formerly blind man offers increasingly bold confessions of Jesus's power and identity, the Jewish leaders increasingly demonstrate their failure to recognize the power of God. No less than the great prophet Isaiah had anticipated the restoration of Israel, saying:

> Say to those who are panicking: "Be strong! Don't fear! Here's your God, coming with vengeance; with divine retribution God will come to save you." Then the eyes of the blind will be opened, and the ears of the deaf will be cleared. Then the lame will leap like the deer, and the tongue of the speechless will sing. Waters will spring up in the desert, and streams in the wilderness.... The LORD's ransomed ones will return and enter Zion with singing, with everlasting joy upon their heads. Happiness and joy will overwhelm them; grief and groaning will flee away. (Isa 35:4-6, 10)

The eyes of the blind are opened in John 9, the restoration of Israel has begun, and the Jewish leaders busy themselves with silencing the song of the restored.[19] These are thieves, outlaws, or at best hired hands who don't care for the sheep. But Jesus is the gate of the sheep, and "the one who enters through the gate is the shepherd of the sheep" (John 10:2). At the end of the Gospel, in its final scene, Jesus sends Peter and, along with him, the rest of the disciples to "feed my sheep" (21:15-19). We saw a similar

---

18. For a similar connection to the northern kingdom made with regard to Paul's argument in Romans 11, see Jason A. Staples, "What Do the Gentiles Have to Do with 'All Israel'? A Fresh Look at Romans 11:25-27," *JBL* 130 (2011): 371–90.

19. For an analysis of the link between physical healing and metaphorical restoration in Jewish tradition (specifically, Matt 11:2-6//Luke 7:18-23 and a text from the Dead Sea Scrolls, 4Q521), see Rafael Rodríguez, "Re-Framing End-Time Wonders: A Response to Hans Kvalbein," *JSP* 20 (2011): 219–40.

dynamic at work in Revelation 2:27, where those who remain faithful will shepherd the nations.

Third, Jesus isn't just the shepherd who leads the people (as in the Synoptic Gospels and, significantly, the anticipations of the Hebrew Bible). He is also the sacrifice that atones for the people and reconciles them to God. John the Baptist offered his testimony to this effect very early in the narrative (John 1:29, 35). The point was reinforced at the end of the Fourth Gospel when Jesus's crucifixion was synchronized with the slaughter of the Passover lambs (19:14).[20] This innovative use of pastoral imagery in the Gospel of John becomes a centerpiece of the presentation of Jesus in Revelation, where the most frequent portrayal of Jesus takes the form of a slaughtered lamb. The Lamb redeems the people he rules, and he rules the people he redeems.

With the Catholic Epistles we encountered something of a potpourri of texts, written by different authors for different audiences for different purposes. The letter of James, perhaps one of the earliest texts of the NT, says very little about Jesus directly; the entire letter mentions Jesus's name only twice! But we saw that James roots the life of faith—not simple "belief" but rather the manner of life that flows from belief—in the pattern and person of Jesus. Moreover, despite the surface-level contradiction between James and Paul on the relative importance of faith and works, we observed a deeper confluence of ideas: both James and Paul associate faithful observance of Torah with Jesus. Paul, of course, rejects that his gentile converts should perform works of Torah; even so, we saw that gentiles who love their neighbor "fulfill Torah." James, however, isn't written to gentiles but to Jewish followers of Jesus (Jas 1:1). His readers don't need to adopt works of Torah; they have always performed them! However, their Torah piety was no better than transgression against the covenant if they practiced partiality. Favoritism takes multiple forms, whether favoring the rich over the poor or blessing the poor in word but not in deed. These, however, are not the footprints of Jesus. Those who anticipate and long

---

20.   In the Synoptic Gospels, Jesus is crucified the day *after* the Passover. The night before the crucifixion he and his disciples celebrated the Passover together, and Jesus imbued some of the traditional Passover foods (unleavened bread and wine) with new significance. In the Fourth Gospel, there is no hint that Jesus's final meal (John 13:2) was a Passover meal.

for the day when they "will be judged by the Instruction of freedom" (Jas 2:12, CEB modified) should put their faith in Torah to work in ways that reflect rather than obscure the ways of God.

The letter to the Hebrews, like the letter of James, was also written to Jewish followers of Jesus. This isn't controversial. But American scholarship especially tended to read Hebrews as an early text, an argument against its readers returning to a Judaic (rather than Christian) faith and worshipping in the Jerusalem temple. Judaism was (so this reading goes) growing increasingly obsolete; not even the author of Hebrews could have guessed that in just a few years the Romans would destroy the temple and prove the wisdom of his words: "if something is old and outdated, it's close to disappearing" (Heb 8:13). The problem with this way of reading Hebrews, however, is that the early Christians don't seem to have stopped worshipping in the Jerusalem temple before the buildup to war between Rome and the Jews. Even the Apostle Paul esteemed the temple as a sacred site where one encountered Israel's God.

Moreover, Hebrews makes its case for Jesus's superiority *through* Jewish symbols and stories, including the Torah, Moses, and the tabernacle cult. Jesus isn't better *than* these symbols and stories; he is the better realization *of* them. As such, even as the temple lay in ruins, smoldering in the aftermath of the Roman war, Israel could be assured of its continued access to God. Genesis 14 tells the story of another priest of YHWH, Melchizedek, to whom Abraham himself gave one-tenth of the spoils of war. Psalm 110 announces to the Davidic king, a Judahite who rules over the tribes of Israel, that God has appointed him through an eternal, solemn pledge: "You are a priest forever in line with Melchizedek" (Ps 110:4). The Levitical cult may have been destroyed by Roman legions, but the God of Israel had already provided a more eternal priestly service. Indeed, the order of Melchizedek antedated the sons of Aaron, and now it seems it had survived beyond them. Here especially we see an interesting example of both the flexibility and the persistence of the past. Even as Hebrews is at its most innovative and creative (viz., casting Jesus in the mold of the Judean high priest), he is also working within very specific cultural constraints, including the tribal identity of Jewish priests and the association of Jesus with the lines of Judah and David.

Finally, we turned to 1 Peter and witnessed our author being innovative and creative not just with Jesus's memory but also with his readers' identity. These were gentiles, former pagans who used to be ignorant and live according to their "former desires" (1 Pet 1:14). The bigger problem facing 1 Peter's readers, however, was that their former friends and family were reacting negatively to their newly professed faith in Christ. To their neighbors, these gentiles appear to have "Judaized," that is to have begun living as if they were Jews.[21] Their new lifestyle would have involved adopting new, Judaic practices (e.g., worshipping Israel's God, reading from the Mosaic Torah) as well as ceasing from former pagan practices (e.g., participating in public festivals and sacrifices, observing holidays). Perhaps understandably, this resulted in interpersonal problems for Peter's readers, and 1 Peter spends some time urging readers not to earn the scorn they receive from others but to bear it with grace and strength.

What we might not have expected, however, is that Peter rewrites his readers' pagan biographies, overlaying the experiences of Abraham and his descendants onto these gentiles and writing them into the story of Israel. From the very first verse, Peter describes them as "chosen" yet in "diaspora," both significant words that draw upon Israel's experience of election and of being chosen by God to be his special and peculiar people. Moreover, Peter refers to his readers as "strangers" and "immigrants" in the world (1 Pet 1:1, 17; 2:11). While Christians have a strong and vibrant tradition of reading these labels in terms of a more permanent home in heaven, our discussion in chapter 4 emphasized that these are biblical words that described Abraham's trust in, reliance on, and faithfulness to the God who called him even in the absence of what God had promised him. In Abraham's story, the experience of being a "stranger" and "immigrant" characterized his life in *this* world rather than his disregard for

---

21. For an insightful discussion of the Greek verb *ioudaizein* ("Judaize") and the related noun *ioudaismos* ("Judaism"), see Matthew V. Novenson, "Paul's Former Occupation in *Ioudaismos*," in *Galatians and Christian Theology: Justification, the Gospel, and Ethics in Paul's Letter*, ed. Mark W. Elliott et al. (Grand Rapids: Baker Academic, 2014), 24–39; see also Shaye J. D. Cohen, *The Beginnings of Jewishness: Boundaries, Varieties, Uncertainties*, Hellenistic Culture and Society 31 (Berkeley: University of California Press, 1999).

this world in favor of the next. Instead, these words—"stranger" and "immigrant"—expressed Abraham's election and the certainty that, despite present appearances, God would give what he had promised. So in the present, Peter's gentile readers could be assured that they, too, had been woven into Israel's election. Like the tribes of Israel assembled in the wilderness at the base of Mount Sinai, Peter's readers were now a royal priesthood and a holy nation. Like the kingdoms of Israel and Judah who were akin to "children of prostitution," their names would be rewritten from Not-My-People and No-compassion. They were now the people of God; they had now seen and experienced the compassion of the Lord. This is the work of the gospel, what Jesus has accomplished and the view of Jesus afforded us by Peter. Jesus not only restores the scattered people of Israel; he also leads the gentiles in triumphant procession to worship with and become a part of redeemed and reconciled humanity.

Memory Incomplete: When the New Testament Isn't Enough

I was raised by loving parents who took my sister and me to church every week, whether we wanted to go or not. We never wanted to go. I didn't embrace my own Christian faith until I was a bit older, still in high school but well after I was made to sit in a pew every Sunday morning.

It has now been twenty-five years since the cold, drizzly weekend in late winter when I embraced my Christian faith. A lot has changed in those two and a half decades. I have earned multiple degrees in biblical studies in both the USA and the UK. I have learned innumerable things not just about the Bible but also about the world of the Bible: the ancient Near East, Second Temple Judaism, Christian origins, the history (or better, histor*ies*) of the church, the Hellenistic/Macedonian and the Roman civilizations, and much else besides. In a lot of ways, the Bible (and especially the NT) is less mysterious to me now than it used to be. This is both a blessing and a curse.

I have spent more than half of the last twenty-five years teaching others how to read the various NT texts as texts from specific times and places. Eventually, nearly all my students want to transcend those specific times and places and just ask what the texts say to them *today*. These are, after all, the word of God. When my students read Romans, for example, they aren't nearly as interested in what Paul was saying to nameless readers in Rome in 57 CE as they are in what God is saying to them in the twenty-first century. I don't fault them for this. Time spent with God should be more than a simple exercise in reading someone else's mail, and the life of faith should be more than simple eavesdropping.

As I see it, however, there are two dangers, and every reader of the NT—myself included—runs the risk of encountering one or the other of them. The first danger is that we ignore the historical situations that gave rise to our texts and read them as universally relevant or universally applicable to all readers everywhere in every situation. These texts, after all, are the word of God, and so they have as their ultimate author the universal God who transcends the times, places, persons, and problems of their original authors and recipients. Some have even found warrant for this way of reading the NT in the texts themselves. For one thing, the Pauline author says, "Every scripture is inspired by God and is useful for teaching, for showing mistakes, for correcting, and for training character, so that the person who belongs to God can be equipped to do everything that is good" (2 Tim 3:16-17). For another, the Petrine author notes, "You must know that no prophecy of scripture represents the prophet's own understanding of things, because no prophecy ever came by human will. Instead, men and women led by the Holy Spirit spoke from God" (2 Pet 1:20-21).

The danger, though, of reading the texts without regard for their generative and formative contexts is that we are able to read them however we wish. Sometimes—not always, but in our worst moments—we wield the NT or the whole Bible as a weapon that serves our own purposes. More importantly, we wield it against others, people with whom we disagree theologically, politically, ethically, or whatever. We stop up our ears against what the Spirit of God would say to us about *our* lives, and we shout even louder what we think God should say to others about *their* lives. This first danger faces every reader of NT texts, but perhaps you can see why I would suggest it threatens lay or nontechnical readers of scripture in particular.

The second danger is one I feel much more personally, and that is the danger of locking up the NT texts in their first-century contexts. Paul's letter to the Galatians, the Gospel of Mark, the Revelation of John, and the other texts of the NT are alien texts; none of us who read them today come from the time or the culture that produced them. This is an unavoidable fact, and it is common for those of us who teach the NT to tell our students that none of these texts were written to or for *them*. All of these texts belonged to or were intended for other people, and we are, often literally, reading other people's mail.

But that isn't all we are doing. We have other letters from the first century CE; we also have other histories and narratives and apocalypses from the same time. With rare exceptions, no one reads these other texts—whether Seneca's letters to Licilius or Josephus's history of the war between the Jews and the Romans or the pseudonymous apocalyptic text known as 4 Ezra—in order to communicate with God. And yet every single day millions of Christians all around the world read Paul's letter to the Romans or Luke's Acts of the Apostles or the letter to the Hebrews for exactly this reason: to learn the will of God, to have themselves chastised and formed into more authentic human beings, to commune with God, and for other spiritual purposes. The twenty-first century might not provide the context in which our texts were produced, but it certainly provides the context in which our texts are consulted for wisdom, guidance, and perspective. This second danger may also confront everyone who reads NT texts, but perhaps you can see why I would suggest it threatens academic or technical readers of scripture in particular.

Those of us who want to understand the NT better must wrestle with the tension between the *fact* of our texts' first-century provenance and the *conviction* of our texts' twenty-first-century relevance.

There is, however, a more fundamental problem facing those of us who believe the twenty-seven texts of the NT are the word of God. *The persistence and relevance of the NT is a sign of the ongoing absence of Jesus.* We remember Jesus in the twenty-first century by reading, studying, performing, hearing, and in other ways immersing ourselves in the NT precisely because Jesus isn't here for us to experience. It is the odd Christian who would prefer to read the Gospel of Matthew rather than to have a conversation with Jesus over a cup of coffee or a pint of beer. In my experience, however, coffee with Jesus just isn't an option (to say nothing of the beer).

I can hear the objections of genuine and earnest Christians who believe that Jesus is with them, "in their heart" or in some other intangible-but-nevertheless-real way. I don't mean to deny the reality of anybody's experience of the presence of Jesus in their lives. But I do want to insist that this intangible-but-nevertheless-real presence is still incomplete, still unfulfilled, still imperfect when compared with the NT's eschatological expectation. One day, Jesus and his followers will be physically, *tangibly* reunited.

Consider a story from Luke's Acts of the Apostles. Luke describes the disciples, standing with mouths agape and staring up into heaven. Jesus, you see, had just ascended into the clouds. Suddenly, two angels appear and rebuke them, saying, "Galileans, why are you standing here, looking toward heaven? This Jesus, who was taken up from you into heaven, will come in the same way that you saw him go into heaven" (Acts 1:11).

Or consider the Apostle Paul, who clearly expected all of Jesus's followers would experience his tangible presence in the eschaton, both those who died and those who were alive "at the Lord's coming" (1 Thess 4:15-17).

Or consider John, who saw a vision in which the people of God walk in the light of God's glory, which emanates from the Lamb (Rev 21–22). Jesus promises, "Look! I'm coming soon. My reward is with me, to repay all people as their actions deserve" (Rev 22:12). Whatever we believe about the intangible-but-nevertheless-real presence of Jesus in the here-and-now, the NT itself promises us that something more, something better, something *tangible* is yet to come.

But if it's yet to come, it's not here yet. This is what I mean when I say the persistence and relevance of the NT is a sign of Jesus's continuing absence. We read the NT in order to know and commune with the

God that, one day, we hope to know directly, without the mediation of a written text. This is the elephant in the room: namely, that Jesus is *not* in the room. We need the NT to bear witness to Jesus precisely because he is absent.

In his first letter to Corinth, Paul contrasts the present situation, marked by Jesus's absence, with his hope for the future. The link between then and now is love:

> Love never fails. As for prophecies, they will be brought to an end. As for tongues, they will stop. As for knowledge, it will be brought to an end. We know in part and we prophesy in part; but when the perfect comes, what is partial will be brought to an end. When I was a child, I used to speak like a child, reason like a child, think like a child. But now that I have become a man, I've put an end to childish things. *Now we see a reflection in a mirror; then we will see face-to-face. Now I know partially, but then I will know completely in the same way that I have been completely known.* Now faith, hope, and love remain—these three things—and the greatest of these is love. (1 Cor 13:8-13, emphasis added)

I am especially struck by verse 12: "Now we see a reflection in a mirror; then we will see face-to-face." Or, if I may paraphrase: "Now we see darkly;[22] then we will see clearly."

It's easy enough, perhaps, to appreciate how Paul's letters show us Jesus darkly. We've already acknowledged that Paul "doesn't give us much information about Jesus."[23] The same is true of James and the Johannine Epistles, while other texts (here I'm thinking of Hebrews and Revelation) say a lot about Jesus but aren't terribly relevant for the kinds of questions historians want to ask. Unlike these texts, the Gospels and, to a lesser extent, the Acts of the Apostles are chock-full of information about Jesus, even if historians of Jesus prefer some of these texts (and/or some of their sources) over others. But all of the NT texts give evidence for how Jesus was remembered by Christians in the first century CE. Isn't this enough

---

22. The Greek phrase behind the CEB's "a reflection," which I've rendered "darkly," is *en ainigmati*, which we might more literally translate as "in an indirect manner" or "in a riddling way." The point I want to capitalize on is that the revelation of Jesus in the present is in some sense obscured, hidden, indirect, or—as Paul says—*enigmatic*.

23. See Ehrman, *Jesus before the Gospels*, 102–6 (p. 106 quoted).

for the average Christian, living an ordinary life, who wants to think about Jesus, to know about him, or even just to know him?

Historically, the church has affirmed the sufficiency of the scriptures for enabling us to know God. We need the texts if we hope to know Jesus, and that's actually the problem. Perhaps an analogy would help. My relationship with my wife depends on the hours we spend together every week, even every day. We not only live together; we work together (her office is across the hall from mine), we have the same friends (with exceptions here and there), and we participate in many of the same activities and events. We not only live together; *we do life together*. If, for some reason, we had to live apart for a lengthy period of time, if we had to write letters and Skype or FaceTime each other to maintain our relationship, those letters and Skype sessions would be the lifeline that preserves and nurtures our relationship. But they would be a poor substitute for time spent together, the hours each day that we currently take for granted.

The NT is like letters and conversations over Skype between Christians and the now-absent Jesus. They are the link between him and us, the divinely inspired texts creating and sustaining the link between Jesus and his body for two millennia. But they hardly compare to direct, unmediated knowledge of Jesus, to doing life with Jesus *tangibly*.

Remember the story of Cleopas and his companion as they walked to Emmaus? The two disciples knew the facts about what happened to Jesus, including the report from the women that he was alive. Even so, when Jesus approaches them on the road, they fail to recognize him. The scene would be tragic, if recognizing Jesus were the point. But even in their failure, they continue to walk with him, step by step, listening to him explain "the things written about himself in all the scriptures, starting with Moses and going through all the Prophets" (Luke 24:27). Even as their eyes fail to see Jesus, their hearts burn within them. It is enough that they walk with Jesus with imperfect sight.

As the three men approach Emmaus, the two disciples urge Jesus to stay with them. Their act of ignorant hospitality keeps them in the presence of Jesus. And walking with Jesus, in this story, is more important than seeing him. In the end, of course, Jesus blesses and breaks the bread, and Cleopas and his companion recognize Jesus just as he disappears from their sight. Again the irony: while they could see Jesus they couldn't recognize him. Once they finally recognized him they couldn't see him.

Cleopas and his companion return to Jerusalem to add their testimony to the women's. When they arrive, they hear from the other disciples that Jesus had appeared to Simon Peter (Luke 24:34). The risen Jesus will appear to the disciples again (24:36-50), only to leave one last time and be taken up into heaven (24:51). In his absence, these men would preach the gospel and bear witness to the things they saw and heard, just as Jesus told them (24:48; see also Acts 1:8). Eventually, the texts that make up our NT would be written, collected, copied, and included alongside the scriptures of Israel as the word of God.

Two millennia later these texts would end up in our hands. Reading the NT today leaves us in a situation something like that of Cleopas and the unnamed disciple. The texts of the NT have explained to us all the things written about him in the scriptures, beginning with Moses and continuing through all the Prophets. Now, having read and listened and learned, we find ourselves seated around the table, bread laying broken, but Jesus has disappeared. Our hearts still burn warm as the memory of his teaching and the presence of his Spirit linger within us. But he is absent. We see him, sure. And we affirm his presence, absolutely. Even so, we see him as in a mirror: indirect, refracted, imperfect.

Today we see Jesus darkly, through the text. One day we will see him clearly, face-to-face.

Index of Ancient Texts

Hebrew Bible/Old Testament

New Testament

Apocrypha

Ignatius, *To the Philadelphians*

6.1 142

Ignatius, *To the Romans*

3.3 142

Martyrdom of Polycarp

10.1 142

12.1 142

Other Christian Texts

Irenaeus, *Against Heresies*

3.1.1 95

3.11.8. 110

Eusebius, *Ecclesiastical History*

2.23.1–19. 137

3.39.4. 95

6.14.7. 110

Non-Christian Texts

Pliny, *Epistulae ad Trajanum*

10.96 143

10.97 143

CPSIA information can be obtained
at www.ICGtesting.com
Printed in the USA
LVHW11s2148181018
594074LV00002B/3/P